ON YOUR TERMS

Discovering a more joyful and
purpose-filled life through
Value Conscious Negotiating

NICK SEGAL
WITH LAURA SEGAL

ON YOUR TERMS

Discovering a more joyful and
purpose-filled life through
Value-Conscious Negotiating

BY
NICK SEGAL
WITH LAURA SEGAL

Book design and text formatting by Ajay Peckham

Cover design by Segal Savad

Illustrations by Elena Lacey

FIRST EDITION

READY FOR SUCCESS?

Creating success is one of the greatest and most rewarding adventures in life.

Many self-help books explore personal growth as a way to make us feel better about ourselves. But then what? How do we more fully engage our expanded self into the adventure of success creation?

There are many books that help you clarify what you want, which is also great. But if they don't teach you how to negotiate the outcomes you want, it becomes difficult to walk into a room and come away with what you're aiming for.

Then there are books that will teach you how to negotiate for yourself. This is great if you have the foundational belief that you are worthy to receive what you are negotiating for. But if you don't feel worthy, odds are you will again fall short in your quest for success.

What makes *On Your Terms* unique is the fact that, finally, there is a working manual that explores the three essential ingredients of success. It gently guides you in:

1. More fully claiming your personal value, then
2. Identifying the success you want to create, and then
3. Empowering yourself to effectively negotiate those outcomes.

Resourcing his own personal wealth of experiences—in business and in life—Nick Segal presents an entertaining and self-revealing exploration of his personal success adventure that will inspire anyone willing to do the work to more fully realize their own heartfelt dreams of success.

Segal's approach is a simple and proven methodology; a "paint by numbers" series of action steps designed to enhance personal confidence and develop practical new skills for creating happiness and success.

His personable, encouraging and often humorous style will naturally lift you into the realization that success is not only possible, but very much attainable. And attainable on your terms.

CONTENTS

CONTENTS

ACKNOWLEDGEMENTS

There are so many people that have influenced my life, both personally and professionally. The content and spirit of this book would not have been made possible without the indelible support from the following dear friends and family that have supported me through every step of my journey.

I begin my expression of gratitude to my parents, Fred and Sandra Segal. And then after their passing, to my second set of parents, Janet, John and George Segal who so gallantly stepped in and showed me compassion and care that will stay with me throughout my life. To my crew of siblings, Gretchen, Harry, Vicky, Johnny, Jeanne, Joanne, and Polly, you've all touched my heart in your own way and for that, I'm smiling with appreciation. And then to Deborah, my dear friend and ex-wife, for your loving, your support and your sweet friendship through my "fuzzy" years of personal exploration to this day. And of course to my dearest children, Annie and Teddy Segal. You both light me up and fill my heart with such joy and loving. I am a lucky man to be able to call myself your father. To Monica and Marty Criswell, I am forever thankful that you would share your lives and your precious daughter, Laura with me as we move forward together in our lives, as husband and wife. Your loving and guidance are part of the fabric of who I am.

I am most fortunate to have been surrounded by so many wise and astute friends with whom I've shared professional victories and partnership along the way. From Alan Long to Richard Stearns, Hugh Evans III and F. Ron Smith with whom we built thriving real estate businesses, to Chatty Arrieta, Scott Carmody, Karen Misraje, Sarah Kosasky and Scott Brown, as well as a myriad of friends who shared the fox hole with me along the way as we navigated our way through the day in, day out trenches of our wacky business. To all of my colleagues at DBL Realtors and then Partners Trust who shared their wisdom, support and allowed me to refine my different workshops and classes and explore the content that became so much of the material for this book. To my magnificent 7 who took a chance with me to join Partners Trust at the very beginning while we figured out how to use the FAX machine, surrounded by boxes in an otherwise empty space, and to all of my Founding Partners as well. Thank you for your trust and faith.

To my dear friends beyond the lines of a real estate transaction, to Mark "Firechief" Updegrove, you make me laugh like no other. To Steve "diapered Spidey" Levine, you've been with me through thick and thin and you are my dear friend. To Lawrence "El Koh" Koh, you've demonstrated the meaning of generosity beyond any human being I've ever known and for that, I love you so much and am so grateful. To my business partner and dear friend, Rick Ojeda, I include no "nickname" simply because I have so many for you that I've lost count. To Shaun Alan-Lee, thank you for sharing your heart and allowing me to see you blossom into a fine man who shares his heart freely. I also thank Mark Werts, for your wisdom and guidance. You are the best player out of any sand trap for sure.

And then there are the angels on my shoulders. John Roger, you've opened the door to your heart with every breath. May I continue to have the wit and wisdom to keep walking through the threshold of your loving and joyous spirit. To John Morton, you are my dear friend and your demonstrations of loving, integrity and support resonate throughout the core of my being each and every day. And to John's Tonto, Leigh Taylor Young Morton, hugging you makes everything in the world safe and sound. To Joey Hubbard & Jsu Garcia, you both are shining examples of what loving looks like demonstrated. Thank you dear Dr. Mary and Ron Hulnick for your sweet encouragement, your loving guidance and sharing your mastery of the expression of the human heart. To David Allen, thank you for presenting the power of effective action and organization through your loving and authentic manner.

And to my support team that helped lead this book to the finish line. Laren Bright, thank you for your tireless efforts in assisting with the crafting of this manuscript. Your talents honored the spirit of what we were looking to achieve and we are so grateful. And to Teri Breir, thank you for your dedication to getting each word in its proper place and spelled correctly. To Jane Dorian, I am so grateful for your astute eye, your encouragement and friendship. To Arissa Bright, thank you for demonstrating your immense talents and sanity with me for 25+ hours in the sound booth to get the audiobook just right. To Shelley Reid, you are one of my champions. Thank you so much for supporting me through this journey with your counsel and sage wisdom. To Jeff "release the Kraken" Morgan, your edits and observations are infused throughout the sum and substance of this book. Thank you! Thank you Steve Chandler for your expert counsel and support. As a seasoned coach with countless accolades and accomplishments, your words of support have great meaning to me. Thank you CFJ for your "check in's" of support, humor and loving. To Deidre Wollard, thank you for your initial encouragement in writing this book and to Brian Cooley, for your steady hand and enthusiasm at every step in getting this book through the finish line.

And to Laura. Your immense talents have brought this book to life through your clear and loving style and grace. Your partnership on every level makes me a rich man and I love you with all of my heart and soul. Thank you for taking this journey with me, in loving accord and making every day feel like a sunny, summer day.

INTRODUCTION

In 2009, I took a risk that most would have called crazy. With the global economy in crisis, fortunes being crushed and a complete distrust of any financial institution, I looked at the landscape and decided I was going to bet on me. Thoroughly disillusioned by the conduct and corruption I saw all around me, I cashed in my pension plan, paid the taxes and decided to go into business for myself. With 20 years in business as a broker, owner and salesperson selling residential real estate in Los Angeles, I set my sights on creating a new company; a company that would play at a higher level of integrity and caring. A small group of us came together, filled with excitement and enthusiasm. We steeled up our nerve and the result was the formation of a company called Partners Trust Real Estate Brokerage & Acquisitions. We opened our doors in September of 2009 with the tagline, "Proudly serving our community since...last Thursday."

Was I concerned that the perception of real estate agents was at an all-time low, blamed for playing a key role in the entire global meltdown centered on mortgage defaults and negligent lending practices? I certainly was. How about the fact that when we opened for business, the number of real estate transactions was at a 10-year low and the vast majority of sales were either distress sales or foreclosures? Oh yes...there were many sleepless nights considering how we were going to overcome that reality. Was I served with a $4,000,000 baseless claim lawsuit from my previous employer within 36 hours of our launch, designed just to slow us down? Of course I was! And yet, none of those, or a myriad of other concerns, stopped me. All I knew was that my heart was aligned with the venture and I was completely committed to make it work, no matter what the world was doing around me.

For some context, I wasn't always that poised and clear. In fact, getting to that point of clarity was an adventure in and of itself. I lost both my parents by the time I was fourteen; my mother to suicide and my father to colon cancer a year later. Puberty came late for me and so while all the boys around me looked like furry animals, I more resembled a hairless cat. Candidly, I'm not sure which experience was more painful as an adolescent boy; the associated sadness and confusion of the loss of my parents or the searing embarrassment of my perceived deformity. I chose the acting profession out of college as a form of masochism, so that I could become fully engaged with rejection, and then transitioned into a career as a real estate agent just to make sure I viscerally understood the experience of "No."

So to have that glint in my eye back in 2009 and to see it culminate the way it did is quite astounding. Eight years later, I can proudly say that risk paid off. And while it was a tumultuous ride with tremendous triumphs and crushing defeats, the statistics speak for themselves. During our eight-year run, we amassed eleven billion dollars in sales and attracted over 250 associates across seven offices throughout some of the best locations in Los Angeles. And to punctuate our success, we just recently negotiated the sale of Partners Trust for many millions of dollars. But that only begins to tell the story. Not only did my risk achieve a great monetary reward, it also showed me something about myself and gave me the opportunity to discover the framework and information relayed in this book. That was completely unexpected and, quite possibly, an even greater win.

Having claimed all of those experiences as my "wealth," I've forged a career and a life that make me very proud. I've helped create two highly-regarded real estate companies in Los Angeles and negotiated their sale. I even made a living as an actor. During that segment of my life, I had the pleasure to spar with Muhammed Ali on a movie set while filming the movie *Breakin' 2; Electric Boogaloo* and appeared in an '80s cult classic called *Chopping Mall* ("where shopping costs an arm and a leg"). I've had the pleasure of creating educational programs within my companies, presenting them to hundreds of individuals who have used those tools and techniques to advance their careers and success. I paint. I write. I have a beautiful, loving wife, two precious children and dear friends with whom I share great love and support. And my greatest daily experience of my living abundance and joy is that I laugh, each and every day.

I consider these benchmark life events to be facets of my success. And what makes them that much sweeter is the knowledge that with each demonstration, I had the courage to take risks beyond my own fears, doubts and the opinions of others. While that hasn't always been easy, in looking back at my life to date, it's always been worth it. And that knowledge and experience has become a foundation of greater trust and faith in myself that I can continue questing, continue risking and going for my next level of success.

But let's be clear. There are still moments during the course of any given week when I deal with a fear or doubt that tries to sneak in to stop me from risking in one form or another. And when that happens, I quickly feel it in my body. My neck begins to tense up and my breathing gets shallow. My mind becomes preoccupied, playing the "what if..." game and oddly enough, every outcome ends negatively. Funny how that works, isn't it?

Having dialogued for many hours with my "fear-based" brain, I've come to appreciate the artistry of my mind and when I allow it, how it can prey upon my energy and focus on moving forward. And when my mind gets going in that crippling direction, it usually comes at me in one of three baseline strategies to try and keep me from risking. In no particular order, my risk-adverse mind likes to question my belief in myself. We'll call it, my "I'm not worthy" mind to realize and/ or be successful. My sabotaging mind also likes to compare me to others as well as get me concerned about what others might think of me. And then of course, my mind can be great at questioning my abilities to negotiate the outcomes I want. Thankfully, because I've been negotiating professionally for thirty years, I'm far less susceptible to that aspect of my fear-based mind, but I'm not immune. If nothing else, there's still a little kid inside of me who doesn't like the thought of rejection.

Now that I more fully recognize how these three "voices" have affected me in the past, it is clear to see how many people are gripped by the same fears that deter them from going for more of what they really want in life. That awareness really bothers me because I believe we are all capable of living successful lives. We are meant to experience joy and experience it more abundantly!

But just because we're meant to experience joy and abundance doesn't mean it's going to be handed to us. We need to earn it, to show up and go for what we want. One of the keys to getting there is being able to redirect our mind and awareness beyond the limiting fear of asking for what we want and our doubts that we're not worth having what we want. Speaking from experience, the actual process isn't hard. Directing the mind simply takes consistency and focus, in alignment with understanding what you want and why you want it. There will be an investment of your time, both physically and mentally. There can also be financial investment, as in potentially all the money in your bank account. Working the day job to pay the bills and then sacrificing sleep to dedicate the time to pursue your dream into reality. Oh, and there will be more than a few moments when you're lying in bed, mentally challenging yourself as you ask yourself, "What in the hell am I doing?" You'll overcome those too.

When you're clear enough about what you want, *why* you want it and allow it to excite and drive you through the damning, negative thoughts of your mind, you can achieve it and experience a level of joy, abundance and gratitude that casts a magical glow on your life. And the quintessential beauty of this reality is that it is available to us all.

You don't need to be born with any sort of advantage. It can help, but candidly, it can hinder as well. Beyond where a person comes from or what their education is, success can be achieved by anyone willing to stay engaged with a clear vision of what success means to them and their ability to sustain a belief in him- or herself until the mission is accomplished. My road to success certainly didn't start with any form of convention or advantage.

This book depicts my road map that guided me to realize the success that I enjoy today. We begin with concepts and actions designed to enhance your awareness of your strengths and gifts. That's your VALUE. From there, we take the steps that will define your clear understanding of what you want and why it's worth going for in your life. You'll be more CONSCIOUS. And once that foundation has been created, you'll be shown nine proven negotiation techniques that will better empower you in NEGOTIATING skills to realize *your* success.

And so I ask you...

"Are you willing to take that first courageous step towards your success?"

If so, I invite you to explore *you* through the pages of this book, more fully discover the beauty and wonder that is *you* and discover how you may more fully experience your many forms of success.

PART I

THE BASIC ELEMENTS OF SUCCESS

You are about to embark on a journey that can support you in achieving profound success. The degree to which you participate will have a direct impact on the value you realize. Some of the concepts that will be introduced will not be new to you; others will. Regardless, consider that you have a fresh start to receive the information and use it to your full advantage. Lean in and check it all out to see what works for you and what doesn't. By "leaning in," I mean engaging in each activity to see how it resonates inside of you. Whether you fully believe me or not, stay "in the game" to explore each aspect of this manual that has been designed to support your success.

I strongly encourage you to start by embracing yourself where you are right now. Whatever mindset you currently have toward your life and ideas about success is absolutely fine. Wherever you are in your process, whatever stories you've told yourself and any apprehensions you've had in the past or currently about your ability to create success is a perfect springboard from which to launch.

Why is that? Because I've never met a successful person who didn't have misgivings about achieving their dreams. The only difference between those who ultimately create their success and those who don't is that the achievers have the mindset and clear focus to work through their apprehensions and doubts.

In this first section, let's explore degrees of awareness and how strengthening your ability to hone your focus specifically serves your pursuit of the success you want to realize.

CHAPTER ONE

MY STORY

My parents divorced when I was one year old, so I grew up living with my mother and older sister, Gretchen, on Long Island, New York. The bond my mother and I formed was steadfast and unshakable. I felt her pure love and support, and it was most reassuring and comforting. While childhood had its ups and downs, overall I was a happy kid. I admit I was a tad spoiled based on the loving my mother showered upon me and I enjoyed my early years of making friends in the neighborhood, playing sports, and learning in school.

We had it pretty good. We lived on a picturesque property in an old carriage house my parents had bought together. My mother was a talented artist; a painter and photographer. Her creativity extended into cooking as well and she had a gift for her native French cuisine. When it came to money, my best recollection was that it was always tight. We relied heavily on the alimony from my father, who lived in Connecticut with his new wife.

As my sister and I grew, my mother wanted a new outlet for expressing herself. So she set out to test her entrepreneurial spirit by building an art gallery where she could showcase works of her artist friends. She also made space in the gallery for a restaurant, where she created spectacularly delicious, simple yet elegant, "café" style sandwiches and salads.

My mother threw herself into this endeavor, using all the resources she had to get it off the ground. She renovated an old two-story Victorian style home on the edge of town to give it her stylistic look and feel. Using vivid colors of canary yellow and royal blue, she transformed that dilapidated old house into Calliope Gallery. My mother was very excited and committed to making her vision a reality. I'd just turned thirteen when the gallery officially opened.

Entering the eighth grade and consumed by my own world, I wasn't aware that business wasn't really taking off. Throughout the fall and winter, Calliope Gallery's performance faltered, and with it, my mother's enthusiasm. Toward spring, I could see her becoming more dejected. She was losing weight and didn't really engage with us at the dinner table much anymore. Being an adolescent, suddenly fascinated with girls and bewildered by the prospects of puberty, I didn't see that my mother's decline was accelerating or that she had an inclination towards depression.

One afternoon, I came home from school to a very quiet house. My mother's car was in the garage. I climbed the stairs and saw that her bedroom door was closed. Knowing that she occasionally got migraines, I figured I wouldn't disturb her and proceeded to my room. Lost in my own world, I suddenly realized that it was getting dark and I was getting hungry. I also noticed that I hadn't heard any sounds around the house.

I went to my mother's room and placed my ear to the door. Not hearing anything, I cracked the door to peer in. The fading daylight coming through a French window revealed my mother lying on the bed, fully clothed. I also heard her breathing, deep and heavy...almost as if she were snoring, but more measured and pronounced.

I walked over to the side of her bed, and gently called her.

"Mama?" No response. The heavy, slow breathing continued. I put my hand on her shoulder and called her name again. Still nothing. I was getting concerned. My contact hadn't broken the pattern of her breathing and she seemed lifeless. I shook her with more force with no result. Noticing a glass of water by her bed, I dipped my fingers into it and flicked some drops on her face. Still nothing.

Now I was scared. I started calling her name and grabbed her by the shoulders to elevate her body. As I lifted her torso, my mother's head fell to the side. Connecting her head to the pillow some three feet away was a thick strand of saliva faintly glistening in the waning daylight. I will remember that image for the rest of my life. As my mother continued breathing with that deep, vacant sound, I laid her back down and started to cry with no idea what to do.

What ensued was surreal. I heard the sound of crunching gravel from our driveway. Gretchen, as if on cue, had arrived home. Next, I remember the ambulance roaring up to the front of the house, with paramedics rushing past me as I pointed them toward my mother.

This became the beginning of the end. The primary source of my loving, protection and caring had just tried to kill herself on that otherwise innocuous day in the spring of 1974.

That evening, my father came from Connecticut to collect Gretchen and me, and bring us to his home. It was late when we finally embarked on the two-hour drive to his place. There was a makeshift bed for us and we fell asleep without a clue as to the condition of our mother. My last memory of her was watching the paramedics carrying her, slumped and lifeless in a wheelchair, down the narrow staircase of our home.

We found out the next morning that my mother's attempt to take her life had failed. While relieved, I was also very scared, sad and disconnected. I didn't have any understanding of what was going on or how to even create a story to tell myself to make it any better.

A few days later, two state troopers showed up. After speaking privately with my father and his wife, they came and somberly told us that our mother was dead. She had convinced the hospital to let her go home to wash her hair. While there, she had slit her wrists.

I didn't know what to say or do. My 13-year-old mind didn't understand how she could be dead when I'd been told just days before that she wasn't. My sister started crying and I just looked up at these two serious and scary men and said, "Thank you for telling me." I was numb.

"Dealing with the loss of my closest ally was beyond anything I could think or feel."

So here we were, no longer living in the home where we'd grown up, suddenly thrust into life in Connecticut with a new family that included a stepmother, my older step-sister Vicky and my younger half-brother Harry. Mother, gone. Friends, gone. Dealing with the loss of my closest ally was beyond anything I could think or feel.

As the days passed, I called old friends from Long Island to tell them what had happened and why I wasn't there anymore. In those moments, I started producing my story of "I'm fine," with an internal dialogue of "Just survive this, Nick." That story included a kid who was working through things on his own. The story reassured people there was no need for concern. I wouldn't cry or feel sorry for myself. That's how I was going to deal with pain. I wouldn't touch it or have anything to do with it. "I'm fine" became my rallying cry.

My story and underlying fortitude were quickly tested again. Five weeks after the passing of my mother, we moved to California. My father was a screenwriter and his work was starting to take off. We needed to be in Los Angeles. Gone were the friendships I'd started to form, and now I'd be 3,000 miles away from the friends with whom I'd grown up.

Landing in Woodland Hills at the western end of L.A.'s San Fernando Valley, I was still trying to make heads or tails of my life while working to fit in with my new family. Through it all, I held fast to my "I'm fine" story. New friends, new school, new job at a summer camp to earn some money—after a few months, I felt like I was beginning to formulate some semblance of "normal" in my life.

My relationship with both my father and stepmother, however, was very strained. They didn't agree with my mother's demonstrations of loving and classified me as "spoiled" —which they decided needed correcting. Though I dreaded even walking into the house at the end of the day, I maintained my stoic disposition, trying my best to survive my life.

During my ninth grade year, my father and stepmother took what was supposed to be a one-week trip to New York for business. While there, my father was diagnosed with colon cancer. It was quite advanced by the time they found it and the doctors felt it needed to be dealt with immediately. One week away turned into eight.

Never having encountered cancer, I didn't know what to expect. We all carried on with our self-consuming lives as best we could. I was still fourteen and dealing with the challenges of being a freshman in a new school. I was completely clueless about the ravaging effects cancer could have, until my father returned home.

My father had left L.A. fit and seemingly healthy, weighing about 165 pounds. The man we saw gingerly step out of the car was a fraction of that person, reduced to less than 100 pounds, literally skin and bones. He'd grown a beard to better hide his frail appearance and looking at this bearded, gaunt person barely able to stand on his own, we all started to cry. We couldn't help it. I remember my father asking us in a faint voice, dulled by a massive dose of pain medication, why we were crying. No one responded.

Six months later, a total of fourteen months after losing our mother, my sister and I found ourselves orphaned. As an adolescent, my feelings of loss were truly devastating. For so many of us, the loving and nurturing that we receive from our parents forms the bedrock of our sense of safety. For me, the loss of both of my parents within such a short time at that vulnerable age created tremendous sadness, separation, confusion and hurt inside.

Staring at my father's closed casket during the memorial service, I had no words to say and I wouldn't allow myself to feel emotion. Not because I was scared of what I would find, but because I didn't know where to start. In the absence of any external guidance, I formulated a plan to "double down" on my survival strategy. My "I'm fine" mantra became my armor, and as I left for boarding school in the fall of 1976 for my sophomore year of high school, I vowed that I'd never let anyone see me vulnerable or hurt.

These events are indelibly etched in the core of my being. But the story I created about them has taken many twists and turns. For years, I carried that "survival" flag. I'd recount my past and the loss of my parents like I was presenting the day's weather report. To me, my casual demeanor demonstrated my strength and stood as proof of my ability to endure anything that could possibly be thrown at me. The story I created was that "I was tough." If I could overcome that type of loss, I'd be impervious to any future pain caused by any situation or person.

As new challenges showed up, I'd see them all through the perception of a survivor who couldn't be touched. And that "survival" lens affected both my judgment and my expression. Most profoundly, I let it affect the way I saw myself. Having lost the most precious love I'd ever experienced, I came to the conclusion that perhaps I wasn't worthy of love. No need for me to consider anything beyond the evidence that my mother and father both left. That was proof enough of my theory. "I'm not worthy of that kind of love" became my understanding about me.

As I've grown and developed, I've had the opportunity to take a closer look at my beliefs about these events in my life. The combination of time, coupled with my desire to feel and express myself more fully and vulnerably, has opened doors of compassionate awareness. I've learned that my journey of healing is a process—one that has evolved to the degree that I've been open to it and capable of working with it. And I've invested the time and energy to explore my pain and grief so that I could learn and grow from it and actually use it for my advancement.

Throughout that journey of healing, I've learned how to better distinguish the events from that time in my life as separate from my stories about those events. This distinction has had a profound effect on me. Because of it, there's a thread that connects the choices, focuses and intentions that I've created for myself from the age of fourteen to the present. I've continued to choose a path that could best assist me in moving toward greater clarity and growth.

Directly after these losses in my life, understandably, it took some time to restore my confidence and to even begin to consider the possibility of living an expanded and bountiful life. The compelling conclusion I've come to about the loss of my parents is this: I may have lost their physical presence but that doesn't mean I lost the love they shared with me while we were together. The loving they blessed me with can live on, in and through me, every time I choose to claim it. And the same is also available to anyone who has experienced loss.

We all have our unique path by which we live our lives. My experiences are not unique or even special. They're simply mine. And you have yours. This book is presented to you from the place of a heartfelt desire to offer anyone a vehicle through which they can step forward and realize greater abundance and success, however they'd like to experience that. And lest we forget...fun is available too!

CHAPTER TWO

PERCEPTION IS *NOT* REALITY

My perception of my lovability as a boy, based on my limited perception of reality, demonstrates the power of a mind that doesn't serve our greater opportunity. It's so easy to see when we know what to look for and blinding when we don't. Telling myself the story that I'm unlovable because my mother killed herself can make perfect sense. But if we expand the awareness beyond my viewpoint to encompass all of the players, including my mother's, we can start to realize a more authentic reality. My mother was in unbearable pain and suffering to the point where she chose not to take it anymore. And as sad as that reality was for her, understanding her anguish gave me greater perspective to realize that her self-pain didn't mean I'm not lovable. Hopefully, this clarification can act as a springboard for you to reconsider certain events in your life from a more authentic perspective. And in so doing, you can evolve your understanding of your abilities and strengths.

We all have events in our lives that shape our perceptions and beliefs. Right now, whether you know it or not, you have an entire belief system influencing your capacity for success. Where you grew up, what you were told, your failures, your triumphs, and the examples set by your primary caregivers and role models all play into the mindset and *heartset* of how you think and feel about your abilities and the success you associate with them.

We move through life and notice patterns; consistencies that repeatedly show up. As much as we "try" to change, we seem to keep coming back to the same place and wonder why we're not creating traction or growth. But what if these beliefs and perceptions are influencing how we think and act? Maybe we need to see how they are affecting our choices and our actions, either for our benefit or detriment. Gaining greater clarity around your beliefs and perceptions is the first step in creating more success and abundance in every aspect of your life. So how do you get clearer?

What does the word "success" mean to you? Do you relate to success as a number in your bank account? Is success defined by what you own in the world? Does it mean your job or title? Perhaps you measure success by the prosperity of your family or your company. Does your definition of success rely on comparing yourself to others? Maybe it means fulfilling your mother's dreams for you or modeling your father's accomplishments. As you consider success, do you think of qualities like joy, loving or laughter as being a component of your success?

Take a moment right now to gauge your current relationship to success. What stories do you tell yourself and others about your success? Does your success story have a negative, positive, or neutral tone?

For anyone who struggles with the idea of success or achievement, the "battle" often stems from a core false belief that he or she is unworthy of success. Accentuated by the stories we tell ourselves over time, living in the perception of unworthiness can be excruciating. I know it all too well. For me, the pain of unworthiness often showed up as a numbing dull ache in the pit of my stomach. If you've ever experienced anything like that, know that I've been there and I have tremendous compassion for this kind of experience.

None of us are exempt from fears and doubts when we consider our abilities and dreams. I believe that's part of the great challenge and opportunity of being human: to come into a greater awareness of our abilities, our value, and our recognition of our true nature. As you read this next statement, notice how it resonates inside of you.

Until you recognize your value and claim your worthiness to achieve success, you'll either sabotage or deflect your opportunities to receive it.

Imagine that a close friend comes to you and presents an opportunity to apply for a new job at his company working in a field that you love. If you look at this from the perception of an "I never get these types of jobs" mindset, guess how you'll probably approach this conversation? Influenced by your perceptions, beliefs and story, it probably won't take you long to push the opportunity away, either by your thoughts or actions. This is the beginning of the "sabotage and/or deflect" cycle that keeps us in our current reality. Conversely, if you receive this opportunity with a positive belief about your ability to receive success, odds are far greater that you will create a positive result that serves your greater advancement.

> **"In these pages, we're operating with the understanding that you are inherently worthy, and that recognizing and claiming your goodness sets the course toward your dreams and desires."**

Recognizing your value and claiming your worthiness is an essential ingredient in creating success. People who realize success know what they offer has value. That gives them confidence to ask for what they want in return. Their focus of value moves them towards greater success. That's why it's so important that you realize where you're placing your focus because that focus has tremendous power. It will either promote greater success or diffuse and repel opportunities to realize it.

However you feel right now, whatever you're thinking, is perfectly fine. My intention in asking you about your perceptions of success has nothing to do with "right or wrong." We judge ourselves enough as it is. I'm simply checking your perception as a reference point from which to begin. As you gain greater awareness about the way you relate to your current reality of success, you'll be better positioned to see how the choices you make affect your future reality.

In these pages, we're operating with the understanding that you are inherently worthy, and that recognizing and claiming your goodness sets the course toward your dreams and desires. If you have any doubts at this point, perhaps all it takes is a slight repositioning of some of your perceptions related to your success and those stories you've been telling yourself, so that you can create better endings that serve your greater success. It all starts with recognizing your value.

I encourage you to read the information in this section and see how it resonates with you. You don't need to act on it; simply read and observe yourself. The process guides you in considering your perceptions of success, money, your past, the stories you tell yourself and why you tell them. It showcases how your desired result can be accelerated through discernment of choice and focus in relation to the way you regard your current reality. And it awakens the awareness of how success can be realized and how "momentum" plays into the equation. Finally, the process helps you look at your attachment to outcomes and why that may actually undermine all your good works toward the results you're looking for.

I recommend that you get a journal where you can write down any awarenesses that show up along the way. We are going to cover a tremendous amount of territory in the exploration and negotiation of your success. And with it, you will be given the opportunity to participate in written exercises designed to clarify and support your successful growth. Having a centralized place to capture thoughts and ideas that may become the foundation for your abundant and joyful outcomes will support your journey. Your journal can also serve as a vehicle to track your progression of growth as you move closer and closer to the life you desire to create.

Ease into these awarenesses with an open mind and heart. And have fun with yourself. We take ourselves seriously enough. If you think you see silliness in any of your current perspectives, smile and even laugh at it, knowing we're all doing the best we can.

CHAPTER THREE

YOUR STORY AROUND SUCCESS

In the previous chapter, I asked you to think about some of the stories you tell yourself as they relate to your success. Here's one from my life that may jog your memory for a story of your own.

I had a friend whose family was very wealthy. We knew each other on Long Island, specifically in Westhampton, because they had a summer house where I was living. They also kept an apartment on Central Park West in New York City when they weren't in Paris at their Avenue Foch residence. As a kid of nine years old, I didn't take much notice. Living in Westhampton all year round, going to the local elementary school, the vast majority of my friends didn't come from money or wealth. My schoolyard friend's fathers performed service jobs for the community. Garbage collectors, schoolteachers, the local dentist, guys that worked at the shipyard, were the types of professionals that I grew up knowing. True working-class folk. So when my friend's family invited me to go skiing with them in Austria of all places, my artist father was not happy and he let me know it.

"No one is buying my son as a play date to go skiing in *Austria*."

I didn't consider that I was being "bought" but that we were just friends and it would be fun. I'd never been skiing, let alone in Europe. The argument that ensued between my mother and father later that evening is when I understood the difference between having money and not having money. And inside of me, I started to feel ashamed and sad that we couldn't afford the life that my friend experienced. That sadness made me feel "less than" for the first time, which started to affect my beliefs around money and whether I was born into a family that could realize wealth.

But wait a minute. Have I taken into account all the players involved in my story? What about my father's point of view and his belief system around success? He's the one who had the strong opinions about what was, to me, a simple invitation from a friend. His feelings and perceptions started influencing my perceptions around wealth and they directly influenced my beliefs around success. Left unchecked, that belief system and my ensuing story about my ability to realize success started to affect my relationship with success, wealth and money.

So is my father the bad guy in this story? Is it his fault? Not at all. I do not begrudge or blame my father for his feelings and perceptions around wealth and how my friend's invitation affected him. I have great compassion for my father and the feelings/beliefs he had. He was doing the best he could, based on what he knew at that time. That said, as you choose to look at the events that may have created beliefs around success and wealth that may not be serving you, I encourage you not to bear any ill will towards anyone who may have impacted your beliefs in a limiting way. The more we understand and have compassion that each and every person is doing their very best, based on what they know or believe, the easier it can be to move into your cleaner, clearer place of understanding for your own benefit and growth.

Any good detective needs clues to discover the truth and find the answers. Our first set of clues can be found in the stories we tell ourselves. But now, let's get a bit clearer and gain some more altitude around that story. How about we engage in a little fact checking?

Do you have a story around your beliefs of your wealth or success? How old were you? Did success seem attainable or foreign to you? How did your family relate to success? Who were the other influential players in your story? Once you have that story, play it out in your mind from your perspective. If feelings surface, let them come up. That could include anger and frustration as well. Whatever is present; just observe it, knowing that you've struck the chord that will assist you in gaining greater altitude and clarity for your advantage going forward. Use your journal to better assist you in capturing the perceptions of the story.

Once you complete the story, consider who was the biggest influencer that affected you and made you start to feel a certain way or plant a seed of a belief in your mind? That awareness is a fantastic first step towards changing that belief system because you now better understand where it came from. I encourage you to now consider shifting the vantage point from where you view the story. Consider how a narrator could or would tell the story. From the perspective of this third person, see what happened first and play the story out from that point of reference. My story would be recounted like this:

Nick had a friend when he was nine years old. The friend came from great wealth. Nick's family didn't. All Nick really cared about was playing with his friend and not his wealth. One day, the friend invited Nick to go skiing in Austria. When Nick asked his father for permission, his father became angry and said, "No one is going to buy my son as a play date to go skiing in Austria." Nick didn't understand why his father was so upset until he heard his father and mother talking later on the phone. It was then that Nick better understood that his family didn't have the money that his friend's family had, and it made him feel ashamed and sad.

Those are the facts of the story without the emotion. Can you notice that the story takes on a more objective tone? That objectivity can be the entrance into your consciousness that can allow you to get a better understanding of what was also going on during the event. For myself, I can see that my father's upset wasn't about me going skiing. From that more neutral place, I can begin asking questions about the event like, "Why did my father get so mad?" "What was it about the situation that made him react with such emotion?" Considering the possibilities with that altitude of objectivity, I started to see that perhaps my father felt ashamed that he couldn't provide for me the way my friend's family could. And perhaps, that shame and embarrassment made him feel that his success didn't measure up to that of my friend's father. What I also realized is that, inside of me, I took on those same feelings as my own and the groundwork was laid for me to start feeling that I wasn't worthy to experience that form of success.

One never knows for sure the exact moment when

> **"One never knows for sure the exact moment when a seed is planted in our consciousness that could be undermining us."**

a seed is planted in our consciousness that could be undermining us. My example may not be the very first time I'd felt shame around my success or that of my father's. But that was the story that came present in my mind, so that is what I worked with. I will say that working with that story definitely assisted me in getting clearer with my relationship to my success. Until I took the time to realize where my shame came from, I couldn't figure out how to let it go.

Now, get back to your story. Take notice as to how you or others involved responded to the event, because there are clues there for your learning. How did this experience turn out? Is there some conclusion that you drew about the characters in your story based on what happened? Is there some conclusion you drew about others in general or about the world based on this story? Moving now towards greater clarity, can you find your own compassion for yourself and those in the story as a way of separating the event from the story you've created around it? Compassion and forgiveness are exquisite expressions of loving that can accelerate your own healing and clarity. Is it possible that you and everyone else involved in the event were doing the best you could with what you knew at that time?

Now consider how this story and negative interpretations of your past might be limiting your mindset toward your future. Whatever memories showed up for you, I invite you to empower yourself by acknowledging that, regardless of what happened, the event is over. It ended, and it is in the past. Gone. Done. Finished. What lives on is what you *believe* about that story—the lessons you took from it— and how you allow those beliefs to perpetuate and influence your behavior. I cannot overstate how significantly working through these stories can support your ability to move forward and create more of what you want.

From this objective, neutral point of view, answer these questions: Is the story you've told yourself in the past accurate, or does it need to be revised? What benefits can you receive as a result of what took place? Are there any gifts, advantages or ways that you can use this story for your learning and growth? From this place of greater compassion for yourself and others, you can now recount your story for your benefit going forward. And so begins the process of creating a new, more supportive belief about your success and your ability to realize it.

Being willing to explore the events of your life and their related stories demonstrates that you care enough about your success to examine what might be inhibiting your greater success. For this true courage, I applaud you.

CHAPTER FOUR

WHAT'S YOUR STORY AROUND MONEY?

The subject of money can be a touchy topic. Some people simply don't discuss it. Others flaunt it. Some hoard it as the most precious commodity on the planet while others can't keep it in their pocket even if their lives depended on it. When it comes to creating success, I have found it very important to have a clear relationship with money in terms of what it represents as a form of success and wealth creation.

In the context of wealth, money is only one of many possible symbols—but it's certainly the one that gets the most attention. If you're going to realize greater success, you're going to need to become more comfortable with all of wealth's associated symbols, including money.

Because our society has bestowed such great importance on money since well before the modern era began, you have had ample opportunity to form your own full-blown belief systems about it, along with its perceived power in such a pervasive societal context. Taking an honest look at your beliefs sets you up to discover and clear out any obstacles that may be limiting your ability to create more of what you truly want; whether it be money or some other form of success that would be enabled by money.

Let's start with this question: How do you relate to money? Notice your first reaction to that word— is it positive or negative? Does it feel joyful, exciting or empowering to think about money? Or do you feel stressed or frustrated or overwhelmed? If you're like most people, you probably experience a mixture of emotions.

You likely have some positive associations with money: Happy memories of purchasing a meaningful gift, earning your first allowance, or receiving money that enabled you to do something special. From these experiences, we come to uplifting conclusions and create pleasant stories. We think money is wonderful, it bestows freedom, or gives us the opportunity to travel and explore.

We can also have challenging associations with money. You might recall uncomfortable memories about not being able to pay for something you needed or wanted. Maybe as a kid, others teased you about how much or little money you had. Perhaps you watched your loved ones exhaust themselves in pursuit of money.

We draw conclusions from these experiences, too. And we create stories like "There's never enough money" or "We don't deserve money" or "Money belongs to other people" to better rationalize our relationship to money.

Beyond these personal connections with money, we've also been handed down all sorts of familial and cultural beliefs about it: "Money is dirty," "Money is only for the rich," "It takes money to make money." And the oldie but goodie, "Money doesn't grow on trees." These adages inform our relationship with money and wealth.

As you begin this journey, it's important to get in touch with how you genuinely feel about money. How you feel about it directly impacts whether you pull it toward you or push it away. If you tend to hold negative associations toward money, then there's a part of your consciousness that will work to repel money. After all, no one wants bad things around them. If you have any underlying beliefs that money is somehow bad or only for those who are *not like you,* then you'll find a way to keep it at bay. This usually happens without your even realizing it.

In writing about money, I also realize that it is not always easy to delve into our unconscious beliefs about it. It takes great courage to examine a topic that is as "charged" for most people as money, and the same parts of you that have kept you from the success you seek may try and perpetuate these hidden beliefs by keeping them hidden.

Try this: Pull out a bill from your wallet or purse. No matter the denomination, hold the bill in your hand and simply look at it. What do you see? Letters, numbers,

"What if your Money Story didn't have any separation in it? And what if, instead of pushing money away because of some beliefs that have likely been handed down to you from someone else, you could simply allow money to come towards you?"

pictures? Perhaps beautiful designs and ornate details. Ultimately, the bill is only a piece of linen paper and ink.

So, what if money is simply...neutral? What if it's just a method and measure of exchange? When I stare at those pieces of paper, they seem pretty innocuous. It is not money's fault that we blame it, crave it, devour it or shun it. It is just money. *We* give it any power that is has.

What if you could remove negative thoughts and feelings from money and start creating an unbiased viewpoint of it? What if your Money Story didn't have any separation in it? And what if, instead of pushing money away because of some beliefs that have likely been handed down to you from someone else, you could simply allow money to come towards you?

For now, be aware of your "relationship" to money. If you have a negative connotation attached to it, are you open to seeing money in a new light? Consider this: Simple awareness is often curative. What that means to me is that once I have the awareness of something, I can naturally course-correct my actions and step onto a path leading toward a better result. I'm encouraging you to test that here.

CHAPTER FIVE

WHO'S CALLING YOUR SHOTS?

One of my favorite comedy skits of all time stars the legendary Bob Newhart playing a psychiatrist. As the sketch opens, he's greeting a new patient. The doctor assures this young woman that no matter the nature of her issue, within 5 minutes at the cost of $1 per minute, he can cure what ails her. Skeptical, the woman agrees to the terms, and begins talking about her biggest fear: being buried alive in a box. She can't escape her obsessive thoughts about this. She starts telling stories about how, wherever she goes and no matter what she does, she lives with this panic-inducing terror. The doctor listens intently and asks some questions. Then he suddenly declares that he has the cure and asks the young woman if she's ready to hear it. Most excited, she implores him to share. The doctor calmly leans over his desk and shouts: "STOP IT!"

Uncertain what to make of this "cure," the patient continues discussing her other challenges: bulimia, childhood issues, relationship struggles and fears of driving her car. No matter what she says, the doctor offers the same guidance—"STOP IT!"— until finally, exasperated, the woman shrieks back, "YOU STOP IT!"

While the skit is clearly a parody, the message is profound: No matter what has occurred in the past and however it's consciously or subconsciously affected our current reality, we have the power and authority to mentally STOP IT and move forward in a positive direction. In your life, you get to call the shots.

One of the great powers we all have is the ability to make conscious choices. We can choose to embrace new empowering beliefs like, "I'm not going to allow my past experience to run my present, which influences my future." John-Roger and Russell Bishop, co-founders of Insight Seminars, put it this way: You create, promote or allow your reality.

"You create, promote or allow your reality."

What does "creating" my reality look like? If I want to create a reality of greater health, I can do so by engaging in activities and experiences like exercising well, eating healthy foods and getting good sleep. If I take action and stay the course, I'll create the outcome I want.

What does "promoting" my reality look like? Sometimes we can be so hell-bent on being right that we take actions or place ourselves in environments that reinforce negative outcomes. Think of the person who walks around saying, "I can't stop eating donuts no matter how hard I try," and then spends every afternoon walking by the donut shop (just to enjoy the smell). Of course, once they get there, they can't resist having "just one." This person is not only promoting their donut-eating reality by going to the donut shop, they're likely to promote the reality of "being right" by reinforcing, "See? I can't stop eating donuts."

"Allowing" reality comes more easily to those who tend toward a more passive or "victim" mindset. This dynamic shows up when we give up on making conscious choices for ourselves and instead allow others to tell us what we "should" do or if we let things happen by not making decisions. We've all seen or experienced this. We let someone else do the cooking and eat what they make. If we get fat, it's their fault. But we allowed it. Or we get together with a friend for a movie. They ask what we want to see and we say, it doesn't matter, you pick. So they do and we hate the movie. But we didn't pick when we had the chance. Consider: if you never make a decision, decisions will keep being made for you. And that is not a model for living that breeds success.

This is the lens through which we'll be considering everything that shows up on the road to your success. Here's an empowering question that I encourage you to ask yourself again and again throughout your quest and growth:

"In this moment, how am I creating, promoting or allowing my reality?"

Asking this question is an invitation to take radical responsibility for your experience. It means that no matter what occurs, you're willing to consider that you've consciously or unconsciously given your energy and focus to that outcome. In other words, you've called the shots. If you're not happy with your current reality, are you willing to take the action steps that will bring you closer to the reality that you want? The more you stay vigilant and diligent in your journey to your vision, the less you'll promote or allow the sabotaging habit patterns from your past to disrupt the good work you're doing to create a life that you love.

CHAPTER SIX

ARE YOU LETTING YOUR GOOD IDEAS DIE?

I have a theory: Any inspired idea that isn't acted upon soon after inception will ultimately become a stupid idea or something no longer worth considering. I've seen this play out time and time again.

Think about it for a moment in terms of your own life. Bring to mind a great idea you've had—one that got you excited and enthusiastic. Did you move forward on it, or did you let it sit idle? What happened to that idea if you didn't act on it? Did you lose interest in it? If so, I bet the energy to carry it out disappeared. And later on when you remembered that great idea, you may have diminished its value or even labeled it a dumb idea.

Why don't we act on ideas that get us excited? In my experience, one of the biggest barriers that block us from actualizing our dreams and goals is not knowing where to start. That ends up extinguishing our enthusiasm for our ideas and we let them go. In fact, our lack of knowing or recognizing the method by which we'll be able to achieve something is one of the primary reasons that we stall out or freeze up on our journey to greater success.

The very nature of new-ness and inspiration is that they contain an element of the unknown. This unknown quotient does not need to stop you. Consider Steve Jobs. His drive to explore new ideas with energy and conviction created one of the most robust and dynamic companies the world has ever known. Do you think not knowing how to get started ever stopped Steve Jobs? Probably not. Jobs' *intentionality* to act on his ideas transcended any desires he had for needing to know how they'd get done. And I'd say the same is true for me and my partners in the creation of Partners Trust. So why is it that most of us fall prey to the idea that we need to know how to do something before we do it?

Wanting to always appear right or in command of a situation is a function of the ego. And egos fear appearing wrong, thinking it means we're somehow inferior. Do you like to be right, or are you happy feeling unsure and making mistakes? Part of this mind chatter of "I don't know where to start" might be our ego creating fear to protect us from any pain of embarrassment associated with making mistakes since we're heading into the unknown.

This ego "protection" is a trap, and does not serve your quest for success. Buying into it results in a two-for-one negative payoff: it stifles our capacity to take action and churns up our limiting stories about the world and ourselves. A common sign of this stuckness is having thoughts like, "If I don't know how to do this, then maybe I actually *can't* do it." It can also show up as perfectionism: "I have to know I can do this perfectly or I can't proceed."

"What if our capacity for awareness could open up pathways for us to take action and then create more of what we want?"

From a more elevated perspective, I recognize that my real growth comes when I'm willing to take risks and make mistakes. If we want to move forward, what's the alternative to getting stuck and bogged down like this? Take the plunge and learn as you go!

Imagine that you start to create a painting and halfway in, you decide that you actually want more yellow instead of all of the orange you'd envisioned. Or picture yourself trying a new recipe and discovering you prefer more oregano and less basil. Taking action and observing helps us get more specific. The more specific we get about what we want, the more it comes into focus for us. And the more it comes into focus, the greater the likelihood that we can then achieve it. Consider this: what if our capacity for awareness could open up pathways for us to take action and then create more of what we want?

Instead of asking myself "How can I do this?" what if I alter the question to "*What* am I going for?" And more importantly, "Why?" In those late-night hours of January 2009, I had no idea how in the world I was going to achieve any of my goals. But I was laser-clear about my intention: To create a successful company that would raise the bar of integrity and service in the real estate industry. This "why" was big enough to drive me past any mental roadblocks that I placed in my own way during my quest to achieve my dreams.

No matter what the idea, your *intention* to complete it is the fuel for the energy that can get the ball rolling. Once moving, you refine your awareness about what you want, and then leverage it to begin streamlining your process to your goal. You don't have to know how or have a plan in place before you begin; simply set an intention and take the first step. When you focus on your intention, the method— the "how"—starts to reveal itself as you move forward.

CHAPTER SEVEN

PROMOTING YOURSELF TO CEO OF YOUR LIFE

Throughout the day and in any given moment, we make choices that impact our experiences and results. If our target is greater success, then it behooves us to become more aware of this dynamic of choosing so we use it to our advantage. This awareness is called "discernment."

The concept is pretty straightforward. If I choose to do something that leads me toward my objective, then I feel good about what I do. When my choice moves me away from what I know will serve me, even if I do so out of habit or without consciously thinking about it, I won't feel as good about the result. The key awareness here is that our short-term choices dramatically impact our long-term outcomes—and we can become more conscious of what results our choices will produce.

Say that I decide to save up some money so I can take a vacation. I achieve my first step: opening a savings account and making a deposit. After doing this, I feel proud of myself and excited about forging ahead toward my goal. A couple of days later, though, after a rough day at the office, I decide I need a diversion and withdraw some cash from my new savings account to take a few friends out to dinner. While I have a great time, I wake up the next morning feeling disappointed that I spent most of the money I was going to use for my trip.

The fact is, sometimes we're not very disciplined. Call it the "instant gratification" principle, wreaking havoc on our longer-term plans and goals. We say we want a grander demonstration of success, but on the way to it we go off-course in favor of shorter-term, more immediate enjoyment. We act impulsively or procrastinate and we justify the choice.

Some would call this justification process a negotiation. We negotiate our choices with ourselves using statements like, "Just this one time," or "I'll get to it later." We tell ourselves a compelling story, and we buy it. Again and again and again. These types of negotiations don't serve your greater purpose or the pursuit of your goals.

I recently put a question to my real estate associates to help them gauge how they spend their time as they create success for themselves. This question will work for anyone, regardless of profession, because in reality, we are all the Chief Executive Officers of our own lives.

I started by recognizing each associate as CEO of their own business. I suggested that, as CEOs, they were in charge of all monetizing activities—self promotion, time management, business development, budgeting and customer service for starters. As they pondered the different facets of their job, I asked them to consider how efficient they were in each of these important categories. Were they attending to all the details in real time? And then I asked them:

"**Discernment is not a skill you magically acquire; it's an ongoing practice that requires continual recalibration and awareness.**"

"As CEO of your business, based on your performance and ability to be discerning with your time, would you rehire or fire yourself right now?"

The room went very quiet as each person considered their performance in creating greater success. That question creates greater self-awareness and a clear benchmark for determining whether someone is making choices focused on their longer-term goals or on their more immediate gratification.

When I refer to "discernment" in these pages, I mean our ability to make the best choice we can in any given moment in alignment with our greater goals and purpose. Discernment is not a skill you magically acquire; it's an ongoing practice that requires continual recalibration and awareness. Practicing discernment keeps you on track and ensures both your progression toward and production of what you want. And you start to become a very effective CEO, guiding your course towards your success.

CHAPTER EIGHT

HOW FAST DO YOU WANT TO GET THERE?

Basic geometry teaches us that that the shortest distance between two points is a straight line. If we apply this logic to the speed of realizing your success, then it makes sense that you'd want your progression to be as direct as possible. The more we use our discernment to align our choices with the success we want to experience, the greater the likelihood that we'll progress in a straighter line, and the quicker we'll reach our objectives.

Take a look at the graph on the next page which represents a timeline to complete a project. When we consider embarking on a task, we generally want to know how long it will take. In our example, in a perfect world without deviation or distraction, the amount of time to finish the project is 10 hours. However, we don't live in a perfect world, so this graph is designed to illustrate how you can affect your completion time, based on your level of focus and discernment.

I've defined four levels of awareness, each of which has an associated amount of time it will take to compete the same project. Every level has specific characteristics that will probably seem familiar; as you look at each one, be aware of how every short-term choice that's made affects the longer-term reality of the pursuit of your goal.

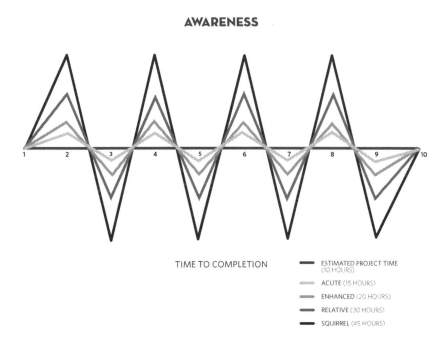

AWARENESS

TIME TO COMPLETION

- ESTIMATED PROJECT TIME (10 HOURS)
- ACUTE (15 HOURS)
- ENHANCED (20 HOURS)
- RELATIVE (30 HOURS)
- SQUIRREL (45 HOURS)

The lightest gray line shows "acute awareness." When you're on this line, you know what you want. You make discerning choices that support your vision and you quickly recognize when you're both on- and off- course with your goals. You're very aware of where you are and where you're heading, and you make rapid and efficient adjustments as needed to keep on the most efficient path to your vision. The key word here is "acute" and the time to completion associated with this approach is 15 hours.

The second lightest line represents "enhanced awareness." You'll notice that this line stretches out longer than the "acute" line. Wandering off-course costs more time and energy to reach the finish line than it does when your awareness is at its peak and your focus is its sharpest. The time if you're exercising this level of awareness is 20 hours.

The medium gray "relative awareness" line shows a more meandering path. Based on the amount of time and energy that it takes to move the ball forward here, it's amazing anyone ever gets all the way home. But some people play in this arena and still somehow manage to achieve results. They're simply exhausted and burnt out by the time they do. Approached from this level of awareness, the project would take 30 hours.

I simply call the darkest line "squirrel" consciousness. This describes the path of those who get caught up in the "shiny object" land of distraction and veer so far off-course that getting to the finish line seems almost impossible. Most folks living in this reality are wandering around wondering why they're still seeking but not finding: "But—oh, look! What's that? Ooooh, shiiinnyy."

Can you relate to squirrel consciousness at all? I can. All of us, at one point or another, will find ourselves going off-track to one degree or another. The question becomes, "Will you return to your path?" One of the important success skills we can cultivate is learning to recognize when we're in any form of "wandering" awareness, then redirecting our energy back toward our intended target as quickly as possible.

I've created this graphic to provide a sense of the relative differences in time it might take to reach the finish line based on each playing field of awareness. For those who want your result as quickly as possible, this graph should clarify that it's to your benefit to remain very discerning about how you spend your time and where you place your focus.

As much as this diagram defines the value of making clear and aligned choices, we know that real life doesn't function in a straight line. The human condition pulls and pushes us in all sorts of directions based on our needs, habits and desires. When life starts batting us around like a tennis ball, staying on-course becomes more difficult. Achieving success depends upon your clarity about what you want to achieve and why.

Creating Partners Trust took tremendous discipline and discernment. Along the way, we faced countless challenges that easily could have derailed us if we hadn't been confident we'd outlast and overcome our obstacles day in and day out. I remember the day I gave notice to my previous real estate brokerage that my new partners and I were leaving to create a new company. I knew my decision would likely be met with disappointment from my employer, and yet I wanted to honor both him and the company that had been good to me. So as a sign of respect, I set up a face-to-face meeting as opposed to simply sending him an email with my news. That meeting was swift and cordial, absent of the drama that can sometimes occur when colleagues part ways. I left feeling very good about my prospects and the future ahead.

My optimism held steady for two days—until I received a registered letter that made my knees buckle and my heart sink to my toes. It informed me that my previous broker was suing me. For $4,000,000. If you've ever been sued for that kind of money—especially if it was money you didn't have—then you know a number like that will get your attention. Remember that this was 2009 and the financial and housing markets were in chaos. In my attempt to evolve and expand my professional life, I'd just positioned myself into a $4,000,000 lawsuit from a Fortune 500 company. Forget the four levels of awareness...I started praying for a fifth level: Oblivion.

But once I picked my heart up from my shoes and put it back into my chest, I remembered why I was doing all of this in the first place. I practiced discernment and brought my thoughts back into alignment with the overarching quest at hand. I called my lawyer, sent him the letter, and got back to moving forward with my eye on the prize of building a company I could be proud of.

Challenging situations are great devices for testing us and taking us off-course because they bring up our fears and concerns. By design and definition, a challenge makes us consider the importance of what we want. If fear kicks in, it can push us off line fast. Once our minds start racing, we can easily forget what we intended or desired in the first place. Anytime you're faced with one of these defining moments, consider this: If you don't act for your growth, you get to stay where you are.

Is that okay with you? If it's not, know that there's a flip side to any challenge that can be used to your benefit: Pressing forward and through the difficulty makes us stronger and more resilient. In my experience, life brings us growth opportunities that offer us a choice to either flex the new positive muscles we've built or to fall back into our old limiting patterns.

Ironically, when we drift away from our dreams and desires, we actually do have a very specific destination in mind. It's called the "Comfort Zone," where everything is familiar and "feels" safe. The plain truth is that the slide into our Comfort Zone is a welcome relief if we're being challenged by our new direction. And change is almost always challenging. Sadly, once we get back to the Comfort Zone, we tend to stay there. Every once in a while, we may venture out and test its edges, but often we scurry right back, telling ourselves, "Screw it; I'm happy in here. I've got what I need." That choice just turns off the engine that's moving us toward the possibility of our expanded success.

Here's the great news: none of this is irreversible to your journey. All of it can be useful. Most of us drift off-course until one day we look around and say, "Wait, how'd I get here? This isn't where I want to be anymore." These are the moments when we realize that we're sick and tired of being tired and sick. That's often what it takes for us to consider heading back towards the Acute Awareness line. Our dream gets rekindled and some part of us remembers where we were going before we stalled out.

These are the moments of redirection in our path. We might go back and pick up the tools we've learned and practiced, we might give ourselves an inner pep talk, or we might simply think, "I've got nothing else to do right now, so I might as well try making a different choice." Whatever gets us moving back toward our success at this point is great. Consider that we do have the opportunity to be smart about our progression. Our goal is to harness the power of discernment to get back into alignment as quickly as we can, so that we can move along in the Acute Awareness zone for as long as possible.

Now, as I mentioned, change is almost always uncomfortable, so be ready to experience doubt. When your doubt surfaces, consider it both a blessing and curse. Sometimes expanding your boundaries means listening to your doubt. Doubt can lead us to slow down a bit to make sure we have enough information to keep moving confidently in a positive direction. In that checking process, new revelations can take place that make our road to success more efficient.

> "Whatever gets us moving back toward our success at this point is great. Consider that we do have the opportunity to be smart about our progression."

But doubt has a slippery side. It can lure you back into your Comfort Zone, enticing your mind to stop taking action and settle back into the habits of your current reality. We often take our doubts as the actual truth without ever bothering to check them out.

When doubt appears for me, I like to consider that there may be some wisdom in that doubt that I can use to my advantage. The best way I know to tap into that wisdom is by actually dialoguing with my doubt as if it is a person with whom I'm having a conversation. I realize this may sound silly, but stay with me for a moment and see if you can find value in it for yourself.

Say I'm questioning whether or not to ask my boss for help with a project. My doubt may be founded on the perception that if I have to ask for help, maybe I don't know what I'm doing and might consequently be fired. I trust you can relate to how quickly my doubt-based mind can launch into full-fledged fear that leads to a draconian ending. In that moment, I have a choice. Either I buy into the fear and allow the doubt to paralyze me. Or...I can engage my doubt and ask it, "Why do you think asking for help may get me fired? Do I really work for such an unsupportive company that asking for help would lead me to being fired? And then I listen to what my doubt has to say: "Well, maybe not. I just get scared whenever I have to extend myself and I take it to the 'worst case' scenario."

Now clarity starts to come in. And with it, a greater understanding and compassion to see how those old fears and "stories" can permeate my thoughts and turn my perception of reality against me. With a clearer understanding of the basis of my doubt and, in this case, fear, I can move more easily through it towards the action of actually asking for help without the doubt. Because at the end of the day, if I don't get the help I need, I'm not going to be able to add value to my job and I'll probably be "course corrected" soon enough anyway. Based on this specific example, I asked and listened to what information the *wisdom* of my doubt had for me and through the honoring of the process, got the clarity I needed to move forward.

I invite you to check out this "dialoging" process for yourself. The next time you feel doubt, try this technique and listen for the wisdom that can come forward from a seemingly very unlikely source.

Whether you try that method or not, the best way to work through any reservations that show up along the way is to focus on fact-finding. Are your doubts really true? What data are you using to verify them? As you work through these uncertainties, continue to give yourself credit for continuing down your path, even if it seems like you're in a slower state of progression. I'll tell you this: After almost getting completely derailed when I received that $4,000,000 piece of registered mail on day three of the Partners Trust adventure, I'm so grateful that I had a clear vision and the pure desire to press forward toward my success past my comfort zone and beyond the legal threats and intimidation designed to defeat me.

Eventually, we resolved the lawsuit in a way that allowed me to keep moving forward. I didn't appreciate the anxiety I experienced in that part of the adventure, however, I can tell you that the learning I gained from it—not the least of which was to check my fears against the facts and to keep moving toward my goal—has served me time and again. I am unquestionably stronger as a result of confronting the doubts the letter brought up.

Meeting challenges, whether they come from our minds or from the influence of others, takes conviction of the heart and discerning choice. We can jump back onto the straight path toward our success when we get clear about why our success matters to us and we utilize our power of choice.

CHAPTER NINE

THE GREAT CARROT MASSACRE

When I was eight years old, I came face to face with death for the first time. It all started out innocently enough, with a package of carrot seeds and a dream. But over the course of six fateful days, that dream shattered, and I was left to wonder how it all could have gone so terribly wrong.

Third-grade science class introduced me to the wonders of time-lapse photography. Witnessing life pierce though the earth in the form of tiny seeds growing into fragile green sprigs that blossomed into an explosion of glorious bushy green carrot tops in less than 30 seconds thrilled and mesmerized me. So much so that I had to recreate the experience for myself and watch it happen in real life.

So I set out to reconstruct the magic that I'd seen in class. I went to the local nursery and bought a packet of carrot seeds. With my mother's assistance, I claimed a small patch of space in our garden. Making sure to allow enough room between the carrots, I pushed each seed into the ground with my thumb and covered it up with dirt as the package instructed. Six seeds in a perfect row. My mother gifted me with a small watering can and told me that my job was to keep the seeds moist.

Brimming with excitement and pride, I prepared myself for the pleasure of

having my very own bushy green carrot tops. As the days passed, I watered...
and waited. Watered...and waited. Watered...and...still nothing. I'd been doing
everything I was supposed to do. What the heck was going on?

Consumed with anticipation, frustration and longing, I'd race out to the garden each
morning and stare down at my blank spot. Where were my green carrot tops? Had I
done something wrong? Did I buy bad seeds? Had I watered them too much? Or not
enough? Every morning and evening I visited the empty space of dirt where my carrots
should've been and grumbled at the garden gnomes, "I want my green tops!"

When yet another day passed with no signs of life, I just couldn't take it anymore.
Something was clearly wrong, and I reasoned that if I could just see what was
going on beneath the topsoil, I might be able to fix it. Using my hand like a bull
dozer, I scraped away the first layer of dirt over my row of seeds. Nothing. I passed
my hands over the row again, digging a little deeper this time. Still nothing. On
the third pass, I took away enough dirt to discover a tiny, fragile web of shoots
extending from each seed.

I stared down at the soil in amazement. My plan had actually been working. My
seeds were transforming! I was ecstatic.

But my joy quickly veered to concern. My digging had dislodged the seedlings
from their beds, and now they lay toppled on their sides, their little roots naked
and vulnerable. Was it possible that, in my impatience, I'd hurt my little guys?
After gingerly placing them upright once more, I reburied them as quickly I could.
Maybe if I hurried, nothing terrible would happen. As I ran to get my watering can
to shower my seeds with sustenance, all I could do was pray, "Dear God, I hope I
didn't hurt my carrots too bad."

So once again I watered...and waited. Watered...and waited. And the longer I
waited, the angrier with myself I felt. If only I'd just waited for those seeds to turn
into happy carrot tops. How could I have done that to those poor little guys?

After three more torturous days of anticipation, I couldn't stand it anymore. I
gently dug up the seeds again. Not only had they failed to grow one single bit, but
their teeny roots had withered. In that moment, I realized that my nightmare was
real. I'd killed all of my fluffy-carrot-top hopes before they could bloom. (Isn't this a
harrowing story?)

Years of carrot therapy and self-forgiveness have since assisted me in
overcoming the tragedy of The Great Carrot Massacre. But the lesson lives on. And

it just so happens that this lesson speaks directly to the very next idea we're working with in our quest for success.

I'm going to go out on a limb and claim that we've all been that 8-year-old kid, eager for results, who may have killed a dream before it could fully take root. Impatience and lack of trust are the culprits in this crime. But with basic awareness, we can learn how to stay more effectively true to our path so that in the end, we achieve the flourishing fluffy-carrot-top outcomes of our dreams. From here forward, consider this journey a No Carrot-Kill Zone.

> "Ninety-nine percent of the time, reaching a goal doesn't happen overnight or in one giant leap. Accepting that many variables and steps go into the pursuit of any dream is the healthiest way to mentally prepare for the quest ahead."

As we saw in the last chapter, creating a path of success isn't a straight-line process. If discernment is the rain that nourishes the seeds of our greater success, then patience and trust are the sunshine. Ninety-nine percent of the time, reaching a goal doesn't happen overnight or in one giant leap. Accepting that many variables and steps go into the pursuit of any dream is the healthiest way to mentally prepare for the quest ahead. I've found that when I overcome my impatience for results, I'm given more opportunities to experience joy and a meaningful sense of accomplishment along the way.

CHAPTER TEN

RIDING THE WAVE OF MOMENTUM

Let's talk about momentum—what it takes to create it and how we can use it to produce explosive results. While the fastest route to get from where you are now to the success of your dreams is a straight line, we've seen how we actually zig-zag our way to the outcomes we seek.

In the graph on the next page, you'll notice two distinct lines that represent pathways toward a result. The first line is straight and travels at a true 45-degree angle upward. On this path, every action is rewarded with an equal measure of progress, represented by the line's steady rise. I apply effort toward getting what I want, and I see a direct reward for my effort. I make a phone call to get a new client, and I get that new client every time. No guesswork or uncertainty involved; pure risk/reward. Doesn't that sound great?

Has that ever happened to you? It sure hasn't happened to me. That's why I call this the "Fantasy" Trajectory; it doesn't exist.

The second line follows a curved trajectory upward. This line represents the process of growth that occurs when we're willing to do the work required to get to our success and when we stay true to what we want. I call this line the Momentum Trajectory.

SUCCESS TRAJECTORY

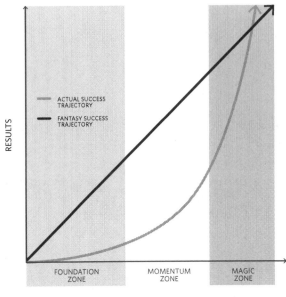

The intention of this illustration is twofold. I want to offer you greater understanding of the process of creating success. And I also want to inspire you to stay the course to fruition and avoid the second-guessing that leads to digging up your seeds of growth before they've fully developed. To do this, I've divided the Momentum Trajectory into three critical stages of progress. My hope is that this will give you a better handle on where you are in your journey to greater success and will help you anticipate what occurs as you move closer toward it. Each stage represents a period of time and your progression toward your goal within that time. As we look at the characteristics of each stage, you'll discover that how you choose to invest your time in each area directly impacts the speed of your progress into the next zone.

The Foundation Zone:

This first zone is the most pragmatic and, some might say, boring or tedious. Here's where you must diligently apply yourself in order to move toward the results you want. You're developing new muscles—paying attention, strengthening your awareness and taking action. As you do, you're building velocity toward your success that initiates the power of momentum. The good work you do in this early stage will bear fruit for you down the line.

Notice on the graph that the greatest movement in this zone occurs not upward but rather more horizontally. Growth occurs by way of the foundation you lay as you create solid roots of stability and strength that, like my fledgling carrots, need time to grow and flourish.

The Foundation Zone can also be the trickiest to navigate. This is where people may stall out because they lack either the clarity or the desire to do what's required in order to keep moving forward. Getting to the other side of this zone demands fortitude and steadiness in ample supply. So many dreams and hopes get dashed simply because we let our inner 8-year-old disrupt the good work that we've initiated.

Bookmark this page so that if you ever feel frustrated or impatient during your journey, you can remind yourself to re-engage and connect back into what you're doing and why you're doing it. Remember: you're in a No Carrot-Kill Zone.

The Momentum Zone:

In the second phase of progression that I call the Momentum Zone, your diligence and consistent effort start taking hold, kicking your movement toward success into a higher gear. Notice that the graph line shifts from a largely horizontal progression to a more vertical one. That vertical ascent represents results. Notice also the amount of time it took to progress upward in the Foundation Zone relative to the amount of time it takes here. This illustrates the return on investment of the groundwork you laid in the first zone—the possibly tedious work that allowed you to transition into this new phase of your trajectory toward your results.

In this zone, you experience the unexpected and it shows up in a host of ways. It may occur as an unforeseen turn of events that happens for your benefit. It may come as a helping hand from a new relationship that you formed when you were in the Foundation Zone. Because you've heightened your level of awareness, you recognize that things are happening with more ease. The pace quickens and you feel like the dream that once seemed so far away is coming into focus on the horizon.

During this phase of your growth, you'll likely feel a renewed drive. The best way to put that positive energy to use is to double-down on your efforts. No laurel-resting here. Take the good you've created so far and work it more fully to your advantage. Continue taking consistent, high-quality action steps to keep on-course.

The Magic Zone:

Now the fun really begins. Check out the explosion of upward movement within this time frame. It blows the previous zones away. The actions you take here catapult you toward your dreams. The energy you spend in this zone pays off exponentially.

In the Magic Zone, the actions you take may trigger a range of emotions from confidence to self-doubt. If challenging emotions show up, know that this is simply the part of you that feels uncertain and scared. You keep your trajectory escalating by calling upon your courage. Be wary of the Comfort Zone, and let any negative emotions be secondary to your focus on moving forward.

> "Your trust, both in your process and in yourself, starts to blossom, realized through the positive energy you begin to enjoy. Events come together with ease, and results rapidly manifest."

The interesting thing, though, is that you probably won't know you're in the Magic Zone until you're in it. But you'll start seeing signs you're there. Your trust, both in your process and in yourself, starts to blossom, realized through the positive energy you begin to enjoy. Events come together with ease, and results rapidly manifest.

Think of the progression through the three zones like the process of moving a boulder that's stationary. At first, the prospect of shifting the rock from its position seems daunting. Because of its mass and weight, it's settled into the ground. With some focused effort, you start rocking the boulder back and forth until it moves the tiniest bit. This is what it's like when you apply your focus, energy and commitment within the Foundation Zone of any project.

You capitalize on the miniscule movement, persevering and eventually getting that rock actually rolling in the direction you want it to go. This equates to the transition into the Momentum Zone. The rock moves more easily now, and as you keep its motion going, you transition into the Magic Zone. Now your cooperative rock almost seems to roll on its own as you guide it to its new resting place. The culmination of your efforts and commitment in the first two zones inevitably pay huge dividends when you reach the Magic Zone.

One last point about our two-lined graph. Check out the Magic Zone again, and notice how much higher the Momentum trajectory finishes as compared to the Fantasy trajectory. This demonstrates the ultimate payoff you get for taking risks without the guarantee of reward. This is what it looks like when you exceed your dreams beyond your wildest expectations. It's also a clue about where the true excitement and wonder reside for you when you're willing to go for what you wholeheartedly want in life.

CHAPTER ELEVEN

START SMALL, GROW BIG

Thank goodness for our evolutionary impulse. Part of our innate intelligence as a species is that we tend to do whatever we have to do to get our basic needs met. But the flip side of that is that once we meet those essential needs, most of us tend to then throttle back until our needs rise up again.

Consider your current bank account balance. If you're like most of us, the amount of money in that account directly correlates to the amount of money you need to pay the bills each month. We'll call that the "need" level. Any money in the account above your need level amount qualifies as the "surplus" level.

Remember how the Comfort Zone is designed to protect us, keeping us feeling safe and in the realm of the familiar? Here's how this plays out with money in terms of our sense of peace and security. The more money we have in the surplus level of our account, the further away we are from our need level; therefore, we feel greater peace and security. Conversely, when our excess level of cash dwindles and we get closer to our need level, we have a tendency to go into fear, feeling tension and anxiety. Sound at all familiar?

Living in this reality is like living on a yo-yo. We go up and down, closer then further away from our need level, but never venturing beyond the length of our yo-yo's string. Considering that the vast majority live paycheck to paycheck, this means that we perpetually operate within a bandwidth of mild to major anxiety.

Here's a cold hard truth about success: This same dynamic of need drives the success we achieve. We cultivate our goals and dreams to the degree that we feel need for them. Building my company had a very high need level, so I did whatever it took in terms of time, money and investment to make it a reality.

But in the absence of a direct need, for the most part, we let our dreams lie fallow. Or at least we don't push for them. Because (let's be honest) most of us don't exactly enjoy taking the emotional and psychological risks that growth and expansion require. That's another facet of the Comfort Zone. Meeting our needs affords us a certain level of security and predictability that we "enjoy" in our lives. But is it really enjoyable? If we want greater success, we've got to be willing to harness the tension between our comfort and the restlessness that we experience when we live in a more static reality.

This brings me to a popular definition of the word "crazy"—doing the same thing over and over, and expecting a different result. While I'm not suggesting that you are certifiable, understand that if you're truly tired of your current reality and want more fulfillment in your life, then you're going to need to summon your courage and take action; i.e., do something different than what you're doing.

If the thought of moving on your dreams makes you break into a cold sweat, here's some great news: You don't have to go out and do something gigantic. Simply put, significant and lasting expansion can occur through microscopic action.

When you consider the word "microscopic," what comes to mind? Most likely something small, right? Like, tiny. Yet, completing a marathon starts with taking the first stride that accumulates into yards and eventually miles. Meeting an annual sales goal starts with dialing one phone number and having a conversation. Sculpting a masterpiece starts with the first chip of stone. That's what I mean by microscopic. Simple, small actions that, when built upon, have the potential to create massive results.

Here's one of my favorite affirmations that speaks to the life-changing power of microscopic action. A dear friend, David Allen, who is the author of the acclaimed book *Getting Things Done,* taught it to me. I've used this affirmation to create just about everything I've accomplished in my adult life.

"Little things done consistently, in excellence, create a major impact."

"Little things done consistently, in excellence, create a major impact."

Let's dissect this statement. We start with "little things." Fairly self-explanatory and, for our collective benefit, not that hard to deal with. When you consider a little thing, does that entail summiting a mountain or slaying a dragon? Not in my reality. "Little things" are more like making a phone call, writing a note, returning an email. That being said, completing little things is one of the quickest and most effective ways I know to expand your confidence level.

"Done consistently." Now we're talking about a measure of focus and commitment. Creating a steady diet of little actions does take some degree of awareness and planning. It also tends to build momentum. With each little success, we're being encouraged to keep going.

"In excellence." Okay, now we're qualifying the action specifically. Whatever the task, small or seemingly insignificant, your commitment to doing that "thing" to the best of your ability in the moment begins to define the measure of quality you're creating and, thereafter, the success that you'll achieve.

"Create a major impact." The results! I like the way the words "major impact" resonate inside of me. If I'm going to invest my time and energy in something, then I most definitely want it to have a major impact.

Remember, no matter where we're starting, we can start small. Making eye contact with the person you're speaking to can be a little thing. Writing a thank-you note can be a little thing. Arriving at one meeting on time can be a little thing. The important qualifications here are consistency and excellence. That's how you reach the rarified air that is so much fun to breathe.

Creating your success, as you define it, is our objective. One simple awareness that momentarily shifts your perspective is all that's needed to begin recalibrating from your current reality to your new, expansive reality. That's how the magic begins.

As you consider leaning into your next adventure, to what degree do you take action in excellence? That question and your answer to it will serve as a clear sign of whether you're on-course or off-course in your effectiveness on the road to success.

CHAPTER TWELVE

THE POWER OF BEING "PRESENT"

As we step into the mastery of success, it's important to understand how your roving mind can hinder your ability to catalyze seemingly ordinary moments into "major impact" moments. The amount of time you spend allowing your mind to drift into fantasies or memories is equal to the amount of time that you risk missing an opportunity. Consider the moment in time when you have an opportunity to get up-to-speed on a new aspect of your job that requires you to fulfill a series of critical actions in precise succession. If you're not fully engaged and focused in that moment, your lack of attention on the facts and nuances of the conversation could result in missing critical information.

Deals are won or lost by the subtlest of details that get relayed in any given moment. One of the marks of a great negotiator is their ability to process information, be it subtle or overt, and use it to their advantage. Oftentimes, that information comes when we least expect it. So if we want to create major impact from any given moment, then it's imperative that we learn to take dominion over our minds and hone our ability to engage and focus. I'm not unique in bringing this perspective forward. Many people, from Zen masters to financial analysts and everyone in between attest to the value of being present if we want to lead richer, fuller lives.

Unfortunately, building our capacity to stay present involves using our minds—those sneaky little devils that don't always cooperate even when they logically know it's in our best interest to stay aware and engaged. Rationally, we may "get" the value of being present. We may understand, in theory, that we can't change the past, and the only way to direct the future is through the actions we take in the present. Yet, in practice, this can be really hard to do. Part of the trouble stems from the mind's proclivity for future fantasy. Whether it's negative or positive, our minds have the uncanny ability to project forward with the thrust of a rocket ship, imagining the wildest of realities and conclusions. We can conjure up future outcomes so seemingly real that we physiologically react as if they're actually taking place.

Earlier in my career, I had a shot at working for a particular client. He was famous and wealthy, and the thought of representing him excited me. In my mind's eye, I started imagining what it would be like to represent him. I could see myself walking into any home with him and spotting everyone there looking at me, envious of how cool I was to be representing this guy. It made my ego giddy with delight.

Then there was the money. Every day I'd think, "Once I sell this client a $5,000,000 home, I'll make $100,000. Oh baby. What I'm going to do with that money." My mind actually started spending the cash that I didn't even have yet.

The more I fueled my fantasy, the stronger my attachment to the outcome became. It grew so strong, in fact, that when the question, "What if it doesn't happen?" popped into my mind, I felt nauseous and clammy. My heart quickened and my stomach tightened with the sickening feeling of dread that maybe my fantasy wouldn't come true. After the 38 seconds it took me to conjure up an entire future reality filled with amazing things, I'd suddenly plummeted into the depths of depression, crushed by the thought of losing something that hadn't even happened. This is what I mean by our "devilish" minds.

But, wait—it gets worse. Spurred by the fear that I might fail to secure this new client and would miss out on living my dreams, I became obsessive. I started forcing the present moment in an attempt to make things happen. With a mind in desperation, I started thinking about all the ways I "had" to stay engaged with the business manager who referred me to the celebrity. I called, I emailed, I texted, always asking when our first meeting would take place. The result? I became a pest and, worse, damaged my relationship with the manager. He started to distance himself from me. From his point of view, the last thing he wanted to do was entrust a valuable client of his to an annoying guy like me.

Consider the outcome that my actions, driven by my compulsive mind, were creating—all based on a future fantasy attachment. Because of my attachment to my own self-serving agenda, I squandered a wonderful opportunity for success, made available to me through a relationship I'd carefully built over time, in a way that could potentially cost me both a new client and my longtime colleague. All because I let my mind create an attachment about what I thought the future should look like. In the end, I did lose the opportunity to work with that client, and my friendship with the business manager was never the same.

I share this with you to illustrate the damaging power of a mind allowed to run rampant. But with practice, we can learn to harness the power of our minds in a way that works for us rather than against us. We can train our minds to pick up clues and nuances that serve us in our negotiations. Our ability to do this hinges on the quality of our focus.

What tends to happen to most of us when the outcome of an event is directly related to our vision of success? Do we zero in, or do we spin out? In my experience, as the stakes go up, most of us start clouding our minds with the attachment to the possible outcomes and probabilities. And in doing so, we lose sight of the invaluable intelligence and information directly in front of us, providing us with the best chance of positive forward motion.

Speaking of "stakes," consider your mind's activity when you meet with your boss to ask for a raise. As you walk into your meeting, where is your focus? If you're not present and aware, you can easily start fantasizing about the future. You might imagine what it'll be like to have more money and what you'll do with it. Or you might start your own inner dialogue about how you're *not* getting the raise before you ever even open your mouth. Or perhaps you go in strong but at the first sign of trouble, you drift off into a negative fantasy. Something like:

"It's not going well. Look at how he's looking at me. Did I offend him by asking for this raise? Is he going to fire me? Maybe I should quit before he fires me. If I quit, I have to get a new job. Where will I get a new job? Who will hire me? Maybe no one. Then what will I do? I'll be out on the street. What will my friends think? What will I do with my cat?"

We've all done this. How long does it take for our minds to start rattling off all our fears? Our brain can take any idea and run with it faster than Usain Bolt sprinting toward the finish line.

Consider how all of this adversely affects our perceptions, our reactions and even our body posture and chemistry. When we drift out of the present moment, we directly undermine our success. When I'm consumed with figuring out how I'll take care of my cat after I inevitably end up living on the street, there's no way I can remain present and accurately digest information my boss is telling me, either directly or indirectly, that can assist me in getting my raise.

"When we drift out of the present moment, we directly undermine our success."

Imagine you're a baseball player stepping into the batter's box. It's the bottom of the ninth inning, your team is down by two runs, the bases are loaded, and there are two outs. Oh, and it's game seven of the World Series. Millions of people around the world and 50,000+ in the stadium all have their eyes on you. How will you perform? Will you get the hit and be a hero, or strike out and be the goat that everyone always remembers as having made the last out?

Where would your mind serve you best in this situation? If you choose the negative fantasy of striking out and living a life of infamy, odds are good that your body will tense up. Your hands will sweat and you'll grip the bat so tightly that your fingers numb. Your eyes may tense and squint as you will them to see the ball more clearly. Your mind might start running the "what if" scenarios: "What if I don't hit the ball? I'll be an embarrassment to the world and myself. Or what if I get a hit and I'm a hero? Endorsements and money and more fame will greet me. I have to get this hit!"

While it might seem like this kind of reaction is inevitable when the stakes are high, I'm here to tell you that there's another way—a kinder, gentler alternative that opens up a much wider doorway for you to enter into success. This concept was introduced to me by one of my mentors, John-Roger. What if you could enter any situation designed to serve your dreams from the mindset of:

100% Participation, 0% Attachment

100% Participation means you're all in. When you fully participate, you're focused only on the matter at hand. There's no luxury of getting ahead of yourself or of dwelling on the past. You enter an environment with a clear intention: to simply stay present and receptive. I've found time and time again that the more I practice directing my mind to stay engaged in the moment, the more I can build the muscle to keep it there. I do this by reminding myself that I stand the best chance of realizing the success I want in my life by being present.

So, if we're 100% focused on our participation in the moment, what are we NOT focusing on? Attachment to the outcome in the future. This is an important awareness. As we better understand the basic working of our mind, we stand a greater chance of directing our focus where it can more effectively serve us. Minds like singular focus. Moreover, when our mind is focusing on one thought, it really doesn't care to focus on anything else. It's occupied and that's what matters to our mind. With that distinction, let's empower our mind with a focus that better enhances our odds for success; in the present moment. Being present also allows our bodies to more fully relax as we focus on what is happening in real time.

Ask any athlete or sports psychologist and they'll tell you that peak performance emerges when we approach challenges from a state of calm. Michael Gervais is a professional in this field who talks about this in the work he does coaching world-class athletes. Taking full, deep breaths creates relaxation, and this allows us to better process the information coming at us and to react optimally. A body in a relaxed and alert state performs better than a body in a tense and distracted state.

This similarly applies to the mind. A mind focused on the present moment is far more receptive to input, it reacts and responds with greater suppleness, and it produces enhanced results. A wandering mind robs us of the ability to focus on the information that can put us in better position to achieve what we ultimately want.

Time is one of our most precious commodities. And so often we think we don't have enough time to do what brings us joy and fulfillment. But how much time do we spend daydreaming about the future or living in the past? We could instead put that "lost" time to use by being present and taking action right now toward our dreams.

I suggest that there's always plenty of time, as long as we choose to focus our awareness in the present. We need to "own" the understanding that the best way to create a fantastic outcome is to double-down our focus in the moment. Your mind will always have its fantasies. I say, give it what it wants—not as daydreaming, but as a reality by actually achieving your dreams.

The more you educate your mind that the best way to attain its fantasies is by staying focused and aware in key moments, the more it will cooperate and support you to stay in the game when you really need that focus. Note that distinction. We don't always have to live in a hyper-state of pure focus (unless, of course, we want to). For our purposes, we're centering on those moments when you're going for more of what you want—whether that is a negotiation or some other creative pursuit. The more we take dominion over our thoughts to the best of our ability and channel them toward using this moment to serve our success, the quicker and more consistently our success shows up.

PART II

CREATING YOUR FOUNDATION OF SUCCESS

As we proceed into this section, your mind and heart are both going to be activated. As a result, you'll discover the rich inner wisdom that resides inside of you. Consider using your journal to assist you in capturing and retaining that wisdom. Journaling is also a great way to support yourself in integrating the techniques you'll learn. It's also fun to use your journal as a reference point for how your growth unfolds along the way. I've reread journal entries from times past and realized how much I've expanded and learned, and that's become a great source of my personal inspiration, acknowledgment and self-appreciation.

With that said, let's jump into Part II.

CHAPTER THIRTEEN

CLAIMING YOUR VALUE

Let's return for a moment to the basic premise that I shared in an earlier chapter:

Until you recognize your value and claim your worthiness to achieve success, you'll either sabotage or deflect your opportunity to receive it.

We're going to make this real for you so that you can gain greater awareness of how it applies specifically to your path to success.

Consider an action that most of us take at least once a day or more: looking into the mirror. When you see your reflection, do you say things to yourself like, "My eyes look puffy. Uh-oh, is that a pimple? What's with these wrinkles? I'm getting old." Or do you look at yourself and see the twinkle in your eye? Do you notice how healthy you look? Do you appreciate the things that you like about yourself—that dimple in your cheek, the brightness of your smile, the shape of your chin?

Almost every one of us goes through some form of this ritual on a daily basis. But how often do we

> **"Until you recognize your value and claim your worthiness to achieve success, you'll either sabotage or deflect your opportunity to receive it."**

actually notice the messages that we heap upon ourselves while we're doing it? Left unchecked, we'll continue ingraining the same ideas, whether positive or negative, over and over until we practically become numb to our own behavior. Are you responding to what you see with messages that incrementally support you or tear you down?

I spent my formative high school years at a Quaker school in Lower Bucks County, Pennsylvania. It was there that I was introduced to the Quaker philosophy of the human spirit: there's a spark of goodness in everyone; and with some you just have to look a little deeper to find it. Holding that perspective in mind, reflect on this question:

To what degree do you currently recognize and claim your goodness, value and worthiness? Accepting the wisdom of the Quakers, how radiant is your own spark? Is it a wooden match or a bonfire? Is there room for you to enhance it? Know that however you find yourself responding to these questions is just fine. You're simply taking note—gaining awareness—of your starting point.

Do you recognize the power within a spark? With a little oxygen and kindling, it quickly becomes a flame. As you now start actively working with the fundamental tenet of recognizing your value and claiming your worthiness to achieve success, I encourage you to try on the Quaker philosophy. Claim your spark and allow yourself the opportunity to nurture it into a glowing flame of growth and expansion.

You can begin this process by acknowledging, as the Quakers do, that you have an inherent goodness. You have positive qualities you can expand upon. You have positive resources that you've developed and can put to good use. You have the learnings you've gathered throughout your life. Whether they've come through a formal education and academic institutions or through the individualized school of street smarts and life experience, you have wisdom and intelligence that you can apply toward your success.

So, how does your spark of goodness, your wisdom, your intelligence show up? If you are ready to participate and put these concepts to work, here's your first opportunity. Open your journal right now and take a couple of minutes to write down your answers to these two questions:

What is my value?

What is my goodness?

Simply spend two minutes writing down whatever comes to mind without slowing down to edit or pondering how to respond. Imagine that your closest, most loving friend is writing you a letter of appreciation. What would he or she say about you? Your answers might range from "I'm funny" and "I'm punctual" to "I care about doing a good job" and "I'm loving of others." No need to make an exhaustive list; just a few positive qualities or traits will do.

Once you've finished that exercise, take a moment to acknowledge yourself. You've just completed a microscopic step towards your success by simply recognizing and claiming your value. You've done a little thing that has the potential to create a major impact. Congratulations! Please know that I'm being quite serious. For some of us, this exercise can feel really uncomfortable, and writing down positive qualities feels like a stretch. If you're a person who was able to tackle that exercise with no problem, consider that your connection to your goodness and value is something you can be grateful for.

Here's an invitation for you as we move forward: Once a day, write down in your journal three things that you appreciate about yourself. For many people, the easiest time to do this is either first thing in the morning after waking up or last thing in the evening before going to bed. By writing these self-appreciations on a daily basis, you're instilling a habit of consciously recognizing your goodness and value. Not just when you look at yourself in the mirror (though that's a great place to start), but all throughout the day. When you recognize and acknowledge these things about yourself, you're actively enhancing your self-image and your sense of worthiness. And as our basic premise states, *it's only when you recognize your value that you can you apply it towards creating success.*

Another way to apply the basic premise is by practicing being gentler and kinder with yourself. None of us wake up in the morning wondering, "How can I really screw things up today? What can I do to completely blow it?"

"None of us wake up in the morning wondering, 'How can I really screw things up today? What can I do to completely blow it?'"

You might be concerned that you will blow it, but that's probably not your intention. Give yourself a break. Stop beating yourself up. Start appreciating yourself. You can accomplish that with the microscopic step of simply claiming, "There's goodness inside of me. I'm a good person and it's okay for me to succeed. I'm allowed to experience success." Because no matter who you are, you are worthy of your dreams. That's not a belief; it's a fact.

Imagine what it would be like to walk into a room fully recognizing the value you're bringing. Imagine walking in with an awareness inside you that says, "I know who I am and that core goodness is with me no matter who I'm speaking to." When we're in touch with the qualities of our unique value, we're empowered. Consider how that can impact your confidence and your negotiations. Do you think you'll have a better chance of achieving the results you want?

Remember that Quaker spark of goodness inside of you. Regardless of whether or not you recognize it or believe it or feel it, it's there. The more you claim that goodness, the more you fan your spark into a brighter flame. The more you claim it, the more you're paving the pathway to your success, and the more you'll begin to believe that you can achieve it. And this means that when you create the next opportunity that can and will promote your success, you can participate in it more fully.

I encourage you to run the experiment and see what kind of results you get. Start acknowledging and claiming your goodness and value every chance you get. This exercise may seem overly simplistic, but this initial step is worthy of great respect and consideration. I know firsthand that it has dramatic and lasting impact. It certainly did for me.

CHAPTER FOURTEEN

REDISCOVERING THE WISDOM OF YOUR WONDER

Claiming your value isn't always easy, no matter who you are. I also know that just because I give you some suggestions that can assist you in positively reframing your mindset, changing thought patterns, in most cases, isn't like flipping a switch. The seeds of your current thoughts were planted in your consciousness before you had any awareness of conscious choice. How and where you were raised has molded how you think and feel about yourself, and a few pages in a book can't transcend that overnight.

When I think of the events in my own childhood, part of me wonders how I even get out of bed in the morning. Yet I do. Most of us do, in spite of the negative mental and emotional conditioning we've experienced along the way. So here's a direction question for you: How do you want to get out of bed going forward? We can't change our past. We can however, learn from the situations that we've "survived" and use them for our advantage if we choose to. That's what I'd like you to consider: your choices right now and going forward. Because just as our past has affected our current reality, our current reality can affect our future.

After my mother passed and my sister and I went to live with my father and stepmother and their two kids, I was in a daze. Whatever caused her to take her own life didn't compute in my mind or emotions, and now I was faced with a completely new living environment in a "family" with which I had little connection. To be fair, we were all thrown into this situation together. Sure I had my confusion and pain, but I wasn't the only one dealing with a new reality. My mother's death had altered the lives of six people all now living under one roof, and each one of us in our own way must have felt the discomfort.

In my new family, I was confronted with a very specific issue regarding my character. Or rather, my father's assessment of my character. His story was that my mother had spoiled me rotten, and he was going to shape me up with "tough love." So he pointed out and emphasized every misstep I made. Anytime I was in my father's presence, I felt like my entire thought process and my identity were being questioned and broken down. My emotions swirled into one big indefinable mass, like scrambled eggs in a blender. I lost all self-confidence and came to believe that I really was the "little shit" that my father said I was.

It was here, at my rock bottom of this time of my life, that I received a gift I'll always remember. The day started like any other. Waking to the same dull ache of futility in the pit of my stomach, I walked down the stairs of our home in Woodland Hills. Only a soft cast of early-morning sunlight coming through the opaque windowpane of our front door lit my path. Filled with emptiness and sadness, I turned the corner at the base of the stairs to make my way into the kitchen, when I heard this little voice say, clear as a bell, "Good things happen to good people, Nick. And you are a good person." The message was so vivid that it stopped me in my tracks.

To this day, I don't fully understand or know where that communication came from. Call it the touch of the Divine or whatever you like, I simply define that voice as me supporting me. In that moment and each day since, I've held that voice and its message in the center of my heart as an affirmation. In the depth of my despair and loneliness, the goodness in me rose up and spoke to me to lift me up. I was good at that time, and I am and have been good every day of my life, beyond whatever circumstances life presented to me.

This experience was as real as anything I've participated in or witnessed in my life. But was it exclusive to me? I don't hold that as true. I see and hear demonstrations of that unique, individual goodness expressed every day by the people all around me. You, too, demonstrate your goodness every day. Even when you don't realize it, it's there.

We are born in pure goodness. Have you ever looked at a newborn and thought, "This kid's no good?" Of course not. You look at that child and, most likely, become captivated by their innocence and purity. Their vulnerability is so profound that if anyone tried to harm that child, you would use everything you had to stop them. From the sweet place inside of you that warms you or lights up as you consider that newborn, remember right now that you, too, were once a newborn baby, filled with the same purity and innocence. That is the foundation of your goodness, and you came into this world with it.

So what happened? How did we allow that goodness, that purity and innocence, to fade? We had help. Help from parents, friends, peers and our environment—all working in concert to "teach" and "position" us about how we're "supposed" to be and act in our lives. While primarily well-meaning, the results of all of this so-called education can block us from remembering the goodness and strength that's inherent in us.

Here's an exercise designed to get you more in touch with the goodness and wonder of the innocent child inside of you. The more you work with it to rebuild your connection with your little child, the more you'll tap into the inner resources that hold the keys to the success you're seeking. There's no heavy lifting here; it's simply a chance to reconnect with that part of your goodness that may just want to play in this field of greater possibility, here and now.

First I'd like to introduce you to someone very special to me.

Check out this dude! What do you see in this picture? I see determination. Confidence. A playful spirit. Oh yes, and of course,

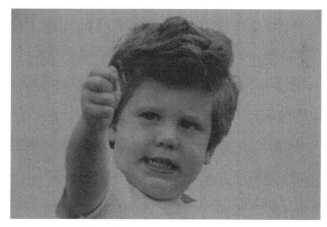

look at that mop of hair!

That's me as a little guy. I don't specifically remember that moment or what was going on around me, but that doesn't matter. As I look at the child in that photo, I see only goodness. I see a kid brimming with life and possibility. There's no condition placed on that little guy about what he "should" do, or what he's not doing, or how he could be "better." The child in that picture is not a "little shit," but a grand and glorious expression of wonder and possibility.

When that picture was taken, I was nothing but the inherent pure goodness of a human being, poised to be whatever I wanted to be. Maybe that little "tower of power" was hearing that same message, "Good things happen to good people, Nick, and you are a good person." I don't know. But what I do know is that that same expression of unlimited possibility captured in this image resides in me today. But that only helps me if I choose to believe it. And I do. That photo, taken some 54 years ago, is a reminder that no matter what's happened in my life, I have a choice about how I want to play going forward.

Will you claim your "tower of power" too? Are you open to visiting an old and dear friend who's been waiting to reunite with you? Are you willing to connect with the goodness of who you truly are, beyond all the "stuff" you may have allowed to consume your life?

If you are, then find a picture of yourself when you were young and innocent—a picture of you that lifts your spirits and showcases your joy. Perhaps your picture lives in your mind's eye, and you can see it as soon as you close your eyelids. That works. Or you may want to rummage through photo boxes, or even ask a loved one or relative for assistance. However you locate this image, I really encourage you to take the time to do this for yourself.

Once you find your picture, take a few moments to slow down and look at yourself as a child. There's a bit of magic that becomes available for you when you do... magic that will serve you as we progress on this journey together. Most importantly, remind yourself of the sweetness you *still* are but may have forgotten. This is a big deal. I want to make that crystal clear. You are still the sweetness, innocence and joy represented in your picture.

You might have lost sight of that (up until now) in favor of the beliefs that others instilled within you. That's the source of so much of our trouble when it comes to seeing and believing in our goodness. We've come to accept what our families, schools, cultures and all those other external "voices" have pounded into us, overpowering our ability to stay engaged with the positive messages of our own internal voices. Know that just as you bought into those external limiting messages, you can now choose reconnection with that sweet goodness of little you. Let him or her come out and play.

There's another bit of magic kids have that you, too, can rekindle through the child inside of you: kids are awesome negotiators. They're really clear about what they want and don't want. And, when allowed to explore and flourish, children have rich imaginations. As we start to look at ways to define and create success for ourselves, we're going to need access to that same clarity, creativity and imagination. What better place to find inspiration than from within us—the most imaginative and creative source possible?

When I started tapping into the goodness and enthusiasm of my inner kid (whom I've come to call "Little Nick"), the adult part of me was amazed by what I could accomplish. If you've ever hung out with little kids, you know that they don't consider "what if" from a pessimistic, limited place of fear and embarrassment. They reach up and go for their ideas and dreams. When I was a kid, I'd find a sheet or towel, hold either end in my chubby little hands, extend my arms as if they were wings, and start running around at a breakneck speed. I didn't care what others thought of me while I was doing this. I was flying! That was pure joy.

Consider for a moment the people in your life whom you most admire. Are they big thinkers, or small? Do you think they stop going for what they want because of other people's opinions or limited mindsets? The people I admire speak their mind, and they do what they believe best serves them based on their knowledge and circumstances. I may not always agree with them, but I do understand and appreciate their "go for it" nature. That's demonstrating liberation and freedom. And that's the child inside. Kids play in freedom. They explore in freedom. They rejoice in freedom. And they go for what they want, in freedom, relentlessly.

Are you open to tapping into the resource of the little child who resides inside of you? Do you realize that you have a choice about how you live your life? The same inner critic who's limited your experience by focusing on fear, the opinion of others or any other narrow-minded approach can be re-educated into a more expansive methodology of joy and fulfillment. This process opens you up beyond your current reality to see a greater, grander reality. From there, you're in a much stronger position to manifest your dreams with ease.

To be clear, I realize that no one is likely to re-program their belief system overnight. However, within the framework of *little things done consistently in excellence create a major impact*, I do know that it can be, and is, done every day. I've done it, and so can you. It requires time and consistent focus to tap back into the strength, freedom and joy of your younger self.

At one time or another, we've all inhibited our authentic and true expressions. We shut down in order to avoid hurt or embarrassment. As a result, there may be a measure of pain when you begin reconnecting with the expression of your little one. That kid inside may be really scared to come out for fear of being hurt again.

I've been there. I remember a time when I shut down my expression because I didn't like the hurt I felt from sharing my openness. It was the first time I can remember being laughed at, and it really hurt. I felt embarrassed and alone with no one to help or protect me. If only someone had been there to assist me when I felt my first pain of rejection and embarrassment. If only someone could've protected me and told those kids who were laughing at me to stop it.

> **"Good things happen to good people, and YOU are a good person."**

This is why I suggest you really ease into this exploration with as much honoring and caring as you can extend to yourself. Consider how old you were when you started quieting that little precious one inside of you. If you're like most people, you've had far more experience shutting down your expressions of wonder and goodness than you've had building them up.

And there's some great news. Protection of your child's innocence is available from now on. You now have your own built-in guardian accessible to you, whenever you need it, wherever you go. And it's you. From your "adult" place, consider that you now have a glorious opportunity to be the guardian angel of your own pure nature.

Imagine what you'd do to keep an innocent child safe. You'd likely expend every ounce of courage to protect an infant, especially your own. This is what I'm suggesting you do here. The strength of who you are now as an adult coupled with the greater awareness that you can protect and nurture your goodness allows you to walk hand in hand with your inner little kid towards the greater realization of your joy and abundance.

That's all kids want when they're young and innocent: loving and joy, and to feel safe expressing it. Your connection to that joy and innocence inside of you can transform into a tremendous source of strength and empowerment, propelling you to move forward towards success. And so I now give to you the gift that was given to me. Please take it to heart:

Good things happen to good people, and YOU are a good person.

CHAPTER FIFTEEN

GRATITUDE: THE ULTIMATE ANTIDOTE

I so appreciate the spirit of the Thanksgiving holiday and how it impacts me and those around me so profoundly. Yes, I tend to eat too much, and that certainly impacts my weight. But that's not the impact to which I'm referring. Thanksgiving gives us the opportunity to consider our blessings. And as we shift our focus to all of the goodness—our families, our health, our abilities and so much more—we fill our consciousness with the spirit of gratitude.

Gratitude reframes our perspective on the priorities in our lives and provides greater appreciation for all that is good and loving. We become softer, more forgiving and more generous. When I experience the feeling of gratitude, my mindset and consciousness are more centered, loving and open than at any other time.

Why wouldn't I choose to live in this reality every day of my life? Remember the concept that we create, promote or allow our current reality? Here's a prime example of how I've allowed myself to wander off-course, away from a choice that makes me happier and more joyful in favor of the distractions that occur every day.

Recently, when Thanksgiving was transitioning to Christmas, I got very depressed. Feelings of dread and obligation arose as I considered what I needed to buy and do as part of the Christmas holiday, and replaced the high that I experienced through the gratitude of Thanksgiving. My discomfort was not because I had to buy presents and deal with all the materialism that can come with Christmas. It was because I had lost the feelings of goodness and purity associated with gratitude. I eventually realized that I was the one choosing to shift my focus away from gratitude and towards a sense of responsibility and pressure. Now, I love giving gifts and celebrating this holiday season. But I realized that what actually puts me in touch with the spirit of Christmas and makes me feel so joyful and abundant is gratitude.

That I have control of my thoughts is a liberating idea. And you have control of your thoughts, too. When we claim that authority, we restore our ability to better create and promote our experience and thus our reality. Breathe that in for a moment and consider the possibilities available to you as you consciously choose more of the experiences you want in your life. This is how we move away from sabotage and deflection and toward opportunity and success.

The power of choice supports us in managing the negative constraints that tend to invade our minds and send us into lethargy or depression. Personally, I've got what I call my "Big Three" distractors. In no particular order they are: Lack Consciousness, Comparison to Others, and Attachment to Outcomes. Let's have some fun loosening the oppressive clamps of Lack, Comparison and Attachment so that you can more freely move toward the receptivity of your success and value. These saboteurs are far less powerful than we imagine them to be.

Overcoming Lack

Lack. Just saying the word makes my head droop a little in defeat. I used to spend a great deal of time living in the consciousness of Lack. Nothing was ever good enough and whatever I'd accomplished could and should have been better. I was so busy looking at where I thought I was supposed to be that I lost sight of the goodness that I'd already created in my life. This consistently depleted me of my energy and happiness. Wins were momentary expressions of joy and losses were all-consuming, marked by stretches of self-deprecation and mental flagellation.

I think it's safe to assume that we've all experienced the grip of Lack. Lack makes us feel less-than, in need, in want, or even in desperation. These negative feelings can consume our minds and darken our current reality. Lack can send us into depression and propel us to do things that we later regret.

But is lack a reality or is it a perception? If our sense of lack were a reality, it would get us thrown out of our apartment if we were in its grip when the rent came due. But that's not what happens. We can feel lack even if we have the money to pay the rent.

In other words, feeling lack merely indicates your *perception* of the reality that you're currently experiencing. That doesn't mean when you're locked in the vise grip of lack that it doesn't feel real—knots in the stomach and chest tightness are real enough. But they are the result of feelings based on how we choose to interpret our situation. Here's the good news: If we can alter our perception, then we can alter our experience of reality.

We've been looking at awareness from the point of view that where we focus our mind either boosts or depletes our energy and influences our choice of direction in which to move. Success takes place through action and movement. The more positive thoughts we have about our success, the clearer our direction and the more energy we have to move toward it.

Considering we're in the business of choice and awareness, let's explore making a new choice in the face of lack. The choice of gratitude. Imagine looking at your current situation from that vantage point. From gratitude, we can assess any reality and give thanks that we are who we are. Be it the reality of your good health, the roof over your head, loving family and friends, your current job, or the car you drive, you can choose to be thankful for what you do have just as easily as you can look over the proverbial fence and consider what you don't have. Therein lies the power of choice. When you choose to make gratitude your focus, you directly affect your mind, your consciousness and your attitude toward what comes next. You instantly transform your reality.

It's been suggested that we don't often change until we become sick and tired of being tired and sick. About 10 years ago, I received a poignant reference point for the power of gratitude and how it can instantly replace Lack consciousness. I was heading into a 10:30am meeting, completely consumed by feelings of lack. Earlier that morning, I'd heard that a deal that I was really counting on had just blown up. Months of hard work were now a big zero. Being a sole provider with two kids and a wife, I immediately felt worried and scared, because the money from that deal was going to pay for my expenses for the month. And beyond the loss of income, the deal falling through made me really feel like a loser. The last thing I wanted to do was head into a meeting and present myself as chipper and confident.

Trying hard to steel my nerves before walking in the room, I noticed that my sixteen-year-old daughter Annie was calling me. I almost didn't take the cell call, but because it was her, I thought maybe there was an issue that needed my attention.

"Hi Annie," I said. "Everything okay?"

"Yes, Dad," she replied, her tone of voice soft and sweet. "I just wanted to tell you that I love you and I'm sorry you had a bad morning." She'd overheard me receiving the bad news, so she just wanted to call me to share her loving.

This expression of love from my daughter so touched my heart that I couldn't help but be lifted. I immediately felt so grateful that I had a daughter who would take the time to call simply to say that she loved me. In that moment, my lack dissolved. Suddenly, I was filled with the spirit of gratitude, and with it a feeling of great wealth. Gone were the money concerns and the worry about how I would make it all work. In that moment, I was clear that my life was working and would continue to work, no matter the immediate circumstance. In the course of three minutes, my whole world changed. I made a new choice to be grateful for my life.

"When I'm residing in the mindset of my gratitude, lack cannot exist, because these two mindsets cannot occupy the same place at the same time."

I walked into the 10:30am meeting fresh, restored and filled with gratitude.

Later, reflecting back on what happened, I had a profound realization: When I'm residing in the mindset of my gratitude, lack cannot exist, because these two mindsets cannot occupy the same place at the same time. Expanding on this, consider that gratitude is light and lack is darkness—polar opposites. When there's only darkness, we have no awareness of how deep the void is or where it ends.

However, as soon as I add light to the environment, I start to see my surroundings and gain greater perspective. The more light I bring into the space, the more the darkness is diminished. Gratitude is the light that mitigates the darkness of lack by dissolving it.

So check this out: The next time you feel any form of lack, bring to mind something that you're grateful for.

The first key is to become aware of when you're in a state of lack. So often, we don't even realize we're in our lack mode. This is why it's really important to be very aware of how you're thinking and feeling. Going back to the four levels of awareness, from Acute to Squirrel, the more aware you are of how you're doing in any moment, the more you can bring yourself into alignment towards how you want to be. This is a very abundant reality and will serve you well as you pursue your success.

Overcoming Comparison

Next, we'll tackle the dynamic of comparison to others. Firstly, let's get clear: It's both debilitating and senseless to compare yourself to anyone when you're trying to focus on your path towards success. As a competitive person, I have a doctorate degree in comparing my worth and abilities to those of other people. And nothing pulls me off-course farther or more effectively. Perhaps it's because I didn't start with much material wealth in my life, and was exposed to those who had it.

Growing up in Westhampton Beach, a very popular summer and weekend destination for wealthy New Yorkers, I was surrounded by people who had tons of material resources. When they'd come out from the city, the cars they drove and the parts of town they lived in served as the evidence of their wealth. My artistic parents, cultured yet without money, had very wealthy friends whose kids became my friends. Here the dichotomy between "have" and "have-not" was most apparent. I'd visit their enormous homes and I'd see the best of everything. Then I'd return home and see what we didn't have. While my mother did her very best to make sure my sister and I had what we needed, there was no way she could have raised our experience of material wealth up to what we'd enjoy at the homes of our wealthy friends.

The story that I made up and told myself was that I wasn't as good as my friends because I didn't have the kind of "stuff" that they did. This caused me to start comparing myself to everyone. In my story, everyone outside of me was perfect. If they had money and means, their life must be happy and content. With every personal setback, all I had to do was think about the apparent purity of the life of one of my wealthy friends, and I'd sink further into depression.

So I started honing my internal fortitude and eagerness to prove I was worthy to claim a seat at "the table of wealth." I watched the way my role models presented themselves with an air of ease and tried to copy them, all the while comparing myself to them. Losing my parents when I did only intensified my determination to fit in. As I mentioned before, my mechanism to deal with my pain became, "I'm fine; don't worry about me." My desire to fit in drove all of my actions and I used the false metric of comparison to gauge my success, both inwardly and outwardly.

Because I'm such an expert in the field of comparison, I can share how much focusing on my gratitude has saved me from comparison's dark trenches. My ability to shift my focus towards gratitude and away from comparison started with remembering to be grateful for all I've created, regardless of what it looks like in relation to other people or environments.

When I began to understand that my path was my path, it started to shake the grip that I'd allowed my comparing mind to have over me. Take my company, Partners Trust, as an example. To an outside observer, Partners Trust was a tremendous and profitable company doing outstanding work. We ranked as a top independent firm in Los Angeles and were a household name in the communities we served. But when I went into my comparison mindset, I didn't acknowledge any of that. When comparing us to other firms, I only focused on the companies that I thought were "beating" us. Gone was any personal satisfaction about the good we were doing. I was too busy focusing on what we had to do to outperform that other company on a playing field, instead of focusing where we were actually performing beautifully.

When I focus in this reality, I'm miserable. I'm blinded by my competitive mindset, and there's no way to relieve the pressure I feel. I'm always looking over my shoulder, concerned that we'll lose more ground to the competition and our company will end up in ruin.

I trust any competitive person can relate to this kind of "mind spinning out of control" phenomenon. The ultimate pain of this self-comparison fantasy is that there's no way out. When I'm in this place, I can never win because I can't control the circumstances or the future. That competitive company may one day fall by the wayside, but another company will take its place, and if I choose to focus on comparison, then I'll remain forever mired in this competitive goo. Cue Gratitude. I have someone in my life who I love deeply and she loves me: my wife Laura. Laura is one of those beautiful people who can look at me in the eyes and shower me with love. The combination of her tone of voice, her touch and her gaze has the ability to stop me in my tracks and transport me to my loving where I truly want to be. We've been together for over four years now and during that period of time she's witnessed me being consumed by my competitive fire to the point where I literally burnt out in exhaustion.

Laura has been one of those external catalysts for shifting my viewpoint; to recognize from a place of gratitude the good work that Partners Trust and I did for our community. From that place, I soften. I gain greater clarity and remember that just as my path is uniquely my path, our company, too, had its own unique trail in the marketplace for as long as it existed. Our only "job" is to focus on what we are doing in alignment with our vision of success.

When it comes to seeking validation of your worth or success, my sincere encouragement to you is to shift your focus from outside parameters inward, acknowledging gratitude for your current reality. I also suggest you consider rewriting any story you might use to compare yourself to others or to fuel your desire to "beat" them. Instead of going into comparison, use your competition as a reference point. Evaluate what they are doing as valuable information you can learn from and use for improving your performance. You can choose to feel thankful they're showing you something you can incorporate for your benefit.

> **"Our only 'job' is to focus on what we are doing in alignment with our vision of success."**

Know this: the more you claim your value, the less time—and inclination—you'll have to compare yourself to anyone else. When it comes right down to it, your only competition is you. Do you allow yourself to be intimidated by others or do you focus on your strengths and deliver them to the best of your ability? When you feel yourself starting to fall into the trap of comparison, practice focusing solely on your abilities and intentions and on letting go of concern about the competition.

The only way you can be intimidated is if you allow yourself to move into comparison. When it comes to this mindset, focus on gratitude for what got you into the game, whatever it is, and stay rooted in that gratitude. Gratitude transports you back into acute awareness and accelerates your journey to achieve successful outcomes.

Overcoming Attachment

Finally, let's look at how gratitude can cure us from attachment to outcomes, especially those relating to negotiation. Attachment to an outcome means that you don't yet have the outcome you want, but you have a story of what it would be like if you did have it.

We've got to start by piercing the illusion of that story. We fall in love with illusions in the first place because our imaginations make them so seductive. Any time you feel yourself in the grip of such a seduction, that's your signal to cue Bob Newhart: "Stop it!"

The only way to realize an outcome is by taking the steps necessary to achieve it. Attaching yourself to a thing or person that doesn't exist outside of your fantasy is a distraction from your focus in the moment—and the present moment is the only place from which you can affect the outcome. This is one of the trickiest Catch-22's ever. My best results *always* occur when I am fully present, perceiving the nuances of a meeting. This puts my chattering mind to rest, and I can participate fully towards the *intended* outcome that I want.

Let's break down the difference between having an intended outcome and being attached to an outcome. Any time we endeavor to do something, there is an intended outcome that we want to realize. Having an intention toward that outcome gives us clarity and shows us how to move toward it. However, being attached to that outcome clouds our clarity, often brings in fear of failure, and inhibits our best performance.

So how is gratitude an elixir and support when dealing with attachment to outcomes? By now, you understand the idea that focusing away from the moment at hand will usually undermine your effectiveness in that moment. Knowing this, what if you simply "suspend" the outcomes and fantasies? You can still enjoy swimming in the warm pool of your dreams and ambitions and basking in the glow of your success. But in those moments when you can actually effect the change that will better create the realization of these fantasies, you put the fantasies on pause and bring yourself present. How can you do that? By moving into gratitude. When you do, the distractions of fear and "what if I don't get..." dissolve. Once free of distractions, what remains is right in front of you: your intended result and a clearer view of the path to get to it.

I get clear by asking myself, "Nick, what are you grateful for right now?" My intention is to connect to the incredible results that are already present in my life, and gratitude reminds me of all of those positive outcomes I've already created. I may not have everything I want in my life, but when I consider that I have what I need in the moment, I tap into my natural state of relaxation and abundance. As you ask that same question of yourself, perhaps it's your faith that comes to mind, your friends and family, a pet, or the fact that you've eaten a meal today when so many others don't have that luxury.

Whatever it is that sparks your Gratitude, cultivate it. Nurture it. Embrace the grace that exists in your life and let that wash over you. When you build a habit of doing this, you position yourself beautifully to enter whatever the environment is and perform better towards the outcomes you want.

To assist you in exploring the power of Gratitude and its ability to support you in creating and promoting the outcomes you'd like to realize, here's an exercise that I developed and have facilitated in my company for an educational course series. It takes only five minutes.

People have shared with me that this exercise has had a profound effect on their minds, their hearts and their results. We start each session of our 8-week series by playing a 5-minute audio message I created specifically for that series. I invite you to download the recording and see how you feel after you've listened to it: **onyourterms.net**.

Most people find it easiest to combine this step with their daily practice of journaling about their goodness, going through the entire process either first thing in the morning or last thing at night. For maximum impact, you can do it at both times. The point is, it's not so important *when* you do it as long as you do it.

You'll discover that the more time and energy you invest in working with this exercise, the more quickly you'll experience positive shifts toward coming more present and neutral and aligning with your success.

Is your success worth this investment of energy and time? Referring back to the Momentum Zone, remember that the steadiness of your upward trajectory toward your dream is up to you. And consider that the only way not to succeed is by ceasing to move forward. Towards your success!

CHAPTER SIXTEEN

DISCOVERING YOUR "WHY"

Let me just start by saying the journey of creating and building Partners Trust wasn't always a piece of cake. The challenges we faced came from conceivable and inconceivable directions. Besides the $4,000,000 lawsuit and the fears it unearthed, as well as other legal challenges, and beyond the financial risks of launching a new business, I suffered through negative opinions of others that challenged my faith in myself. I witnessed how the seduction of money can fracture years of goodwill and loyalty in a matter of moments. I questioned my strategic choices at times, having relied on others to guide me based on their expertise, only to find them to be not-so-expert. I worked through internal company conflicts that stretched my tolerance to the limit and caused me great pain on a number of occasions.

My saving grace throughout all of these challenges was my bigger "Why"—and I do mean "Why" with a capital "W." When I started Partners Trust, I knew that if I wanted to turn a vision of such magnitude into reality, I had to connect with a higher purpose than making money or having the title of company President. For me, saying yes to my dream meant saying yes to sharing my best self, both personally and professionally. And it meant saying yes to creating an environment that nurtured and fostered a commitment to professionalism and service on a daily basis.

Through all of the discomforts, doubts and challenges, the defining key that sustained me and kept me moving forward was my connection to why I started that whole thing in the first place. No matter how hard or frustrating it became in any given moment, when I had the wit and wisdom to remember why I started Partners Trust, I was able to regroup and restore my faith in what we were doing and how we did it. I truly believe that without that connection, we wouldn't have sustained our company to become attractive enough for acquisition.

In order to build a solid trajectory for your success, it's imperative to begin by exploring your personal "Why" that connects you to what you want to achieve in your life. Similar to my challenges with Partners Trust, you can count on obstacles impeding your own ride toward success, designed to test your commitment and connection to your goals. Going for what you want takes great resilience— physically, emotionally and mentally. Empowering your "why" is essential to overcoming challenges and achieving success.

Simon Sinek illustrates the concept of "Why?" eloquently in his TED talk, "How Great Leaders Inspire Action," which is available to watch on YouTube. Sinek examines the way that most of us approach our lives from the perspective of asking "What?" and "How?"—that is, what we want to do and how we can accomplish that goal. However, he turns that paradigm on its ear, inviting us to instead look at our lives from a "Why?" point of view.

Think back to your first waking moments this morning. As you considered the day ahead, from what perspective did you see it? Most of us automatically go straight to the question of "What?"—"What's on my schedule? What do I have to do today?" But instead, how about making your first question, "*Why* am I going to do what I do today?" Or try this one on for size: "Is what I'm doing in alignment with my greater 'Why?' for living my life?"

A life of meaning and purpose is available to you. But it can only take shape if you first spend some time considering what's most important to you and *why*. And I mean truly, authentically important to you—beyond the opinions of others, the past, and the preconceived notions. That's the ultimate driver. You can choose a life of success on every level. Doesn't that sound like a life worth living?

For me, my "Why?" centers on sharing my joy and my loving in service to myself and everyone around me. Money is a fantastic thing and I love the freedom it provides. But whether I have money or not, nothing can stand between me and my expression of loving and joy unless I allow it. And when I'm living and expressing my "Why?" I've discovered that loving and joy are returned to me.

There's a great saying I love to share with those walking the path of their chosen success: "If it were easy, everyone would do it." These words offer me solace in the face of challenge; they remind me that I'm going for the greater qualities that I want to experience in my life. They're also a reminder that not everyone chooses to strive for the greater good that's available to them, and that spurs my competitive spirit to stay my course.

At the same time, don't assume that your path to your dreams has to be "hard." Going back to the beginning of the book, how you define something becomes its reality. Whether it's "success" or "money" or "peace on earth," these are all simply words on a page. You bring your own meaning to all of it. I am suggesting that by connecting to "why" you do what you do, you will discover great support and the fortitude to stay on course towards the end you desire.

This is where we're heading together in the chapters to come. Everything you do, everywhere that you go, you'll have the opportunity to be aware by asking yourself this all-important question: "Why am I doing what I'm about to do?" or "Is what I'm about to do aligned with my personal 'Why?'" The more you're in alignment with that, the more easily you can fire up the machine that is you, knowing that you're stepping into situations and environments that are leading you to your success. The clearer we are about "why" we do what we do, the easier it is to align with it and to discover "how" to do it and identify the actions we take to make it happen.

> "Everything you do, everywhere that you go, you'll have the opportunity to be aware by asking yourself this all-important question: 'Why am I doing what I'm about to do?' or 'Is what I'm about to do aligned with my personal 'Why?'"

CHAPTER SEVENTEEN

UNLEASHING YOUR INTELLIGENCE

At this point, you might be thinking, *How in the world do I figure out what my "Why" is*? The technique we're about to explore will help you discover the "Why" of your success as well as "how" you can realize it. There's great power of awareness available to you here. I encourage you to play with this and see what shows up for you.

Introducing Mind Mapping

Mind Mapping is a powerful tool that shows us both *what* we want to achieve and *how* we can achieve it. It's a process that taps into our inherent intelligence and allows our mind to partner with the wisdom of our instincts. As we mind map, we move from the conceptual all the way down into concrete next steps, bypassing the plague of Paralysis-by-Analysis. It is also the single most powerful tool that I've ever experienced toward creating the outcomes that I want. As a reference point, Partners Trust was entirely created and executed using Mind Maps. Just ask my partners.

> **"Mind Mapping is a powerful tool that shows us both *what* we want to achieve and *how* we can achieve it."**

More clinically presented, a mind map is simply a

visual representation of ideas that occur to you related to a central topic or theme. It was popularized by Tony Buzan as a tool for brainstorming or idea generation. For more details about the method (how to do it, how to use it and the research proving its efficacy), take a look at Tony's website: **www.tonybuzan.com**

Most people find the process user-friendly and simple to do. You take a topic or idea that you want to explore and write the name of that topic in the center of a blank piece of paper. Then as thoughts about that topic occur to you, draw lines radiating from the central idea, adding to each line the words or images that represent your thoughts and concepts related to that topic. Each sub-topic may, in turn, have its own set of branches with thoughts and ideas related to it, and this process can continue as far as you'd like to take it.

Let's walk through the process using an example. Say that tomorrow morning I'm taking my weekly trip to the grocery store, and I need to decide what to buy. What are all of the things I might need to think about in order to draft my grocery list?

First, I remember that I have a couple of lunch and dinner engagements this week, so those are some meals I won't have to prepare at home. Then I look at my calendar and see that I invited our friends, Kailani and Keith over for dinner on Friday night. I'll want to make sure that I have food for them, and I think Keith is a pescatarian, so I'll need to pick up some salmon to grill. I remember that last week I ended up tossing out a few things from the refrigerator. This gets me thinking about what I'm actually eating most often these days. Lately my staples are avocados, eggs, protein bars and grapefruit. And then I think about what's fresh right now. We're in the middle of summer, so peaches and nectarines and corn are all in season. That reminds me that I probably want to check out a couple of recipes for the week ahead so that I can make sure I get any other ingredients I'll need. I'll check a couple of websites for ideas.

So there you have it. I literally just write down whatever pops into my mind that seems relevant to the topic at hand. This technique mirrors the associational way that our brains tend to process information. Notice that I was never thinking about a structure or order for my thoughts. It's only *after* we allow ourselves to generate and write down our ideas that we then start considering how to organize and prioritize what we've come up with.

I clocked this, and that whole process took about three minutes. Is there more to add to my map? Sure. But what did I do in those three minutes? I captured plenty of information, and I can now pull back from it and start to assess my next action steps. This activity gets me well on the way to creating a fairly solid game plan for a successful trip to the grocery store.

Beyond the obvious benefit of moving us into action, mind maps offer an even bigger payoff that I've discovered. In my experience, this tool aligns my awareness with all of the things that show up on my map so I start training my brain and intelligence to focus on and create those things.

Here, then, are some mind mapping guidelines:
• The process generally takes no more than 3-5 minutes.
• The only supplies needed are a timer, a piece of paper and a pen.
• The goal is to capture any thoughts that "pop" into your mind concerning

your topic—what it means to you, what's needed to fulfill it, people to talk to, its qualities...really, it could be anything you find relevant.

• Your objective is to write down as many ideas as you can think of. There's no editing and no judgment allowed. That means no evaluation at all about what you're writing; there's simply writing.

That last "no editing" guideline is critical to the process. Because you're going to be accessing information from both your conscious and subconscious mind, you don't want to filter or judge any of your ideas. Consider that your internal wellspring of ideas may actually be smarter than the part of you that edits your thoughts or thinks things like, "That's a stupid idea."

Also note that there's nothing high-tech here. Want to use a white board or a digital tool that you like? Great. Just write the word or phrase representing your topic in the center of your page, circle it, start your timer and begin writing. It's that simple. The more you practice this, the more you'll access the intelligence inside of you that creates pure magic. Let's start putting this concept on its feet. Now that you've seen this in action, it's your turn to take a crack at it.

CHAPTER EIGHTEEN

DEFINING YOUR SUCCESS

Let's now give you a shot at mind mapping on your own. This technique is absolutely critical to your journey to success, and it forms the foundation of pretty much everything that we'll do in the pages that follow. You'll want to allow 25–30 minutes to complete the exercise in this chapter. If you're not able to do that right now, block out 30 minutes on your calendar as soon as possible so you can come back and do it.

Our goal is to better define what success looks like for you by exploring eight different aspects of your life that give you a holistic picture of your success. In the first diagram, you'll see eight areas I've chosen to include in this exploration of Success, which work well for me. If there's another category that you'd like to include or if you want to delete a focus or two, go right ahead. Whatever categories you choose, as a whole, we'll refer to all eight areas as your "Balance of Success." As you review the categories, consider them equally at first. They all have value as part of your success experience.

There's a lot of cultural conversation these day about how we can bring more balance into our lives. In the United States, we tend to focus on work and family.

DEFINING SUCCESS FOR YOU

Looking at each of these aspects of your life, how would
you define what success would look and feel like
if you could have it any way you wanted?

Self-care and play often get pushed aside with the justification that we don't have time
for such pursuits. I'm going to suggest taking a "what-if?" approach to your success.
What if we could create the time to honor all aspects of our lives in greater harmony?

As you look over the first diagram, imagine that you could participate more fully
in each of the eight aspects, and think about how your experience of success could
expand. We're going for success as YOU define it.

Imagine what your life would look like if you were honoring these eight aspects
of your success. And by honoring them, I mean engaging with each of them on a
day-to-day basis. What if you could acknowledge in your journal at the end of the
day, "Today I touched and experienced success in eight different aspects of my life?"
Think about how wealth and fulfillment will naturally come forward as a result.
That's the opportunity here.

The purpose of the following process is to engage in a free-form capture of
thoughts that come up related to your personal definition of Success. Each aspect of

DEFINING SUCCESS FOR YOU

Success defined around . . .

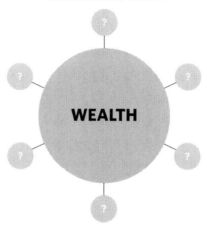

your Balance of Success will reside in the center of its own page as your main topic, and around it you'll write down all of your ideas.

Take a minute right now to get your supplies: eight pieces of paper and a pen (or, if you prefer, a digital device or whiteboard and markers). Don't forget that your journal can be a great place to capture what comes present. If you have a timer or alarm handy, set it for three minutes. We'll be spending that amount of time on each area, totaling about 24 minutes.

Starting with **Wealth**, take a piece of paper, write the word WEALTH in the center and circle it. You are about to have the opportunity to explore what the dynamics of Wealth would and could be for you. No need to pre-think this or have any idea of what you're going to write down; in fact, it's better if you don't come in with pre-conceived ideas. The process itself is going to bring you an enhanced awareness of *your* definition of "wealth."

A few considerations: Remember to avoid editing or judging whatever you write. For now, we're just exploring all possibilities. You can focus on what you want to achieve in this area of your life. And you can also include how you want to feel or what your inner experience would be like if this aspect of your world operated optimally. Again, all you're doing is capturing ideas. What you write down doesn't even have to be true or make sense.

DEFINING SUCCESS FOR YOU

Success defined around . . .

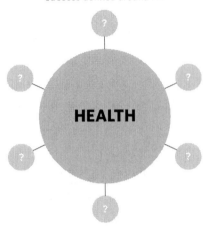

While you're doing this, your mind may get stuck. If that happens, I suggest you close your eyes and ask yourself, "What else is there for me here?" Relax into it and trust—the answers will come. You might even imagine a role model or someone you respect, and consider what wealth looks like through their eyes or how they might experience it. Play the "what if?" game and ask yourself what new possibilities might be available to you in this area of your life. You can write down whatever you want, with the understanding that before we can create something, we need to define it.

Before you dive in, take a moment right now for you. Enjoy an easy, full breath and gently let it go. Experience the sensations in your body right now—feel yourself sitting in your chair, or if you're standing, feel your feet on the ground. We're stepping into the field of play and imagination, so invite your inner kid to dream with you for a few minutes. This can actually be fun! When you're ready, start your timer and begin writing down whatever comes forward in response to this question:

"If I could have it any way I wanted, how would I experience greater Wealth in my life?" Write about what you'd be doing and how you'd be feeling about your wealth.

Once you're complete, take a look at what you've written. Really take it in. Now close your eyes for a moment and get in touch with the feeling of what it would be like to achieve this personal definition of success in the area of your wealth. Breathe

DEFINING SUCCESS FOR YOU

Success defined around . . .

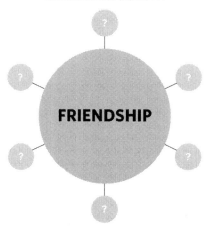

that in for a moment. When you're ready to move on, step off your yacht and come back to this page.

Now set that mind map aside for a minute while we look at another aspect of your success: **Health**. Take out a fresh piece of paper, write Health in the center and circle the word. Now take three minutes to explore what Health looks like for you in your life, the same way you explored Wealth.

This can go beyond the purely physical aspects of your health to address the mental and emotional aspects as well. If you get stuck at any moment, consider what your personal definition of well-being or vibrancy looks and feels like. Does it mean flexibility? Does diet come into the equation? How are you taking care of yourself on an on-going basis? Is regular exercise a component of your Health? Does it mean setting up an appointment with a physician? What would you be doing, what would you have, and how would you be feeling?

Once you're done, take a moment to reflect on how you've just defined greater health. What does that feel like inside? What is the quality of your breathing as you consider this possibility? What's your heart rate like? Realize that you are already creating this reality, simply by directing your mind toward your upliftment.

Friendship is next. New page, new word. Circle it. Set the timer for three

DEFINING SUCCESS FOR YOU

Success defined around . . .

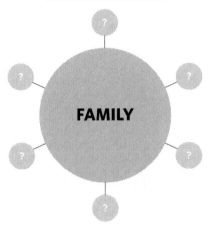

minutes. What does friendship mean to you? We spend a lot of time in social connection in our lives. Are you excited about how you're spending that time, or does it feel like obligation? What are the qualities and the caliber of friendship that you want in your life? If you could have friendships that look any way you'd like, how would you create them? And what would you love to do with your friends? Spend the next three minutes fleshing this out. If you get stuck, consider whether or not you have any friends whom you haven't spoken to lately and would like to reconnect with. Or, conversely, think about any people in your life who make you wonder, "Why am I friends with this person?" Is there some pruning you may want to do? Time to explore.

Once you're done, take a moment to consider what you've just written down. Imagine this taking place in your life. You're defining your ideal reality in this exercise, so take a moment to experience it.

Now let's look at **Family**. You know the setup drill. What's the relationship you'd like with your family? Have you noticed that families can have a tendency to pull us in directions that may not be our personal authentic direction? Now's your time to create this any way you want it. What does your ideal family dynamic look like? What kind of experiences would you like to have with your loved ones on a more

DEFINING SUCCESS FOR YOU

Success defined around . . .

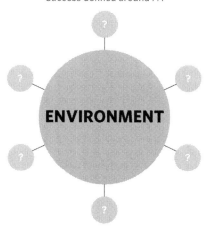

regular basis? How would you like to feel in their presence? Maybe you're at the point in your life where you'd like to create a family or expand your family. What would that look like?

If you get stuck, consider what qualities you'd like to have in your family. Ask yourself if there are friends you consider as family and what those relationships might bloom into in the future? Animals can be family, too; if that's relevant to you, ask yourself what you'd like your life with your fluffy friends to look like. Spend the next three minutes fleshing this out.

Now breathe in that feeling of realizing this ideal definition of success for your family. Let yourself experience fulfillment in this area of your life.

Next, let's consider your **Environment**. With this aspect, I'm referring to your home, your office, your car—anywhere you spend your time. How can you define your success in and around your environment? This doesn't need to involve a widespread overhaul. Perhaps there's some fine-tuning to do? Are you getting what you need in your workplace? What will assist you in creating the environment that supports you best? This question can tend to result in long to-do lists of improvement projects, but I invite you to also consider how you want to feel when you're in your home, office or transportation environment. This can be about inner

DEFINING SUCCESS FOR YOU

Success defined around . . .

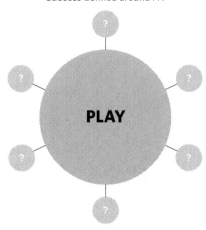

qualities as much as outer embellishments.

Again, don't edit; just write. If you get stuck, ask yourself again, "What else?" and take a breath. Consider whether there are things you can change in your current environment to make it more uplifting. Perhaps there are some things that need to be cleaned out of your basement or your garage that would make those spaces feel fresh. Maybe there's a room you've wanted to paint, or a piece of furniture that's been broken that you'd like to get fixed.

Once you're complete, breathe in the awareness that you're creating an environment that supports you and is a part of your definition of success. Enjoy that feeling.

How are you doing so far? Do you feel a sense of possibility? Are you recognizing that there are wonderful ingredients in your life that you've already created that you can use as building blocks for your next level of success?

Now let's look at **Play**. This might also be called Recreation or Re-Creation. Does this re-frame your sense of the value it could have for you? How often does play get sacrificed for all of the other "stuff" that we feel we have to do? What if this area of your life was thriving? How much tennis or golf would you be playing? How often would you be taking out your boat or drawing in your sketchbook? If you get stuck,

DEFINING SUCCESS FOR YOU

Success defined around . . .

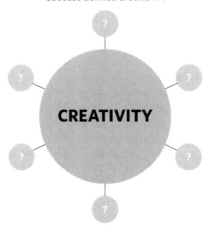

imagine yourself as a little kid, saying "I want to play." What would that look and feel like if Little You were getting the playtime that he or she wants? What brings a smile to your face? What feels like a reward and a pleasure to do? How do your friends and family get incorporated into that? How does your wealth support this aspect of your life? Spend three minutes exploring this right now.

Once you've finished, take a few moments to savor the playful aspects of you. Imagine yourself at age five and invite that child in to participate in your success.

Now let's explore your **Creativity**. How are you expressing your creativity? How could you do that more in your life? And what do you want to feel like when you're engaged in your creative pursuits? To what degree do you express your creativity through your work or any of the other aspects of your success? Your creativity may show up through how you market your business or how you problem-solve. And then there's also your artistic expression. If you get stuck, ask yourself what most inspires you. Is there an instrument you'd love to play? Have you had fantasies of writing poetry? Is there a dish you've always wanted to learn how to prepare? Is there a part of you that's always wanted to do something, but just didn't feel like there was time? What would it look like to put that into motion?

DEFINING SUCCESS FOR YOU

Success defined around . . .

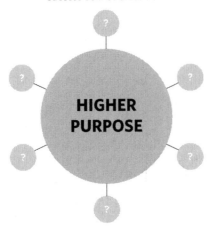

Once you're done, breathe in this enhanced awareness of your creativity and inspiration.

Let's look at the final area: **Higher Purpose**. What does Higher Purpose mean to you? Is it being of service in some way? Is it a dedication to a spiritual practice? Is it raising your children? Or perhaps it's the ways that you nurture and honor yourself on an ongoing basis.

What do you do when you need access to perspective and wisdom, and how could you be doing more of that? If you get stuck, imagine what it would look and feel like if you were expressing your higher purpose. Perhaps it means enhancing your connection with your source—whatever that means to you. There are no right or wrong answers here. Take a few minutes to be aware of that and define it.

Once you've finished, take a moment to breathe in the quality of connection with your Higher Purpose.

Now take a look at what you've written for all eight areas. There's magic on those pages in front of you. Magic that you created by taking the time to consider the possibilities for your life. Consider how each aspect of your success has the potential to complement the others, forming a foundation to build upon. What if you achieved all of these things? How would that make you feel? Once I started realizing that I could take my "possibilities" and make them "realities," I got really excited. Is "excitement" part of your equation right now? I hope so.

In the journey ahead, you're going to have the opportunity to further explore each of these eight aspects—to build upon and realize them. You're going to create an architecture to support achieving what you want. We'll bring in resource vehicles for this vision of success, designed to address the quality of your experience as well as the results. We're going to define timelines for when and how you achieve your levels of success. And beyond that, we're going to look at your schedule and determine the daily and weekly steps you'll take to infuse all aspects of your success with energy and focus.

As you build new habits that support you in realizing these visions, each layer of your success can become much easier to achieve. Realize that you completed an exercise designed to assist you in defining what and how you'd like to experience eight key aspects of your life. Your clarity and awareness will help bridge the gap between where you are currently and where you want to go. Now it's time to mold these ideas into a greater, more vivid vision of success so that you can experience it.

CHAPTER NINETEEN

DEFINING YOUR "WHY"

Now that you have more information about your personal definition of success, let's get back to your "Why." In my experience, moving towards something takes support and encouragement. *Defining my "Why" in relation to realizing any goal has been the most powerful tool in fueling my success.*

Looking at all eight mind maps of your Balance of Success, you're now going to sort everything you wrote on them into two basic categories. The first category relates to feelings and emotions as you achieve your success; this will include anything that has an experiential component to it. The second category relates to the outcomes, results and actions you identified.

Starting with your Wealth mind map, do you notice certain elements of your writing have more of a "feeling" quality, while other items are more action-oriented? For example, "Freedom" may be a quality that you'd like to experience as a result of creating greater wealth, whereas a specific amount of money you'd like to achieve, such as "$50,000 in sales this quarter," is more tactile or action-oriented in nature. When you look at each of your maps from this perspective, it will quickly become apparent which phrases fall into each category.

Here are some examples of "feeling" words that would go in the first category: Joy, Freedom, Abundance, Loving, Appreciation, Humor, Trust, Respect, Calm, Focus, Inspiration. These are all feelings or experiential qualities that I've heard many times expressed by my associates as they work through this exercise.

Now review each mind map. Look for any nouns or adjectives that describe how you want to *feel* in each area of your success. Each time you identify one, write it down. You're creating a "quality scorecard" for yourself. If you run across a quality that shows up more than once on any of your maps, make a mark next to it on your list; no need to write it a second time. In doing so, you're acknowledging that this quality or feeling lives in multiple areas within your Balance of Success.

Take a few minutes right now to review all eight of your maps and capture the qualities that show up for you. You can either use your Journal for this exercise or you can write your list of qualities below:

QUALITIES

What are the qualities or feelings that consistently show up throughout the various aspects of your defined success? As a reference point, from my personal tally, "Joy" showed up four times on my mind maps, and so did "Loving." "Abundance" and "Caring" showed up three times. As you look at your list, are there any words that have similar meaning and thus invoke a similar feeling based on that word? For me, I had qualities such as "Supportive," "Safe" and "Nurturing" on my list. When I considered those three words, I found them all similar enough to me that they could be distilled into one word that best represents the resonance of all three. I narrowed them down to the quality of "Nurturing" as that word best honored the sentiment of all three ideas for me.

Your intention as you review your list of qualities is to distill it down into, ideally, three words that encapsulate the essence of how you'd like to experience your Balance of Success. Review your list one more time and consider the top words that you keep coming back to that best articulate and represent the feelings you want to experience as you move towards your success. Identify your top three words and write them down.

_____, _____ and

_____

Notice how you're feeling inside right now. There's a physiological and psychological recalibration that takes place inside of us when we open ourselves up to expanded possibilities and reimagine what's available to us in our lives. Consider that each of your three qualities has an energy, a power to ignite. And when you combine these qualities, their power becomes exponentially greater.

Let's now start to package your discovery so you can put it to work for you. We're going to use your qualities to create a statement of empowerment designed to keep you in alignment with your success. It's called your Statement of Purpose, and it goes like this:

"I am creating my success because I want to experience more

_____, _____, and _____

in all aspects of my life".

Insert your top three qualities from the list you've just made into the blank spaces. Congratulations! You've just created a tool that reinforces the quality of the experience you'd like to enjoy as part of your success and realigns you with your definition of success. This statement is powered by you and the qualities you personally want to experience. There's nothing preconceived here. This is you, authentically expressing and honoring yourself.

Remember the statement in Chapter 12, "Little things done consistently in excellence create a major impact?" In the spirit of this pithy wisdom, let's break down your Statement of Purpose so that you may better appreciate the power of the resource

> **"Consider that each of your three qualities has an energy, a power to ignite. And when you combine these qualities, their power becomes exponentially greater."**

you've just created.

"I am creating...": It's happening in the present. It's active, right now.

"...my success...": this language is, by design, personal. It's also authentic to you. You are claiming the success that you want to experience and your internal motivation to keep driving forward. Ultimately, no one motivates you better than you. Outside inspiration is eventually fleeting, but you always have direct control over how you motivate yourself from within.

"...because I want to experience more...": this directs you back to your "Why." It also allows you to consciously redirect your awareness in any given moment.

And then we have the three qualities. Each quality that you've chosen becomes activated and experienced as you consciously focus on it.

"...in all aspects of my life.": This reaffirms that it's inclusive, supporting all eight aspects of your Balance of Success.

Here are a some examples of Statements of Purpose:

"I am creating my success because I want to experience more Joy, Freedom and Abundance in all aspects of my life."

"I am creating my success because I want to experience more Power, Connection and Mastery in all aspects of my life."

Now read your Statement of Purpose to yourself, either out loud or silently. How do you feel as you do this? Do you feel more connected to those qualities you've selected? Do you realize that these are your organic qualities and not some "canned" words on a page? These qualities are aspects of your life that you'd like to experience more often.

Consider now, the ancillary power of your Statement of Purpose:

Each time you make your Statement, you tap into the qualities you want more of in your life, which means that you are experiencing those qualities more fully right now.

Because every thought that we think has a residual impact, each time you make your Statement, you're actively building a resource that can support you in staying on track during moments of self-doubt or self-sabotage.

Each time you make your Statement, you engage in self-encouragement. That's the fuel that moves you forward towards the success you desire.

Each time you make your Statement, you automatically become more aware and discerning of where and how you're spending your time and energy. It gives you the ability to gauge on a moment-to-moment basis whether you're moving closer to the success you desire or further away from it.

Most importantly, each time you make your Statement, you define "Why" you're doing the tasks of the day.

One of the great misconceptions we labor under is, "I don't have enough time to create the success that I really want." I challenge that. Most of us have time— probably not as much as we'd like, but we do have some measure of it. Often we've just been devoting it to things that don't support our goals. It's all about priorities. At some point, we wake up to this—some part of us recognizes, "I'm running out of time today, and I haven't put any effort toward what I really want." When this happens, we experience a sense of lack in relation to how we spend our time, which leads us to reinforce the idea that "there's not enough time." And from there it takes about twelve seconds for us to start believing that the goals we're aiming for ultimately aren't going to work out.

Understand that the clearer you are about your priorities in the eight aspects of your life, the more likely it is that you will start filling your time with the things that matter to you—the things that bring you closer to your success. When you have a healthy connection to your priorities and natural discernment, you're going to take charge of your time. And a person who takes charge of their time completes whatever they want to complete.

Connecting to "Why" you do anything in your life brings greater purpose and authority to how you lead your life. Remember back to when you were lying in bed in the morning and considering your day from the perspective of, "What am I doing today?" Now you have the perspective in relation to your greater success to ask the question from the "Why" point of view. "Why am I doing what is on my schedule today?" And now answer that question with, "I'm doing it because I am creating my success and want to experience greater (insert your three qualities) in all aspects of my life."

Let's look more specifically at how your Statement of Purpose may better support achieving your goals of success. Say that your primary goal over the course of the next three months is to lose 10 pounds. Every time you're presented with an opportunity to ingest calories, you can make your Statement of Purpose. For example, "I am creating my success because I want to experience more beauty, vitality and well-being in all aspects of my life." Does the cupcake in front of you support your goal or sabotage it? As you connect to your goal through your

Statement of Purpose, you'll be more conscious with your choice. Saying your statement gives you an opportunity to reflect prior to taking action. And that's a valuable moment in time.

Consider this Statement of Purpose that you've just created as if it were a newborn baby. What does a newborn need? It needs constant nurturing, loving, care and attention. Your Statement of Purpose now needs that same attention so that it may grow in your consciousness and awareness. The best way to nurture your Statement of Purpose is to say it, again and again. Remember that you designed it based on the Balance of Success you want to realize.

The stakes are high here. You have a glorious opportunity to start stepping into the greater empowerment of your life. I recommend to my associates that they say their Statement of Purpose to themselves at least 100 times per day, every day. I encourage them to use "trigger" reminders—everyday events that they already partake in, such as brushing their teeth, answering the phone, getting in the car, going to bed, arising in the morning—as signals to energize and integrate their Statement of Purpose.

Be creative. Have fun! Remember that each time you say your Statement of Purpose, you move along your trajectory of Momentum to bring you closer to realizing your dreams, your success. I'd say that's a worthwhile reason to engage and nurture your Statement of Purpose, that newborn consciousness that is poised to flourish inside of you.

PART III
PREPARING FOR YOUR SUCCESS

In this third section of the book, we're going to build upon the solid foundation of success you've created. We'll look at how you prepare yourself for the actions you'll take to realize your success. Be on the lookout for how your confidence grows as you engage with these tools. This is a powerful consciousness that will propel you forward in achieving your definition of success.

CHAPTER TWENTY

BRINGING YOUR "WHY" INTO FOCUS

Up to this point, we've been developing and energizing resources that will powerfully support you in creating your true success reality. Now it's time to get moving!

Pull out your mind maps and have another look at the eight areas of your Balance of Success. Which aspect do you want to focus on first? Which one seems ripe with opportunity for greater success, or has the most "juice" for you? Most of the folks I work with typically want to address Wealth or Health, but you may focus on whatever priority is most present with you.

Let's begin creating the road map to achieving your successful outcome for whichever aspect you've chosen. You used the "Feeling" ingredients of each aspect of success to create your Statement of Purpose. Now we turn our focus to the action items related to your success.

One key element you'll need in order to create your ultimate vision of success is clarity. Accordingly, your next tool is a simple five-category grid designed to help you define and refine your goals. Let's take a look at it on the following page.

ASPECT	DEFINED	CURRENT REALITY	GRATITUDE FOR MY CURRENT STATE	IMAGINING THE GOAL REALIZED

Let's break this down with an example from my world of real estate sales.

ASPECT:
Simply identify which of your eight areas you'd like to focus on first.
I've picked WEALTH as my sample aspect.

DEFINED (what & by when; date-specific)
In this section you'll review all of the items you wrote down on the mind map pertaining to the specific aspect you've chosen to work on. (In my example, the Wealth mind map). What most draws your attention out of everything you wrote down? Take a minute to articulate the result you desire and your timeline for creating it. For example:

I want to realize $100,000 in income within the next 6 months.

CURRENT REALITY:
This step is about painting a clear picture of where you are right now in relation to the result you just defined. Why is this important? We've got to know our starting point so that we can measure our progress.

At the moment, I don't have any active sales opportunities in my queue. To date, the most money I've ever made in one full year is $100,000, so to create that within a six-month time period is most assuredly outside of my current comfort zone. I'm going to need to apply myself in both mindset and strategy to achieve this goal.

(Suggestion: After you've completed this step, repeat your Statement of Purpose as a way of positively reinforcing where you're heading.)

GRATITUDE FOR MY CURRENT STATE:

Once we identify a dream or vision of our success, some of us might look at our current reality and feel discouraged about the gap between our vision and where we are. Discouragement and self-doubt drain our energy from creating what we want. Fortunately, there's an antidote: Gratitude.

Remember: when you focus on gratitude, lack cannot exist. The idea of this step is to align with your gratitude for wherever you are right now. This helps us avoid the trap of lack and mitigates the dampening effects of thoughts that focus on the "how" of our goal rather than on the intention of our goal. Be grateful for where you are and the opportunities afforded to you.

I'm thankful I have an opportunity to create this wealth in a profession that allows for it. I'm thankful for the resources that I have such as this book, my network of support, my intelligence, and my health that are all assisting me with making my goal a reality.

IMAGINING THE GOAL REALIZED: PRESENT TENSE

This step is designed to raise your energy and create the enthusiasm to engage and move forward. Write about achieving your goal as if it has already occurred and you're experiencing the results right now. Imagine that you're talking to a friend whom you haven't seen in a while, and she asks what's been happening in your world. Describe this as if it's already a reality in your life: "I did it! It's fantastic! I feel so good about myself."

Creating $100,000 in 6 months demonstrated to me that I can make infinitely more money thereafter. I feel empowered in my abilities, and my confidence level is skyrocketing. I feel a level of freedom that I've rarely experienced, and I'm really proud of myself for my hard work. I'm grateful for all the support I've received in creating this goal and for my courage to get there. And I'm enjoying the fruits of my labor—I paid off my car and I'm now in a position to save up to take a vacation.

Why does this step matter? Because it sets you up to accept the reality of your goal, and even more.

The second phase is to create a new and specific mind map about the goal you've just defined. This process is modified from David Allen's "Natural Planning Model" for our specific purposes. Here's where you'll uncover some of the steps needed to make your goal a reality, and your order of priority for taking action.

We'll continue with the same example so you can see the logic and flow. Later, you will do this exercise using your own mind maps for as many (or all) of the eight aspects. That's up to you. If you're unfamiliar with the world of real estate, you may not understand all the actions outlined here, but don't worry about it. The key is to understand how the process works. That's your focus.

Always begin with a leading question about what you want to create. A great way to start is to ask, "What are all the things I can think of that would help me realize this goal?" For this example, I would state my question as; "What action steps do I

need to take in order to make $100,000 in the next 6 months?"

Let's see what I came up with:

As I share with you about the various items on this mind map, I'll refer to them by their location on the page as if they're on the face of a clock. We'll start with "Economic Equation" at 3 o'clock on the mind map.

If I'm going to realize $100K in the next six months, then I want to know what I need to gross before taxes each month in order to achieve that objective. In real estate, we have something called a commission split between the broker and the agent. It's a percentage equation. I've factored in my commission split with my company, and I've determined that I need to sell just over $1 million in inventory each month. What I'm doing here is working my goal down into bite-sized, attainable pieces. I could break this down further into weekly goals if I wanted. These kind of metrics allow me to know if I'm on- or off-course in achieving my success.

Around the 4:30 mark on the diagram, you'll see my ideas for "Networking" and the people I might want to reach out to. Near the 6:30 mark, I've jotted down thoughts about my "Sphere of Influence"—the people I already know. When I consider "Added Value" as it pertains to that topic, I'm thinking about what I can give to those people that will keep our connection strong and healthy. In terms of identifying where my potential opportunities live, I know that in my business 80% of my opportunities come from the people I already know. That's something I really want to pay attention to. The "Education" spoke around the 8:00 mark is about considering what assistance I might need with anything related to this goal—be it getting up-to-speed on technology or policies or current best practices. I might want to consider whom I can reach out to for support if I'm feeling a gap in any area.

Only after I've completed my mind map will I start prioritizing it. One of these items will organically rise to the top for me in terms of its importance or significance. I might even ask myself, "What's the most important or valuable thing to me on this map as it relates to my goal?" It will become obvious. Then I'll start to discover my second and third priorities on the list.

My final task is to take my top priority and further flesh it out by mind mapping about what I know and what I need, related to that part of my business. Let's say I recognize that my top priority is Open Houses, from the 10:00 spot on my mind map. I'll then stick that topic in the center of a new map and start shooting off all the components of that priority.

What we're doing is essentially deconstructing something that's been achieved so we can see how we got there. Then we'll go back and take the steps we identify. To be practical, we need to get the steps small enough so they're doable.

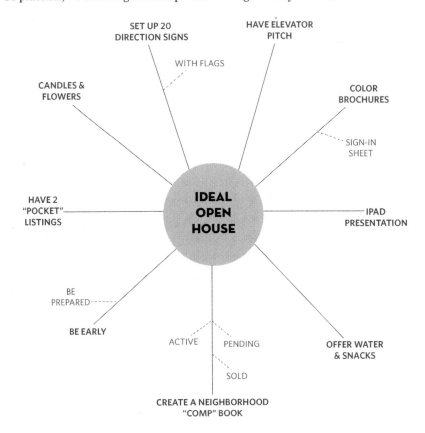

Maybe I have some ideas about my ideal Open House strategy and what that looks like. Or I might want to interview top listing agents in my company to find out what techniques they use to be successful. Maybe I want to write about what my preparation is before I walk through the front door of an open house. My mission is to consider both what it is about this area that works and how I might do more of that, as well as what kind of support I might need related to this area and how I can get that.

This process is typically pretty easy to understand when it comes to our concrete goals. But what do I do if my priority is more of an inner or experiential goal? What if I want more relaxation in my life or a higher quality of friendships, for example? How do I incorporate some of the more tactical aspects of this grid, such as adding a completion date, for topics that don't have a visible finish line to cross?

The first step I'd suggest is to get crystal clear about what it will look and feel like when you're making progress on your inner goal. Clearly describe what it's like when you're in the first stage of realizing your experience. To do that, you might create a checklist.

A colleague of mine who took one of my workshops determined that his primary goal for enhancing success was to experience greater peace in his life. Is peace a finite goal—meaning, once I've achieved it, then I don't need peace anymore? For most of us, probably not. Most of us would want peace to be an ongoing thing. So I invited my colleague to reflect on each of the eight aspects of his success and to get very clear about what it would look, sound and feel like if peace were present in each area. How would his health be impacted if he experienced greater peace? What would his closest relationships be like, and how might they transform as a result of experiencing greater peace? What kinds of shifts might he see in his professional life?

For those of us motivated by metrics, a great suggestion for working with quality-of-life projects is to try using percentages. I might start by gauging what percentage of the time I'm experiencing peace in my life right now. Let's say it's 20%. I'd then determine my goal for six months from now (or whatever timeline that I determine works best for me). I might decide that I want that number to be at 50% or 80% within that prescribed amount of time. Then I start a practice of checking in with myself over the course of the day and asking, "What's my peace quotient right now?" I might track this data in my journal or use digital tools so that I can see my progression over time.

If tactical deadlines don't work well for you, there's no need to add a completion date for the goals that relate to your quality of life. Consider that rather than going for completion, we're going for evolution.

As you go through this process, you may bump into other kinds of how-to questions. If this shows up for you, I encourage you to access your inner wisdom to discover your own answers. In my experience of facilitating people over the years,

99% of the time the person with whom I'm working has the answer to any question that they ask me. If you are willing to trust your inner guidance, then all kinds of exciting things can show up.

One way to practice accessing our own wisdom is to simply ask the question, "What else is there for me to consider related to what I'm thinking about? What else do I already know about this, or what else might I need here?" Referring back to my colleague who was seeking greater peace, one question he might have asked during his mind mapping process is, "How will I know when I've realized more peace in my life?" If we pause for a few moments and wait attentively, often amazing things pop into our minds. Know that at any point in this process, you can take a moment and allow space for answers to arrive. They usually show up.

Having defined your objectives in alignment with your greater intention for success, we're about to put what you've written down into motion. Consider for a moment that you're about to start walking a path that you've created for yourself. This is a dynamic moment. It's also a time when your apprehensions and negative "Yeah, but what if I can't?" or "I'll never get all of this done" concerns can bubble up in your mind. Remember that no accomplished person in any field of play—whether athletic, creative or in business—achieved their success because they believed the "naysayers," either internally or externally. Any time you catch yourself thinking these kinds of thoughts, I encourage you to slow down, say your Statement of Purpose and simply consider the new reality that's waiting for you.

Now that you have the explanation of this process, fasten your seatbelt and get ready to take off .

CREATING YOUR ROAD MAP

Now that you've seen the overview, it's your turn to take a shot at these exercises. As was true with the mind mapping assignment, the more focus and attention you invest here, the better your results will be. If you can't stop and engage in this moment, then schedule 15-20 minutes with yourself sometime during the next 24 hours to complete the following exercises.

If you haven't yet decided which aspect of your success you want to focus on, do that now. If you feel stuck, go with the area you feel most attracted to or repelled by— either one will generate great opportunities. Take 5-10 minutes to work through the five-category grid, clarifying your vision and direction for this aspect of your Success.

ASPECT

DEFINED (what & by when)

CURRENT REALITY

GRATITUDE FOR MY CURRENT STATE

IMAGINING THE GOAL REALIZED (present tense)

Once you've completed your grid, take this goal you've selected and write it in the center of a blank page. It's time to mind map about this topic. Take another 3-5 minutes to capture as many thoughts/ideas/questions as you can about it. What are all the simple, practical, wild, and hare-brained ideas that you have about how you could achieve your goal within your defined timeline? Remember the ground rules: **no editing and no judgments.** Any idea is fair game. If you get stuck, take a deep breath and ask yourself, "What haven't I thought about yet related to this goal?"

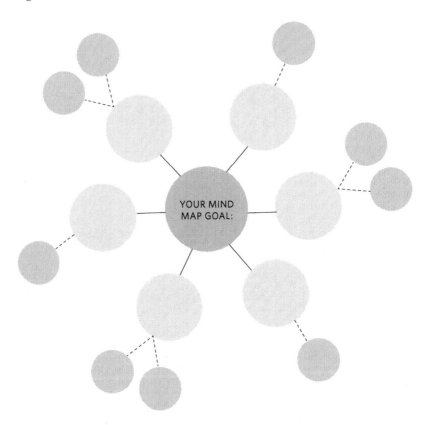

Once you've finished, look over your new map. What do you see? What keys begin to surface that can help you realize your overall goal for this aspect of your Success? Are there resources, such as people who can assist you or education that you might need, which you can access to support you? Take a minute or two to review what you wrote and capture any other ideas. What you've just created is your road map for the journey to your defined Success in this aspect of your life.

Let's gut check for a moment. Any thoughts showing up for you that sound something like, "Where am I going to find the time to actually do this?" Most of us feel like our lives are already completely consumed and that there's no time to do all the things we have to do. The thought of trying to do *more* may be daunting—even really frustrating, given that your definition of success probably includes a higher quality of life. I get it.

But what if you created more time and energy to finally do the things that support you and your quest for success? Remember all the things you wrote about on your mind maps? Does the thought of actually realizing your goals excite you? Can you imagine what it will be like to actually do it? And how expansive that will feel? If you like what you've seen so far, just keep reading and participating as fully as you can.

> "But what if you created more time and energy to finally do the things that support you and your quest for success?"

Now it's time to prioritize. Ask yourself, "What's the most important thing to me on this map?" Or, "What's my best sense of where to focus my energy right now in order to achieve this goal?" Consider the ingredients that have shown up and see what stands out. Does an order of priority start to appear that better directs you in your pursuit?

Take a moment now to circle any action steps on your map, and then label those in terms of their priority. If you don't find any steps on your map, just ask yourself, "What one little thing can I do to lean further into this aspect of my defined goal?" Specificity is our friend in this process. All of this is driving you toward clarity about the "how" for your ultimate intention to experience more of your success.

Do you begin to see the foundational action steps that you could take to begin walking toward your goal? After identifying priority one, you might then consider whether there are things that need to be further fleshed out related to it. If so, then one small next step could be to do a "mini" mind map about that priority. Each branch of your map could (and likely will) become its own micro mind map that you'll use to continue to flesh out all of the elements and timing necessary to complete that component of your bigger-picture goal. The bottom line is that you're looking for clarity and direction. "Mini" mind maps are quick, almost doodle-like diagrams designed to further expand your thinking. No heavy lifting; they usually only take a couple of minutes. Taking full advantage of this stage in creating clarity will pay huge dividends. Reminder: it's okay to enjoy this—you're creating your success. And that is FUN!

Now that you've got a working road map, let's add one more tool for the journey ahead. We've been working with the foundational tools of practicing gratitude and saying our Statement of Purpose. And now, thanks to your mind maps, you've got some clarity about things that you could actually begin doing that will take you closer to your success. Next up: a playlist. Because every good road trip deserves one.

We've all had the experience of having a song play over and over again in our minds, like it's stuck on repeat. That can be maddening. But whether we like it or not, we all have active minds that are constantly looking for stimulus. Now, we're about to take hold of this dynamic and use it for our benefit. What if the songs running in your head were songs of upliftment that supported you to focus your mind and thoughts in a positive direction?

I encourage you to create a playlist of songs that make you feel good and strong; songs that align with the qualities of your Statement of Purpose. For example, at the top of my list is "Here Comes the Sun" by the Beatles—just thinking about that song gives me goosebumps and puts me in a good mood.

Which favorite songs belong on your uplifting playlist? Name your top five favorites that make you feel good. Rounding out my list are: "You'll Be in my Heart" by Phil Collins, "Go Your Own Way" by Fleetwood Mac, "Thunder Road" (acoustic) by Bruce Springsteen and "September" by Earth, Wind and Fire.

Do you have your favorites on a playlist somewhere? If not, load them onto a device so you have them available at all times. As you take the steps to realize the number-one goal in the center of your mind-map, why not have an awesome soundtrack playing in the background that makes you feel good? You could listen to your songs while you're jogging in support of your Health aspect, or while you're cleaning out the garage in support of creating a more beautiful Environment around you. Play your songs while you're on a hike feeding your Higher Purpose or while you're having a meal with friends and cultivating Friendship. Discover whether or not this music impacts your mood or your expression if you play these songs on a more regular basis. (Here's a hint: It will most likely work out to your benefit.)

When I introduced this idea to my company, many people rallied around it. There was so much enthusiasm for it that a group playlist of songs was created. Hundreds of songs, shared within the group, fostered a synergy and bond between us all and it was so much fun. That's what's available here.

As you complete this task, you're practicing another form of discernment. You're directing your mind to stay as positive as possible as often as possible. That's fertile ground for creating greater success. Be smart and give yourself more of what supports you and makes your life better.

DARE TO BE SPECIFIC

I realize that the approach we've taken in the last couple of chapters can seem exacting. It might feel uncomfortable, or you may experience resistance to being that specific. It's helpful to think of this approach as if you're an athlete in training. The results of athletic competitions are measured in very specific increments; $1/100^{th}$ of a second can mean the difference between a Gold and Silver medal in the Olympics. Specificity matters. And those who truly want to realize their success must be specific in their approach. In the spirit of learning from "the information" instead of "the experience," I share the following story with you.

Kurt, one of my associates, has attended my workshops a few different times. The first time he did, he was clear with me about what he wanted. "Nick, I'm all about creating a happy, safe, loving environment for my kids and my wife," he said. "That's what success is for me."

As the weeks passed, I watched him engaging with the exercises and utilizing the tools he was learning. He faithfully showed up to meet with a small group of colleagues who gathered once a week to encourage and support each other. Every time he met with that group, he had new wins to share: the family was now regularly eating dinner together; there was a lot more laughter in the house; the kids were opening up and sharing more of their thoughts and feelings; they were making some changes in their living environment and it felt cleaner and lighter. From my perspective, things were shifting radically, and I was thrilled for Kurt and his family.

But as soon as we completed the final session of the workshop, Kurt walked into my office in a state of distress. "It didn't work the way it was supposed to," he said. "I put all of this effort into doing this, Nick, and I didn't get what I wanted."

I said to him, "Tell me about your vision of success when you started."

"My goal was to create a happy, safe, loving environment for my kids and my wife," he said. "I've probably said or written that 500 times over the last ten weeks."

I was puzzled because that's just what I'd been hearing him describing for the last ten weeks. So I recounted to him all of the successes that he'd celebrated each week—all of the transformation that occurred in his life.

He nodded and agreed with me: He had in fact created a great home and a thriving environment for everyone. The family was happier and more harmonious than ever. And all of those shifts took place exactly the way he'd envisioned.

"So, I don't understand, Kurt." I said. "What's the issue?"

"We don't have any more money. We're still stretching to make ends meet."

"Did you want to make more money?" I asked.

"Of course I did. I mean, I have to be making more money if I'm going to really have the kind of home life that I want."

As we talked more about this, I learned that, for Kurt, more money was implicit in his intention and vision of success. But it wasn't articulated. Kurt assumed that one of the obvious by-products of success in this area of his life would be having more cash to spend.

"Well, first of all, is it true that you need more money to fulfill your vision?" I asked.

"Yeah," he said. "That's my vision of success."

"But didn't you end up creating a happy, safe, loving environment for your family? Did you need more money in your life to achieve that goal?"

There was a pause as Kurt mulled that over. "I guess not," he finally said, shaking his head and smiling.

"Exactly. Sometimes we can create exactly what we want without having to accumulate more resources. We don't always need more money to solve our issues."

"I get it," he said.

"Second of all, you weren't specific enough. If the quantity aspect—in your case, a higher income—of your success really matters to you, then going for *quality* without also defining your *quantity* can lead to hazy outcomes. You didn't articulate that you wanted to be generating more money, and you didn't identify an amount of money you wanted to bring in. So you didn't specifically direct yourself toward that outcome."

His eyes lit up and a big grin spread across his face. "Can we start this workshop over again?"

Rest assured—during the next workshop, Kurt was back again. He said to me, "I have that other stuff. I just want more money now. I get it. If I take the action steps that line up with the map of success that I've defined for myself, it's a pretty simple process. If I get clear and take action, it's going to happen."

> "Dare to be specific about what you want. Make sure you're not expecting something to automatically manifest just because you assume it to be part of your vision. Name what you want so you can gain it."

Let this inspire you to engage in your own refining process. Dare to be specific about what you want. Make sure you're not expecting something to automatically manifest just because you assume it to be part of your vision. Name what you want so you can gain it.

And, by the way, at the conclusion of our most recent class, Kurt had created more money in one year than he had in the previous five years combined. His annual net income reached $350,000.

That's the value of clarity and precision.

THREE

SCHEDULING YOUR SUCCESS

Let's talk about schedules. If you're someone who wilts at the very idea, think of using a schedule as a way to consciously choose to make certain people, events or experiences in your life important. Putting something in your calendar is like saying, "I'm declaring that what I'm inserting here matters to me, and I want to honor myself and my priorities by actually doing it." When you consider your schedule from that point of view, whatever "stuff" it contains becomes something to look forward to. We might even feel excited about what we "get" to do next. If you detest scheduling, I suspect you might not mind it too much if the scheduling involved something like planning a vacation (a great example of having something to look forward to). Imagine having that same kind of anticipation and excitement as you're scheduling and engaging with each step of your defined success.

When we hit this stage of the game in the workshops that I teach, I start hearing comments like:

"Nick, I'm absorbing so much good stuff that I want to incorporate into my life, and I really believe in what we're doing. But I just don't have the energy right now to do anything about it."

Or...

"Nick, it's really important to me to implement this stuff. But I'm feeling really frustrated. I can't seem to carve out the time to engage with it."

Or...

"Nick, on two different days last week I woke up half an hour early so that I could spend some time with this material. But both days, I never actually got to it. There was always something that needed to be dealt with or a last-minute emergency that showed up."

Ah, the time/energy/focus conundrum. This is the spot in the journey where we'll often bump into that. If any of those statements resonate with you, know that you're right on track.

My response to all three of these comments is the same: "Have you scheduled any time in your calendar to work on this material?" Most of the time when I ask that question, I get a blank stare. Occasionally, someone will nod their head yes, in which case I'll ask, "Then what are you making more important than working on it?"

Scenarios like those are symptoms, not causes. When we start talking and thinking about how little time we have, experiencing a sense of overwhelm, or feeling as if we're at the mercy of our circumstances, that can be a signal that we're simply not prioritizing the tools and practices that lead us into growth and expansion. However, it's those very tools that are the ticket out of our identification with time poverty, overwhelm and a sense of limitation.

> **"When we start talking and thinking about how little time we have, experiencing a sense of overwhelm, or feeling as if we're at the mercy of our circumstances, that can be a signal that we're simply not prioritizing the tools and practices that lead us into growth and expansion."**

Here's the thing: often when we make a deeper commitment to our goals and dreams, we may start to discover truths about ourselves that are uncomfortable to see. And the more we engage with the kind of awareness work that we're doing here, the more likely it is that we'll start to have revelations about our patterns with how we spend our time and energy. We may be confronted with the truth about our work ethic or about what we actually do with our time every day, and sometimes those truths can be unsettling. As in, "Wow, I really do waste a lot of time and energy trying to be everybody else's friend. Or doing tasks I don't really care about just to feel productive. Or distracting myself on the web when I meant to put time toward my success."

Know that it's normal for these kinds of realizations to show up. As we move forward, one of the most powerful commitments we can make is to be honest and transparent with ourselves about who we really are and how we spend our day. This is an internal process—you don't need to share it with anyone if you'd rather not. You simply need to look at your current reality and be aware of what you see. As you gather data about where your time and energy go, the key question becomes, "To what degree am I willing to microscopically change the course of my 'normal' day and transform it into a new kind of normal?"

This is all about practice. We're in the game of practicing positive habits and getting closer to our success. In Chapter 8, we explored the concept of discernment. We're now going to focus on applying discernment in our lives on a daily, hourly, and moment-to-moment basis. When dealing with the realms of time and energy, practicing discernment becomes vital in our journey toward success. I invite you to start practicing greater discernment by building the positive habit of scheduling your priorities into your life. Consider it an experiment. Your task is simply to gather data about what works best for you.

What I've seen over the years is that when we schedule the time to engage with this material and then actually do what we say we want to do when it shows up in our calendar, we build consistency. And, by extension, we also build our sense of trust and faith in ourselves because we're showing up for ourselves and doing things that move us forward. The more we build the muscle of scheduling, the more we discover creative solutions to begin shifting our time- and energy-related challenges. As we implement those solutions, we develop even more trust and faith in ourselves. And when that happens, we start naturally recognizing new kinds of steps we can take toward our dreams—steps that we may have never even considered.

FOUR

USING YOUR ENERGY EFFECTIVELY

Change takes movement and movement takes energy. If you're looking to create change, there's a "next level" of discernment that I encourage you to use as you manage your schedule. Learn to recognize when you're more and less energized during the course of your day, and use that awareness to your advantage. Your goal is to schedule the time to take the steps that fulfill your vision of success during the periods in your day or week when you're most likely to have the capacity and energy to get them done.

If we want to experience a new reality in our lives, our creativity is one of our most powerful allies. When does inspiration flow more naturally to you? I'm typically at my most creative first thing in the morning. That's the part of the day when I schedule time to write, create instructional materials and design new campaigns. If I engage with my work early in the morning, three hours can pass in a heartbeat for me. In contrast, I'm rarely creative right after lunch. That's the time of day when I tend to bang out emails or take steps that move the ball forward on a more tactical level.

Energy levels vary throughout the day for everyone. In doing this work, there are times when your advancement will call for creative expression and times where you operate very effectively in a methodical mode. You can maximize your efficiency by aligning your schedule of activities with the times of day that best support your accomplishing them. Being sensitive to your unique biorhythms gives you the best opportunity to move forward in strategic ways.

"Energy levels vary throughout the day for everyone. In doing this work, there are times when your advancement will call for creative expression and times where you operate very effectively in a methodical mode."

For instance, it's probably less-than-effective to schedule writing time at the end of an evening when I know I'm usually wiped out from the day. It's also probably not optimal to schedule my writing sessions in the morning when the kids are getting ready for school and I inevitably end up running around looking for shoes or lost homework or something to take to show-and-tell. This journey is about practicality. Our aim is to schedule time when we know the odds are good that we'll be able to put some solid effort toward the things that we've designated as valuable to us.

FIVE

YOUR "NON-
NEGOTIABLES"

We all have certain commitments in our lives that are either ongoing (meaning, they're never "done") or that rise in importance to us based on new circumstances that show up along the way. These commitments take a variety of forms, but their common characteristic is that they matter deeply to us and clearly need to be honored. I call these "non-negotiables." One example of a non-negotiable is our children. I've got to have breakfast on the table for my kids at 7:00am, five days a week. Morning workouts from 6:00 to 7:00am can certainly be ongoing events that are essential. While there are a handful of universal non-negotiables, most non-negotiables will be unique and personal to your life.

Organizational meetings could be a non-negotiable for some. Regular spiritual or religious practices may be non-negotiable for people of faith. It might be family holidays or even your weekly basketball game that you "must" attend for your sanity. The hours of your job are certainly non-negotiable if you want to keep it. Beyond that, there are windows of opportunity that can be mined from your schedule so that you can start creating the time to do more of what brings you closer to your success. To address this, we start with a blank canvas.

WEEKLY SCHEDULE

	SUNDAY	MONDAY	TUESDAY	WEDNESDAY	THURSDAY	FRIDAY	SATURDAY
7AM							
8AM							
9AM							
10AM							
11AM							
12PM							
1PM							
2PM							
3PM							
4PM							
5PM							
6PM							
7PM							

This schedule is meant to be a neutral space, uncluttered by all of the things you think you're supposed to be doing right now. It contains 91 boxes, representing 91 hours of the week when you're potentially not sleeping

On the following page is a sample of my personal schedule. It shows where I need to be when. It also represents what's non-negotiable for me throughout my week. You'll see I've allotted time for meditation, working out and breakfast in the mornings so I get my day started off right. I've also included critical meetings for me, along with the travel time I need when I'm visiting our various offices for regular appointments. You'll also see blocks of time that are completely open.

Your first step is to use the blank sample schedule to block out time for your current personal and professional non-negotiables. So, take out your weekly schedule now and transfer the non-negotiable events onto this sample schedule. You can use the page in this book, however if you do, I suggest you go old-school and use a pencil. You can also make a photocopy, or go to our website to print out a blank schedule.

Mentally walk through your daily routine and designate on the worksheet the

WEEKLY SCHEDULE

	SUNDAY	MONDAY	TUESDAY	WEDNESDAY	THURSDAY	FRIDAY	SATURDAY
7AM	Mediation, Exercise →	→	→	→	→	→	
8AM	& Breakfast →	→	→	→	→	→	
9AM		Partners Meeting	Pasadena Malibu Meetings	Susan Meeting			
10AM				Bev Hills Office Mtg			
11AM		Office Mtg	Property				
12PM		Lunch	Touring	Lunch	Lunch	Lunch	
1PM			Caravan		La Canada Travel		
2PM					La Canada Office Mtg		
3PM			BH Broker Mtg		Nick Time		
4PM			Team Mtg				
5PM							
6PM							
7PM							

days and times when you engage in the commitments that are a "must" for you. No need for great detail; just a key word or two is fine. More important is that you block out the time you think you need to be successful with each of these actions, including travel time to and from. Office meetings, carpools, exercise, client conferences, weekly family gatherings...whatever it is for you, take a few minutes and fill that in now.

Next, consider the power of the empty spaces on that schedule. When you really get honest with yourself about where and how you spend your time, you get to discover how productive your day and week really are. If you're an entrepreneur or independent contractor with flexible hours, free time can produce either great glee or great panic. I've noticed that many of us who run our own businesses can tend to get a bit languid in those undefined slots. For some of us, getting social (in person or virtually) is an easy way to fill open space. No problem, except it tends to be a bit of a slippery slope into lost chunks of time. Some people simply drift off-course until they bump into the next defined scheduled moment or the next emergency. And then of course there are the two "Black Hole" time sucks: e-mail and social media.

Instead, imagine that you are inserting into these open spaces the next action steps you've defined as valuable to your success. You've already got your vision, and you've created a tangible goal for one important aspect of your Balance of Success. You've attached a definitive timeline to that goal and broken it down into a series of projects or components. Now, visualize breaking those down further into a series of action steps that you insert on your schedule.

Consider what your schedule then starts to mean to you. See yourself waking up in the morning and connecting to a purpose that you've defined, secure in the knowledge that you've set the table beat by beat over the course of the day to achieve the success you desire in an aware and balanced way. Now we're talking!

Go back and take a look at that scheduling worksheet where you accounted for your non-negotiables. Did you include time for play or to pursue your creativity? If not, consider allotting time to honor these as non-negotiable events. Once you've made any additions, take another look. Do you have any time left over to create more of the success you've defined for yourself? Consider blocks of open time as "Opportunity Time" that's ripe to be filled.

Finding Your Opportunity Time

Here are a few stats from my personal schedule:

91 total hours available

Daily Non-Negotiables:

Meditation/Exercise/Breakfast: 1.5 hours x 7 days	= 10.5 hours
Lunch: 1 hour x 5 days	= 5 hours
Monday	= 2 hours
Tuesday	= 7.5 hours
Wednesday	= 2 hours
Thursday	= 3.5 hours
Friday	= 0 hours
Total	30.5 hours

91 total hours

- 30.5 hours

60.5 hours to create my definition of Success

The fact is, I have a lot going on these days; my weeks are pretty busy. Yet I still have that much elective time to fill in as I desire. Most of those hours go toward individual client meetings and strategy sessions and things of that nature. But I make sure my non-negotiables are honored before I allocate the balance of my time toward whatever else I choose to do.

Take a minute to do your own calculations based on your current schedule of non-negotiables. How many open spaces do you have? There can be something really liberating in acknowledging the number of hours you have to devote to whatever you choose.

"There can be something really liberating in acknowledging the number of hours you have to devote to whatever you choose."

Remember that concept called "overwhelm?" Not enough time? Still feel that way now? When you're ready to take the next step forward, start filling up that space with action steps, as defined by your mind map work to create your success.

BUILDING YOUR ARCHITECTURE OF SUCCESS

Let's start with one of your eight Aspects and the pursuit of the priority goal that you've already defined. Here's how this works!

Step 1: Claiming Your Goal Realized

Review the primary goal of your aspect and start by reviewing **your goal realized.** (Remember the grid exercise from *creating your road map?*) Picture yourself enjoying and celebrating the completion of this goal. Experience the feeling.

Our inner child loves this step, by the way. Kids love to pretend and dream and imagine themselves as a hero or heroine. Think about what it can do for your levels of energy, focus and enthusiasm when you invite your inner kid to participate in this step.

Now ask Little You if this is something that you *both* want to experience. There's really great power in this step. Take full advantage of it.

If we refer back to my example of making $100,000 in the next six months, the realization looked like this:

Creating $100,000 in 6 months demonstrates to me that I can make infinitely *more thereafter. I feel empowered in my abilities and my confidence level is skyrocketing. I feel a level of freedom that I've rarely experienced and I am really proud of myself for my hard work. I'm grateful for all the support I've received in creating this goal and for my courage to get there.*

Now it's your moment to claim your vision realized. Enjoy it for as long as you want!

Step 2: Appreciate yourself for your dedication

Now appreciate yourself for taking the time to map out the steps to achieve your goal. You can even acknowledge, "I don't know how this is going to turn out, but I'm really happy I'm on the journey." This is your *Big-Sister/Brother You* encouraging you forward. You've created some actions that will move you toward your success. Have confidence that you'll know "how" to get this done as you keep trekking forward because you recognize that you've now defined the road map and created the time to make it happen.

Step 3: Remembering your "Quality Control"

"Little things, done consistently in excellence, create a major impact." This is your internal reference for playing at the highest level possible. After any step you take, ask yourself, "Did I do that with excellence, based on my capacity right now? Or did I half-ass that one?" The intention here is to inspire you to higher levels of quality and efficiency as you move into action.

"Reviewing your primary goal within the aspect you've chosen, what's the first step you can take toward getting there?"

Step 4: Time to get going!

Reviewing your primary goal within the aspect you've chosen, what's the first step you can take toward getting there? A friendly reminder that action steps are typically pretty small: a phone call or digital communication, reading through some information or showing up at a meeting. I'm talking about an incremental step; one I could watch you physically do if I gave you a few minutes right now to complete it. Be mindful of whether or not you need assistance from anyone else to get this step done.

What is your action and how long will it take to complete? Review your new schedule, factor the level of energy you'll need to get it rolling and insert your action step into your schedule. Yes, this is really happening.

With reference to my example of making $100,000 in six months, the first project for me was to create the Ultimate Open House. The first step toward creating that larger project was to have quality promotional materials that express my value proposition in attracting Loyal, Gracious and Qualified clients. The first step toward this would be to brainstorm with my manager ways to better communicate that message. The intention of the meeting would be to come away with clear points that articulate what I'd give each client in the way of my graciousness, loyalty and expertise so that I may in return, receive gracious, loyalty and qualified clients. So the next action to be scheduled would be to sit down with my Manager.

Step 5: "Making it happen"

Insert the initial action step or steps into one of the open spaces on your weekly schedule, allowing enough time to complete the action. Based on the timeline you defined for completing this goal, when do you want to take this next step? In most cases, the first action does not take long and can be completed efficiently—maybe 15-20 minutes. Once you've defined this and inserted it, you may want to consider any actions related to it as a new Non-Negotiable. This is, after all, a step that's moving you closer to your definition of success.

So on my schedule, I'm adding call manager to set meeting to "ideate" my messaging campaign.

Recognize two key things here:

1. You've just created the first building block of your goal made manifest. Congratulations!

2. You'll know your next action step once this first one is complete.

When your first action is done, make sure you insert into your schedule the next step that has shown up as a result of completing the action step that preceded it.

Again, this is the approach that works for me. Once you've practiced and become confident with it, you may find you want to tweak it for working with your schedule.

Gut check: How do you feel having now scheduled this first step toward your first Success goal? Empowered? Still Overwhelmed? Is there any excitement or enthusiasm about having taken action to create more of what you want? Is there any apprehension? (Hint: If so, your self-talk might sound something like, "Now that I've defined my first step, do I have the staying power to take that action toward achieving my dreams?")

Whatever your thoughts, feelings or considerations, I encourage you to trust the process and allow it to unfold. Proactively say your Statement of Purpose to keep you aligned. Honor wherever you are and whatever you feel right now. Change often feels foreign, and in moments like this it can seem like a great idea to revert back into our protective shells. Keep leaning in. Keep participating. Know that as you're ready to expand, this material is available to you.

HONORING ALL ASPECTS OF YOUR SUCCESS

If you're ready to incorporate more, here's your next opportunity.

Let's harness the momentum that you've already generated. You've now defined eight different Aspects of your Success. You've created and scheduled an action step for your primary aspect. Do you see that you have more time in your schedule to craft road maps for the seven other aspects of your success?

If you have the time and appetite, you could schedule the time to complete this same set of steps for each of the seven remaining aspects of your Balance of Success. I realize this is a big "ask," but it is simply a suggestion for those who would like to touch on all eight aspects right now. If you just want to stick with one at this time, that is absolutely fine. Start there and build up your muscles by completing one Aspect, then add in the additional areas as you continue to get a better grasp of the exercise. I support you however you want to lean in. And for those willing to focus on all eight aspects in unison, here's a checklist:

Identify the primary goal for each of your remaining seven Aspects.

Fill out the five-category grid for each goal.

Do a mind map about each goal, capturing everything you can think of that relates to it—e.g., its components, your best sense of what's necessary to complete it, etc.

Determine what specific action step you can take right now to launch you toward realizing each goal.

Making your best guess about how long it might take to complete each step, insert your actions into your weekly schedule. Refer to your schedule for open spaces to craft architectures for all eight of your Aspects of Success, and invest that time wisely.

Consider the reward. Imagine what it would feel like to have eight different components of your Success identified and inserted into your schedule. Imagine how empowered you'd feel at the end of your week after taking those steps, in alignment, that move you closer to your dreams.

I encourage you to pull out your Statement of Purpose right now and re-read it or say it out loud to yourself. Here's a variation on the question: ask yourself, "How long have I wanted to create greater _____, _____ & _____(your three qualities) in my life?" In identifying a goal and mind-mapping it out, you're paving the way for this experience. Claim the fact that, right here and now, the possibility exists for making your dreams a priority in all aspects of your life.

"Claim the fact that, right here and now, the possibility exists for making your dreams a priority in all aspects of your life. "

Now look once more at your seven-day schedule. Identify the opportunity time that's available and how much time you think it will take you to complete this assignment. Here's a rough estimate for completing your remaining seven Aspects of Success: approximately 7-10 minutes to identify all seven of your primary goals; completing seven mind maps at the rate of 3-4 minutes per map—that's another 21 to 28 minutes; add another 10 minutes to insert all seven action steps into your weekly schedule. Recognize that by completing one 45-minute session of time (or two 20–25-minute sessions), scheduled in alignment with your creative biorhythms, you're launching the journey to success in all aspects of your life.

Once you've finished this assignment, you may prefer to transfer all of this scheduling information to a digital calendar if that works best for you. If you're a more kinesthetic learner, you may enjoy keeping your own master copy of the blank schedule so that you can print it out and physically write in your commitments from week to week.

What's the potential upside for you for diving into this level of participation? Many people find that they discover a lot about what matters to them as they begin to clarify their next steps and put them into their calendars. I was speaking with someone and they shared this:

"I've been finding that some of the things I thought were non-negotiables actually aren't so important to me. I'm saying 'no' more. And as I do, I'm discovering that I have time to address new things that are showing up in my life that really are priorities."

How many of us get sucked into other people's emergencies? That's natural. When we follow a schedule that is designed as a tool that aligns us with creating the success we desire, we still have times when we can be flexible in the day. I'm not an advocate of every moment being accounted for; just the times that support the alignment of me moving towards my success.

Another insight I often hear is, "I'm discovering that what's non-negotiable and what isn't evolves." That's my experience, too. Change is always floating through our lives. Which means that our priorities are dynamic as well. Our commitments and our schedules need to adjust accordingly.

Some people build the habit of starting and ending their day with their non-negotiables. As one of my participants shared with me recently, "Spending time on my non-negotiables allows me to bookend my day and leaves me with the feeling that I've accomplished what I wanted." For those of us who work for commission instead of being paid a salary, we don't have the validation of a regular paycheck as a way of acknowledging the work we put into our professional lives. Starting and ending the day with non-negotiables is a great way of creating self-validation by building in acknowledgement of each day's work.

THE ELEPHANT
IN THE ROOM

If we're going to look deeply at incorporating our priorities into our lives on a daily basis, then we've got to address the elephant in the room when it comes to productivity (or lack therof). I'm talking about the great time-suckers: any device you possess that has a screen. Specifically, let's have a come-to-Jesus chat about email (including any other type of digital communications).

Many of us begin our workday by turning on our device or opening our inbox, and start responding to the most recent communication that's come in. Go to the freshest ones, right? Then as soon as we start replying to those messages...people reply back. So we reply to their reply and the hamster wheel starts rolling. We end up stalling out on this top-line level of communications. And since we can only get to so many messages at one time, the incomplete communications from weeks ago that we haven't wrapped up just get buried deeper at the bottom of the pile. Are you identifying with this?

This is about much more than simply managing the volume of stuff to be dealt with that shows up in our lives (although that's important). What we're actually looking at is how we handle distractions and how we take responsibility for

> "What we're actually looking at is how we handle distractions and how we take responsibility for ourselves and our priorities."

ourselves and our priorities. We're programmed to immediately respond to whatever comes our way. But once we engage in that game, it drains us of valuable time and energy that would be better spent moving toward our vision of success. As most of us know all too well, digital distractions are among the most prevalent time-sucking culprits in our culture.

What compels us to immediately address these kinds of communications? First and foremost, we've got the instant-gratification and novelty factors of receiving something new and the addictive loop this creates in our brain chemistry. On a more conscious level, we sanction this behavior because we want to be regarded as responsive to the needs of our clients and colleagues. That's a benevolent motivation, but let's examine this dynamic a little more closely in service to creating greater discernment.

When you send a communication to someone, what's your expectation of how quickly they'll get back to you? Do you presume they're like a panther waiting to pounce on whatever you send them? How frequently do you typically get the response you need or want within the timeframe you expect it? For me the answer is, "Not very often." If that's true for you too, then recognize that there's no need for perceived urgency when it comes to responding to the needs of others.

We all have the ability to manage our day based on our priorities. Learning how to communicate appropriately with others is a significant key in that pursuit. My professional life is often like a ping pong match that I'm playing with potentially 900 different people at any given time. If I want to avoid being overrun by written or verbal conversation all day long, then I've got to be strategic about how and when I communicate.

One way to start practicing strategic communication is to say to people up front, "My intention is to respond to you within a certain period of time," – however long makes sense for you. It could be 4 hours or 24 hours or one week. It requires a little forethought and effort to do this, but the payoff is that you're managing the expectations of those whom you serve. This gives you more space and time to produce a high-quality result.

What I've found in 28 years of negotiation is that when I'm in the middle of a fast-and-fierce deal, ultimately what people really want to know is that they're being taken care of. (More on this later.) They want to know that I'm there for them. In that context, utilizing this communication key demonstrates my trust and faith in our relationship. If I tell them, "I'll be back in touch with you by 5pm," knowing I can do that, then my clients almost always give me that latitude. Occasionally people ask, "Is there any way you can get to me sooner?" and then we negotiate that. But those instances are few and far between.

I'm a big fan of designating specific times in the day to deal with digital communications. Instead of imagining yourself as "always on-call," experiment with allotting three half-hour-long periods of time in your day to respond to emails and digital messages. That's what I do. Because my creative energy is highest first thing in the morning, I do one 30-minute round of handling messages in the late morning after I've completed any creative work I have to do. Then I do a second round after lunch in between meetings. And I use my last 30-minute segment near the end of my day to wrap up anything that can't wait until tomorrow.

If you want to try this, schedule just one small period of time in your day to deal with digital communications. Given your schedule and your role, maybe you only need 15-minute periods of time. Customize this based on whatever makes sense for you.

Use technology to support your life, not the other way around. If you schedule times to complete your communications, then you don't need to worry about immediately addressing everything that pops up on a screen. You can actually turn off your phone (gasp!). Be smart and take care of your day. As you hone your ability to take charge of your schedule and manage your day by managing others' expectations, I suspect you'll be delighted by the way people organically fall into place with you.

PART IV

ESTABLISHING YOUR CONFIDENCE
FOR ANY NEGOTIATION

Consider the foundation that you've laid for yourself in pursuit of your success. You now have a Statement of Purpose to support you in greater alignment to go for what you want. Via Mind Mapping, you have created a clear direction and path, demarcated by the action steps you now know to take and the time you've identified to actually do them. You have your *intention* (Why) and your strategic *methodology* (How). Bravo to you for your great work to date!

For perspective, consider that the nature of the work that you've done so far is more on the "internal" side. Its focus has been to define success for you and build your inner foundation.

Now it's time to put all your truly good work into a more "interactive" mode, which means dealing with the people who will assist you in realizing your success. So, the next level of your preparation is designed to support you in the interactions to come, the negotiations you'll engage in to ask for what you want. This preparation will build your confidence to walk into any room or environment poised to honor yourself and the success you wish to achieve.

There's an expression that my partners and I have employed during our entire run at Partners Trust. It's a simple statement that expresses, in an understated manner, our confidence to succeed:

"I like our odds."

Inside of us, we know we've got what it takes to make "it" happen, with the tools and resources behind us. At this point in your journey, I offer this statement to you for your use and enjoyment. To those who've traveled with me this far, I say to you...

"I like *your* odds."

THREE KEYS TO CREATING CONFIDENCE

With this book, and particularly with this section, my intention is to assist you in mastering a new set of skills designed to powerfully accelerate your success in realizing your dreams. At this stage in our journey, we're delving into the aspects of Success that come into play more directly when we're actively engaging with others. There are three key elements to our new skillset, and each one is essential to creating positive outcomes.

The first element for successful interactions starts with your relationship with yourself; recognizing your worth, your value. Remember the core premise at the outset of this book.

> "Until you recognize your value and claim your worthiness to achieve success, you'll either sabotage or deflect your ability to receive it."

Recognizing your value and claiming your worth is a proclamation to yourself that you "belong" in any situation or environment that you choose before the event even occurs. Wouldn't that be refreshing and offer you a feeling of great strength? It's available.

Promotional marketers call the individuality of a product or service a Unique Selling Proposition (USP). The fact that the product or service is without equal, is why the consumer needs this specific product or service. The first job of the marketer is to recognize the USP, then create a narrative around that product or service, and finally convey that message to the public.

Consider that you and I are both Product *and* Service. Therefore, we need to recognize our individual USP. For me, that's nothing more than defining your worth in what I call your Value Proposition. As with the USP, once you establish your Value Proposition, you can then share the narrative that describes your unique talents and skills, and convey that message to whomever you are speaking. That, to me, becomes your Value, *recognized* and *claimed*. It's also a prescription for great confidence.

In this section, we utilize the concepts associated with the wonder that still resides inside of you through your Little Kid, your Statement of Purpose, and mind mapping to further explore and create your Value Proposition. Once it's established, you'll begin to realize the power and authority you possess and how you can put your Value Proposition to work for you in any environment or situation. You do this not from an ego place but rather from a consciousness that you offer your value in genuine service to those ready to recognize and honor your value in return. That consciousness shift can actually enhance the quality of your life and create dynamic, lasting relationships that better serve your Statement of Purpose.

The second element is what I call "Proper Preparation." This encompasses gathering information through due diligence so that you feel confident, relaxed and ready to engage with others. Proper Preparation asks the question, "What do I need to prepare to make this interaction as successful as possible?" Here's an example from my world.

Let's say that I have an appointment to take a new buyer out to see some homes. One step I might take to ensure greater success is making sure I have a thorough understanding of the buyer's needs so that I'm not wasting anybody's time when we get together. For that, I ask my buyer qualifying questions as part of that preparation. Another step might be analyzing the properties I intend to visit to make sure they match up with my client's needs. The most effective way to achieve this level of preparation is to schedule the time to review all the properties on the market and see which ones best align with the buyer's needs. A third step could be to map out the route I'll drive to get to those properties so I feel most confident in how I transport my buyer while showing him or her these properties. Proper preparation is critical to instilling confidence.

The third element of my trifecta for any interaction is Clear Intention. I introduced you to the basics of this element earlier in Chapter Seven. In this context, Clear Intention is all about clarifying what we want our personal outcome to be as a result of engaging with others. Clear Intentions can be quantitative, as in, "My intention is to reach out to ten new prospects today and to share about the services I have to offer." And they can also be qualitative, such as, "My intention is to feel joyful today." And there's a broad continuum of possibilities in between. Utilizing intention gives you the ability to continually hone your sense of whether or not you're on-course, in real time, toward your vision of Success.

Visualize walking into your next meeting armed with these three elements:

1. You're connected to your Value Proposition: you're so in touch with your innate goodness and value that you're completely relaxed, present and at ease.

2. You're Properly Prepared: you've done your research and have what you need to maximize this opportunity.

3. You have a Clear Intention: you've identified your desired outcome for the meeting so that you may stay more present and aware, ready to handle whatever unfolds.

When you enter a room solid in who you are, properly prepared and with a clear intention of what you want as a result of that meeting, you become very, very effective.

CHAPTER THIRTY

YOUR VALUE PROPOSITION

Remember that how you think about yourself directly affects your actions and attitudes. As you build your Value Proposition, it is imperative that you think kind thoughts and speak kind words to and about yourself. That means no more self-deprecating remarks. This takes discipline and awareness. Considering that the enhancement of your Success is what's at stake, I'd say discipline and awareness are worthy prices to pay. Refining your awareness in this area is best supported by the context of "little things done consistently in excellence create a major impact."

I remember playing golf one day with three other guys. I'd been working on my awareness around my self-talk, attempting to think more positive thoughts than negative. If you've ever played golf, you know there is ample opportunity to analyze specific shots during 18 holes. For me, that's about 95 opportunities. We were on the first hole and one of the guys hit a bad shot off to the right and out of bounds. Immediately, he dropped his club and proclaimed out loud, "What an idiot!" His body posture slumped and he continued muttering negative assessments of the shot as he teed up another ball.

As I watched, I saw myself in him. How many times had I hit that same shot and immediately started hammering myself with negative thoughts? Too many to count. From my more positive vantage point, I recognized how that didn't serve me in the past and how it wasn't serving this guy in the moment. My ability and willingness to see what he was doing was probably the best reinforcement to keep saying positive things to myself because by doing so, I was able to have a far better time during that round of golf.

As for my foursome buddy, he duck-hooked the next shot into the adjoining fairway and ripped into himself with renewed vigor. He ended up getting so mad at himself he couldn't even finish the round. He literally worked himself into a negative frame of mind and stormed off after nine holes.

The first building block to creating your Value Proposition is to say and think positive thoughts to yourself. This starts with awareness. We know we can't change the past. The best way to use the past is to learn from it. Beating yourself up for what you can't change is a waste of energy and will most likely continue to yield more negative results. "STOP IT!"

Who enjoyed getting scolded as a child? Not me. But every time you beat yourself up, you scold that little person inside of you as well. When I look at it that way, I shudder at the thought that I had ever been so mean to myself.

Consider a dog that's been beaten repeatedly. After a while, that dog becomes so gun-shy that it never fully relaxes or allows itself to be free. It's always looking to see when it will be beaten again. That's what we do to ourselves with this negative talk and it diminishes the innocence and wonder of who we are. This is counterproductive to owning your value and claiming your worth.

A powerful, dynamic attribute we possess as individuals is our vulnerability and the ability to express it through our most authentic voice. I realize this concept may be far-fetched for some, and that's okay. If you scoff at this idea, consider one time when something touched your heart and it melted you for a moment. It could have been the caress of a loved one, a gesture of kindness extended to you or seeing a movie that choked you up inside. You didn't cry because you'd never let anyone see you cry, but it did move you. I'm suggesting that's the authentic part of you that got sparked in that moment and it moved you. That's the part of you that relates to softer, gentler experiences. For this section, I invite you to consider allowing that softer part of you to receive this information and see what shows up. No one is watching you. This is just for you and your awareness.

Each and every one of us was a little kid once, filled with wonder, excitement and innocence. Life was filled with possibilities, sparked by our vivid imaginations. But as we've gotten older, the wonder and enthusiasm that we felt as a kid can have a tendency to dissipate. Experiences of disappointment and heartache can take their toll on us; a toll that causes us to shut down and hide that innocence. I fought my innocence after my parents died. That fight created a shell that protected me from pain. It wasn't until I realized that it was also blocking me from experiencing my sweetness, my innocence and my vulnerability that I was able to start breaking that shell. That started with a choice to reclaim my innocence and I encourage those of you who may be resistant to lean in and see what's present for you here.

One last reminder before you explore your Value Proposition. If you're wondering "how" you're going to do this, remember that when you start with a clear intention to do something, the "how" follows and the action steps more readily reveal themselves. Intention vs. Method is our friend. Breathe in and trust.

I invite you to do a mind map to explore your uniqueness, your gifts and your talents. To prepare for this, get out your journal and open to a fresh page. In the center of the page, write, "My Goodness, Talents and Skills" and circle it.

Begin by remembering your Statement of Purpose and say it a couple of times so that it resonates inside of you. You've created your Statement of Purpose to align you towards your Balance of Success. Better defining your Value Proposition will empower your Statement of Purpose so that the two forces can better support each other in moving you forward.

Next, invite Little You to come play. Either in your mind's eye or by looking at a childhood photo, see that young version of yourself. See the preciousness of you. If any sadness or negative distraction comes in, let it go. Sadness or other forms of negative association are feelings based on judgments of your past. They will not serve you now in the rediscovery of your goodness and value. Stay present, looking only for the goodness, wonder and innocence of that child. As that goodness starts to materialize, ask yourself these simple questions: "What is my goodness? What makes me uniquely me? What are my talents and gifts?"

As you consider your answers, here are a few questions to activate your mind. Did you play sports as a kid? Were you good at any of them? Were you a team player? Were you creative? How did you express that? Are you steady? Dependable? Funny? Kind? Are you considerate? Thoughtful? Sensitive? Focused? Honest? Trustworthy?

As you dive into this mind map, remember no editing or judging allowed. Let the good things bubble up naturally, uncensored. This is the time to explore and enjoy you, for your gifts, talents and abilities. Take the next 3-5 minutes and have fun celebrating YOU!

When you're complete, look at what you've written down. Does it bring a smile to your face? Were you aware of being good at so many things? As you review your goodness, talents and abilities, is there a theme or thread that starts to show up? Perhaps your dependability is demonstrated through many talents. To what degree does your heart show up? Maybe it's better defined through your caring, the quality of your friendship, your loyalty. Consider the qualities before you as flexible resources you can apply towards each and every situation you move into from this moment forward.

What if, before your next meeting, no matter what the importance, you claimed, for example, the value of your loyalty and dependability as part of your Value Proposition? How would that affect your communications during the meeting? Do you think there would be an opportunity to express your defined qualities as the meeting unfolds? It may be in the quality of your listening, the suggestions you offer or the commitments you are prepared to make that serve the greater interests of all parties.

I am a firm believer that we do ourselves a tremendous injustice when we don't acknowledge our strengths and further add to that injustice when we don't share our gifts with others. We all want to be better. You, reading this right now, have that ability as you claim it. It starts by recognizing the goodness of who you are.

Now review your mind map. Circle the top three qualities that really resonate to you. Whether an action or trait, do you think any or all of these qualities could add value to any situation? As a parent? A friend? A colleague? A boss? An employee? The answer is YES!

Your unique goodness, once empowered, is part of your authentic YOU. Do you get that? As you step into claiming your goodness, you step forward into claiming the unique and innate strength of who you truly are. From that place, I share the pearl of wisdom that was given to me when I needed it most: "Good things happen to good people. And you are a good person."

As you claim your worth and your value, you allow your goodness to shine forth for all to see. Let it SHINE!

ONE

APPLYING YOUR VALUE PROPOSITION TO EVERYTHING

Like having a Swiss army knife in your pocket, your Value Proposition is infinitely useful and applicable. Once you're clear about it, you can apply it to anything as a way of getting closer to your Balance of Success. Whatever you're doing next is your next opportunity to practice infusing your Value Proposition. I mean that: *whatever you do*.

I recently shared with one of the groups I lead that I brought my Value Proposition to driving my new car. Before I turned on the ignition, I sat there for a moment, reflecting on the core qualities of my Value Proposition—my loving, caring and sweetness. I took a few breaths and just allowed those qualities to bubble up inside of me. And then I thought, "That's how I want to drive today." Of course a guy in our group immediately asked, "Is your new car a Prius, Nick?" I said, "No, I'm driving a gas-guzzling beast of a car. But I'm driving it very sweetly."

I share that story for two reasons. First, to give you a sense of the wide range we have when applying our Value Proposition in our day-to-day lives. And second, to demonstrate that even when it seems like applying it has a negligible impact, that's rarely the case. Applying my Value Proposition to my driving affects the way

I drive because now I have a clearer intention as to how I choose to drive. And from that place, I'm less distracted and more present. It also affects how I feel while I'm driving. I'm more relaxed and at ease on the road. It affects how I relate to the drivers on the road with me and to the people I'm talking to on the phone during my commute. Because I'm connected to my own goodness, I have more space for other people's emotions and humanity. All of those people, places and experiences are affected by my connection to my value and my intention to empower it.

This practice of applying your Value Proposition to everything you do is a way to start putting the goodness of you to work for you, while building that muscle of familiarity. Whether I claim my value out loud or not doesn't detract from my intention to express my value. There are many ways to do this non-verbally. I can infuse my value in my listening, my eye contact and my empathy. Regardless of the situation, there's a good reason to stay engaged with your Value Proposition: It will impact everything about your conduct and demeanor. Imagine how it will start to affect relationships, business and personal. Can your Value Proposition add value to the way you speak to your children when you've come home from a really challenging day at work? Or to the way you respond to the customer who's just walked into your office red-faced and screaming? You won't know until you experience it for yourself whether or not it works. I will tell you, it works for me every day.

Wait. Back up a second. Is it really possible to express my Value Proposition in the face of someone else's upset? I grew up believing that anytime someone confronts me it's time to put my fists up, assume fighting stance and say, "Let's go!" I've gone that route and ended up bloody. But we don't have to operate that way. We have the option of staying centered in our Value Proposition even in the face of challenges. When you play at that level, do you think you give yourself a greater chance of diffusing the situation? In my experience, when I want a fire to go out, I don't throw more wood on it.

In the best-selling book, *The Four Agreements* by Don Miguel Ruiz, there is an agreement that speaks directly to dealing with the upset of others: "Don't take anything personally." As I practiced integrating and applying this one simple concept, my conflicts with others started to dissipate. If you haven't read Ruiz's book, here's my take on his philosophy. It becomes much easier not to take others' actions or statements personally when I consider:

1. I will never have as much information as you do about your issue because I have not been in your body and mind having experienced all that you have that leads you to think and feel the way you do in any given moment.

2. You are entitled to feel however you want. However, just because you feel the way you do doesn't mean I have to accept your opinions and thoughts as true for me. That awareness is most liberating.

The point here is simple: Carry forth your Value Proposition into any and all situations with the understanding that you are doing the best you can in any given moment. If you make a mistake, you can claim it in your authenticity and focus on doing your best to make it right. End of story.

One last note on this. Recently, I was speaking with a person who had what we'll call a "big" personality. The stakes were high and this person was challenging my perspective as in, "You're wrong." Instead of taking it personally, I looked at him and simply said, "Okay." Well, he didn't like that answer because there was no "fight" in it. He quickly responded back, "That's it?" To which I responded "Yes. You're entitled to your opinion and no words will seemingly change your mind, so let's just let it go." I walked away while he stood there dumbfounded.

Here's the really cool part about all of this. The more you practice reminding yourself that who you are is valuable and worthy, and the more you apply your Value Proposition to everything you do, the more momentum you create on your journey to greater success. You'll also be less inclined to dwell on failures, foibles, badness, or ideas like "They'll never like me," that, in reality, serve zero purpose towards your growth and well-being.

> "The more you practice reminding yourself that who you are is valuable and worthy, and the more you apply your Value Proposition to everything you do, the more momentum you create on your journey to greater success."

In service to keeping things practical, let's take a quick look at what applying our Value Proposition to everything we do might look like in a professional setting.

Recently I had a meeting with a guy who'd just become a Realtor. The upshot of the conversation was that he wanted to ascertain everything there was to know about real estate, and he wanted it right then. He was looking for any-and-all information he could get from me about what he "should" be doing so that he could dive in and immediately make a "ton of money." When he finally paused to draw breath, I said, "You're approaching this whole thing backwards by focusing on what you need to get from other people. You'd be better served by figuring out what you can give to them. Once you've discovered that, you'll be able to interact with clients and prospects in a way that communicates, 'I'm here to assist you' as opposed to communicating, 'I'm here to get something from you.'"

Here's what "I'm here to assist" might look like in my world. Imagine that I'm a real estate agent hosting an open house for the very first time. And while I've never held an open house before or even sold one home, I *have* studied the real estate contract. And I'm prepared to offer value from that study. And from that contract, I know what the top five protections are to better protect buyers. I know they include inspections, contingencies, seller disclosures, details about the buyer's ability to gain financing if they need it and title insurance protections. So I create a placard that reads "Do you know the five protections in the real estate contract?" and place that question next to my sign-in sheet. Whenever someone walks in the door, I welcome my guest, and then I ask them, "Did you happen to see the question next to the sign-in sheet?"

If they respond that they haven't, I can then use my contract knowledge as an education vehicle by asking, "Would you like to know the five protections of the contract for your benefit? Because no matter what house you view, you may want to know what your protections are when you begin your negotiation to buy it. If you'd like, I'd be happy to share that information with you."

What does this person know about me that they didn't know before? Simply an element of my Value Proposition. Do you think that by opening our conversation in this way, I might have value to them immediately? Sure! Forget about the fact that I've never sold a house before. Or that I've never even held an open house before. I've taken the situation at hand and offered my intelligence, my caring and my "go getter" attitude for their benefit.

To be clear, in the land of Partners Trust, this agent would never move forward without the immediate supervision of a professional mentor to shepherd him or her through this transaction. We're not just hooking unsuspecting clients with someone with less than professional acumen and service. This story is meant to showcase the fact that you can add value to any situation, no matter what your level of experience if you understand what your value is and how you can demonstrate it.

That's the inside-out approach to negotiation and success. It's founded on sharing your Value Proposition. Does that example inspire you to generate your own ideas about how you could do something similar in your current role or profession? What's the source of those ideas? Your strong, solid sense of the value and goodness that you offer. And that's how you actively start to put the beacon of your Value Proposition to work for you in new and expanded ways.

Here's a fun example of a deal that was secured by the Value Proposition alone. This story came from a new associate of ours who'd just begun working with a team in one of our offices. Here's what she told me.

"We were talking with a client who's based in London. In the midst of a great conversation about some potential properties I'd found for him, the topic of Gratitude came up. I was moved to tell him about the five-minute Gratitude exercise we use at Partners Trust. I shared that 'At our company, we use this tool to reflect on gratitude, and it's part of a workshop series we're doing on the topic of Value-Conscious Negotiating.' The guy was impressed and wanted to hear more, so we had a deeper discussion about it. At the end of the conversation, he said, 'I'm not only interested in buying this property. I want to purchase more. I so love what you and your company are doing, and I've decided that I'm only going to work with you.'"

Remember: the more you recognize and claim your value, the better you'll be able to articulate and share it. And the more you share it, the more you'll attract people who like what you do.

One of the oldest precepts around is "What you put out, you get back." Given the truth of that, my strong encouragement is to practice infusing your Value Proposition into everything you do. In the process, you'll reinforce your upward focus and enhance the possibility of outcomes that align with your Success.

TWO

PROPER PREPARATION PAYS DIVIDENDS

How many of us have only fantastic habits in our lives? (I'm not raising my hand.) Probably all of us would be well-served by focusing some time and energy up-leveling our habits. Proper Preparation is about creating empowering habits that support your Success. Preparation increases the odds that the next steps toward your success are effective, leveraged ones. Poise, relaxation, fulfillment—that's what's available as a direct result of practicing Proper Preparation.

Let's start exploring this concept in a real-life scenario. Right now, think about an upcoming appointment you have scheduled. Go for one that makes you feel uncomfortable or that's nagging you in some way. Next, ask yourself: "What action steps would I need to take in order to feel properly prepared for this meeting?"

Take a minute to consider the things that you know you'll need in advance. Here are some ideas to get the wheels of your mind turning:

• What resources do you want to have available during this appointment?

• Do you need information? Statistics?

• What might you offer that could build your credibility or demonstrate your value?

• How can you present that information so that it will be best received?

• What questions do you need to formulate to ensure that you and the other person are clear about your collective next steps?

Take a minute or two to identify any next steps you want to take that can help you show up for this meeting at the top of your game.

Proper Preparation isn't restricted to the realm of meetings; we can use it to support us with any action we take. What if, prior to making your next call or writing your next message, you asked yourself: "What information do I need to make this action as productive as possible?" The three seconds required to ask that question could dramatically impact your outcome. Too often, we rush into our actions without first considering what we want to realize as a result. Rushed actions create haphazard results.

"Proper Preparation isn't restricted to the realm of meetings; we can use it to support us with any action we take."

Let's explore this further by applying it to our defined Success. Back to my $100,000 in six months goal:

After mind mapping about my Wealth aspect, here's what I know: I'm going to generate the money I'm striving for by creating a better open house experience. And I know that if I want to do that, I need to create a more robust strategy so that I walk into the open house with an enhanced degree of confidence. This will allow me to make the most of each opportunity.

Given all of that, bearing in mind my goal of making $100,000 in six months, here are three ideas from my mind map that I could choose to develop and pursue:

1. Conduct interviews with my peers who consistently get results in this area.

2. Hone my skills as an ambassador, strategist & negotiator on behalf of my clients.

3. Understand the markets in the area where I'll be holding these open houses.

While each of those avenues has multiple actions, all three can work in concert with each other, so long as I'm efficient with my time and plan out my course of action for each objective.

Let's take a look at the first action: Interviews with top associates. This is something I definitely want to do. I haven't moved on it yet because I'm worried that these folks are too busy to talk to me or that I'm going to bother them. I tell myself, "They don't know who I am, so why would they take time to share information with me?"

When I ask myself the Preparation question, "What support would I need to offer in order to maximize this opportunity?" I suddenly have the idea to reflect on what I could offer these associates in exchange for the small amount of time and energy they'll spend answering my questions. There could be a myriad of gestures here. My starting place may be simply asking the question: "What can I offer you to sit with me for 15 minutes and tell me what makes you a great agent?" That feels like a solid next step to me, and I immediately think of two people I could reach out to. And so into my schedule this next step goes.

While there's a host of ways I could get the ball rolling toward my goal, the key is this: Taking the time to consider the additional resources I'll need in order to complete an action in excellence better ensures maximum reward and return on effort.

While it may seem counterintuitive, Proper Preparation often makes the biggest impact when it comes to elements that may seem most inconsequential. We can trip ourselves up when we assume that certain appointments in our calendar are more important than others. Have you ever shown up at a meeting to handle something minor and been surprised by what actually took place? Sometimes unexpected information arises as a result of the preparation we've done which impacts the way we listen, the questions we ask and the way that we engage with others. And that information can lead to much bigger opportunities.

In the business of real estate, I've experienced this many times. Case in point: a friend and client owned a house in the Hollywood Hills. I'd sold him the house about three years earlier and as friends, we'd stayed in touch, having an occasional lunch or a phone call.

One day, he called me up and said, "Got a minute for a quick question?"

"Of course." I replied, not knowing what he wanted to know.

"What's my house worth?" was all he asked. In real estate, that simple question is usually the precursor to "I want to sell my house."

Because I actively stayed in touch with this client *and* I was keeping aware of the sales activity in his market as part of my realtor's due diligence, it was easy to answer his question by referring to other area homes for sale. Having that knowledge at my fingertips instilled in my friend immediate confidence in me, demonstrating to him that I was on top of my game. The next thing I knew, we were listing his home.

Considering this from the point of view of Proper Preparation, two things came into play:

1. I stayed in touch with my friend.

2. I kept up with market conditions in his area as part of my job to know my markets.

Staying engaged with what you do, no matter what your profession, will better prepare you for opportunities that show up as you position yourself to receive your success.

One of my associates at Partners Trust was referred a client from Bogota, Colombia. This client's company was relocating her to "the States," and she needed to find a home for her family within two weeks. The typical protocol in this situation is to call the client and ask a standard series of questions like, "What do you like? What are you looking for?" But after taking a few minutes to reflect on the Proper Preparation for how to engage with this new client, my associate chose to take an additional track.

Before initiating a conversation, she first researched the client's current culture and environment. She got more information about price point in her client's current neighborhood in Bogota and gathered resources that her client's family might need to streamline the process of making an international move. Because the associate had done so much preparation, what could've been a five-minute cursory chat ended up as an hour-long conversation filled with meaning and connection, solidifying her relationship with this new client. She maximized that opportunity and transformed her relationship from realtor to trusted and valued resource.

Let's look at one more tactical example of how to work with Proper Preparation. Before any meeting, I ask myself three questions.

1. "Where did we leave off the last time we spoke?" What was I supposed to do? And what did the other person commit to doing?

2. "What information are they looking for in this meeting?" Is it statistics? Qualitative information? Where are we in the process right now, and what does this particular person need?

3. "Where can I truly add value?" This loops my Value Proposition into the equation. Are there any aspects of this meeting where we might need more traction? Is there something I can offer—through my expertise or skills or talents—that might grease the wheels a little bit?

What I love about human nature is that most of us enjoy helping each other. When we offer service to others in the fullness of the "100% participation, 0%

attachment" principle, it's amazing what kind of opportunities present themselves. When we understand and start trusting this premise, we stand a much better chance of maximizing these opportunities when we give ourselves the gift of preparation time. Creating the habit of Proper Preparation simply takes the awareness to ask yourself key questions that can better assist you in being ready and then acting on the answers that come forward.

THREE

DEFINING YOUR PREPARATION

We start this process by reviewing the action steps you identified from your first Aspect of Success mind map. As you do this, reflect on these questions:

• Do you see that you'll need support for your actions?

• Does that support involve additional information, materials, resources or education?

• If so, by when do you need it?

With those answers in mind, identify your primary Aspect of Success and your priority goal: _____ + _____

Using the example we've been working with, I'd write:

WEALTH + Focusing on creating my open house

Now, list the **action steps** you want to take, the **form of preparation** required in order to take your step, and the **completion deadline.**

ACTION STEP	PROPER PREPARATION	DEADLINE
_____,	_____,	_____
_____,	_____,	_____
_____,	_____,	_____

Your preparation directs how and where you focus your energy for each action step and the completion deadline builds in accountability. Otherwise you can drift away from your goal with every new notification or message that shows up in your life. Incentivize yourself by creating a timeline that allows you to win. That's how you build internal confidence and great trust in yourself.

My list would look like this:

ACTION STEP / PROPER PREPARATION / DEADLINE

Call Aaron to set up a meeting / Consider what I can offer him in exchange / 1 week from today

Call Felicia to set up a meeting / Research her 5 most recent sales / 1 week from today

Research latest sales stats for Brentwood / Call David to ask where to start / Wednesday

Why does this work? Because:

Action Steps = the road map to completion

Proper Preparation = the installation of greater confidence

Deadlines = the built-in accountability that demonstrates that your goal matters

One more note about a benefit of Proper Preparation: the "Pause." Consider that whenever you take the time to ask yourself "What information do I need prior to moving forward?" you're giving yourself time and space to slow down. So often, in our eagerness to perform, we rush into situations. This tendency can lead to less than positive results.

> "Consider you're going into battle. The imprudent person impulsively barges onto the scene with a knife in hand only to find himself staring down the barrel of a gun. "

Consider you're going into battle. The imprudent person impulsively barges onto the scene with a knife in hand only to find himself staring down the barrel of a gun. The prudent man asks, "What sort of weapons will I be facing?" before he enters the fray. So, slow down, take full advantage of the "pause" that inherently comes from asking preparatory questions, and enter your next environment better prepared to win.

From here forward, declare a moratorium on rushing into the next action step without first considering how you can make that step as meaningful as you can.

Ready to try it?

Schedule a 20-minute window of time in your week in which to take the following steps.

1. Identify the priority project or activity that's in alignment with your goal.

2. Consider one to four action steps you're willing to take to create and complete that priority project. You may even want to mind map about this. Once you've identified your steps, write them down in your journal or calendar.

3. Ask yourself what additional information you need to maximize each action you'll be taking. How can you set yourself up to win as you take this action? Write down that information.

4. How long will it take you to complete each "Proper Preparation" step? It could be as little as 30 seconds of "pause" time, or you may require a larger amount of time to fulfill these needs.

5. Consider your deadline to achieve each of the actions you've identified. The sequence and timing may be quick and easy. And some of your next actions may hinge on someone getting back to you. Consider deadlines for all of it.

6. Add into your schedule whatever preparation time you think you'll need, keeping in mind your deadlines.

Now you're ready to engage far more effectively. Is your confidence level higher now, even before you've taken action? Are you more relaxed? Do you feel more Properly Prepared?

We're now turning the corner and applying your new mindsets and tools to go forward in action. In action, we create our success. To what degree are you giving yourself every opportunity to win right now? And by winning, I mean experiencing your Success. My personal wish is that you always give yourself every opportunity to win. Proper Preparation leads to more productive outcomes. Proper Preparation positions you to win.

FOUR

TUNING IN

Sometimes I'm asked how I can stay on the healthy side of the line between being thoroughly prepared and overthinking things. Your best gauge here is your internal gauge. Your biggest asset in developing that gauge is expanding your capacity to feel comfortable moving forward based on what you know, and then seeing what shows up. Realize that you're never going to have all of the information; things are always going to evolve.

I accept that I have enough information if, before I make a communication, I experience a degree of confidence that I know how to make progress. Having a sense of clarity about what I want from the other party and what I'm willing to give them in return, is all I require. I don't need to have every single detail worked out.

In service to strengthening your internal gauge of clarity, I want to introduce another question that I consider to be a power tool in my preparation practice. It's inspired by the Imaginary Council exercise outlined in Napoleon Hill's classic, *Think and Grow Rich*. Take a moment to read through the following exercise, then close your eyes and test-drive it for yourself. You might even record it so you can do it with your eyes closed.

Imagine that you're about to begin a meeting. It's a type of meeting that you have frequently in your life—maybe it's an introductory meeting with a new client, or a financial discussion between you and your partner, or perhaps a one-to-one with one of your direct reports. Because you have this appointment on a regular basis, you know what your normal course of action is, right? Just take a couple of moments to review that right now...what is it that you generally do and how does that typically go?

Once you have a clear sense of your standard procedure for this meeting, just let that go, and come present. Now take a moment to consider the answer to this question: "If I were a Master at having this type of meeting, what additional steps would I take to create the consummate experience for everyone involved? What would a Master at this do?" Take a few moments to reflect on this and observe what shows up. If you've closed your eyes to do this, open them when you're ready. If you need to, grab a notepad and pen and jot down anything noteworthy.

Did any insights pop up as a result of that exercise? Was there something extra that was available to you, something perhaps, unexpected or surprising? Interesting, right? Consider that there's a Master inside you, and all you need to do is resource it. Invoke it. Invite it to show up.

I close my eyes and ask, "What would an expert do in this moment?" With 90% success, I get at least one pearl of wisdom. You can do this anytime—all you need is 20–30 seconds. You can use it before any type of meeting, regardless of your profession or walk of life. You could also use this same visualization considering, instead, one of your role models or mentors. There may be someone whose life or career you aspire to emulate. The question, then, might look something like, "How would (person's name) handle this situation?" or "How would an expert at this prepare for this next step?" You'll get the same type of intuitive insight.

Every sound bite of information you receive is registered within either your conscious or subconscious mind. You overhear a colleague mention something exciting they did, a new technology they're using, an innovative way of doing sales forecasting, even a new ingredient they're cooking with. You think, "That sounds good. I want to remember that." And within 30 seconds the idea disappears. Ever have that experience? But did it really disappear? No. Actually, that idea gets filed as part of your information data resource and it lives on inside your subconscious mind. As you enhance your ability to quiet your mind enough to allow the relevant information to filter in again, you'll be amazed at how those ideas will come back and support your natural intelligence.

If you gained any insight from the exercise above, you now have a tangible experience that this works and that you can use again to serve you as you access it. Some people prefer to think of it as simply trusting their instincts. That's fine; it doesn't matter what you call it. If something works, I'll use it. From my point of view, it's more important that we empower this concept than try to define it. I don't want to spend my time trying to figure it out; I just want to use it. If you're giving me a hammer, I don't need to know how the hammer is made. I see a nail, and I'm just hitting that thing.

"As you enhance your ability to quiet your mind enough to allow the relevant information to filter in again, you'll be amazed at how those ideas will come back and support your natural intelligence."

The exercise of mind mapping about your primary goals works off the same principle. We don't necessarily need a therapist, coach, guide or mentor to unlock the doors to our wisdom (though I'm a big fan of all of them, and they can provide great value in our lives). When we plug ourselves into this, a bigger picture can drop in.

One of my associates had the intention to create more business. Part of the strategy was to reach out to specific people in his sphere of influence. Part of that subset strategy was to quiet his mind and ask for any intuitive guidance. When he did that, he got an intuitive nudge to reach out to another broker he knew in the area to ask if he could be of service to her.

Then his mind, that self-judging filter that can influence us to stay safe, chimed in: "That's a stupid idea! She is a broker in her own right. She doesn't need my help."

But my associate followed his instincts and made the call anyway. The other broker's response was, "I'm amazed that you called me. I've been handling all of my deals myself, but now we're about to have a child and my life is changing. I don't want to be representing myself anymore. You're my *sign* (yup, she said that) saying that I should have someone represent me. I want you to do it." And just like that, he secured a new client.

That could be happenstance, or it could be absolute creation. Guidance comes from all sources. We simply need to open ourselves to call it forward. Give yourself permission to play at this level, and see what shows up. Less noise...more awareness.

WHAT IF THERE WERE NO "TOUGH" QUESTIONS?

We must ask questions of ourselves and others to gain greater insight, clarity and understanding. We need to ask questions if we want to progress, grow and learn. In the context of this work, I look at questions as one of our most empowering tools to create the success we want to achieve.

Some folks take full advantage of their ability to ask questions and others do not. For some, based on upbringing and/or the mental filters we've imposed on ourselves, we don't always feel it is "appropriate" to ask certain questions for fear that they could make us or others feel uncomfortable. The truth remains that in any relationship, we get asked all sorts of questions. Some come with easy answers and others, based on filters, can cause us to stammer, pause, sweat, wish we were invisible. These types of questions come with the label "Tough."

Being a student of the game, I've done my own analysis on this. While I realize that society has imposed its influence over which questions we ask and how we ask them, ultimately, I've concluded there really are no "tough" questions. Only questions we hope we don't get asked or questions we don't want to ask others for fear of how we might make them feel or how they may in turn respond.

Sometimes we'd rather not even ask a question for fear of hearing an answer that we may not be able to deal with. "Do you love me" is a great example of this type of question. However, we're dealing in success here. Part of the pursuit of success is having information; as much information as we can. We need to ask questions of everyone so that we can learn, grow and gauge our course to check that we are heading in the right direction. That means we can't be afraid to ask questions or be too concerned about the "appropriate" nature of the question.

This conversation may test your comfort zone of "safety" around the whole topic of questioning. If that's the case, take a deep breath and just consider that this section may have some value for you. My intention is that you have greater freedom to ask the questions that serve your higher purpose and growth.

The truth is, everyone has a "get out of jail free" card when asked a question: We can always respond, "I don't feel comfortable answering that question." That response is usually honored. The Fifth Amendment of our U.S. Constitution affords us that legal luxury in the context of not incriminating ourselves, so clearly, this is an "acceptable" answer. That means we can get over worrying about the "appropriate" nature of questioning and recognize everyone has the opportunity to simply abstain from answering any question we may ask.

My focus here is to get to the questions that incite fear in us. Say you walk into a meeting that could advance your career and you're really nervous. You're so distracted that you feel like there's a marching band parading through your brain. In the room all you see is adversaries. Your defenses are up and your eyes dart around looking for the quickest escape. In other words, this is not the environment you want to create to progress your career in that moment.

"What if the 'unknown' associated with those fear-creating questions is actually your answer to creating more of the positive outcome you want?"

What is the real cause of this distraction? Pertaining to the questions we ask or answer, consider that the root of your concern and your sweaty arm pits is simply your dread, your consuming fear that you are going to be asked a question that you are not prepared to answer.

Time for a perception check. You know the questions that are creating your fear, right? What if the "unknown" associated with those fear-creating questions is actually your answer to creating more of the positive outcome you want? What if, as part of your proper preparation, you considered the three questions that, if asked, could freak you out the most and took the time to answer each of them? You'd literally strategize your answers prior to the meeting and come up with tangible, logical responses that put you in the best light to win in that situation. You still may stammer a bit as you find your rhythm during the meeting, but at least you'd have a much more solid foundation of responses upon which to stand that would support you far more effectively than a cotton mouth and a "deer in the headlights" look that doesn't instill confidence.

If you take the time to consider any environment prior to walking in, you can provide yourself more ammunition to win. Otherwise, you might as well just pick up that knife and hope that your adversaries' guns take you out quickly and without too much pain.

At Partners Trust, I encouraged our associates to write out a list of the top five questions they pray the other person won't ask them during a meeting. Full Proper Preparation requires us to answer those questions before the meeting ever arrives.

As a realtor, one of those questions that I might not want to hear could be, "Why should I go with you when Jane Smith sells all of the houses in this neighborhood?" Some other greatest hits include: Why should I hire you? Why should I pay you? Why would I pay your fee when someone else will do it for much less? If I want to create outcomes that line up with my Success, I've got to be prepared to respond to those.

My preparation starts with how I craft my answers. My response begins with the full support of my Value Proposition and in accordance with my Statement of Purpose. I rehearse my responses enough that when I'm in the room, I'm authentically articulate with my answers. This gives my answers more authority. Furthermore, I'm far more present to see how my answers are being received.

From this vantage point, consider the concept of a "tough" question. Can there really be a hard question if you are prepared with an answer? Not in my experience. From that perspective, the only "tough" part of this equation is choosing to make the investment of time as part of your Proper Preparation. If you can instill this pre-game habit of Proper Preparation, your confidence will surge and you'll start looking at these types of questions with the attitude of "Bring it on!" simply because you're ready.

SIX

ARE YOU HAPPY?

Sometimes the questions we don't want to be asked are more personal. They're not strategic points that need to be clarified; they're more revelatory and reflective. One of my colleagues shared with me that the question he hoped no one asked him was, "Are you happy?" "Nick, I never know how to authentically respond. I just shrug." He confided that the truth was that he wasn't so happy. And every time he was asked that question, he was forced to confront that reality along with a certain level of social awkwardness around not knowing what to say.

While this is a different type of issue from the ones we've explored so far, the process of creating Success in this area plays out the same as our $100,000 goal. My guidance for my colleague was to create a Happiness mind map. I asked him to take 5-7 minutes to consider, "What are all the ways that I create happiness for myself?"

Next I invited him to look at what he'd come up with—the people, the experiences, the environments that evoke happiness—to identify which ones give him the richest doses of happiness and make those his new priorities. Happiness becomes one of the non-negotiables.

Following that, I suggested he identify happiness action steps and drop those into a schedule. "When you do that," I told him, "you're committing to engaging more often with what makes you happy." I also recommended he consider whether or not he needs any kind of preparation for those things—what could amplify his experience of happiness even more when he's doing the stuff that makes him happy? As a result of taking these steps doing those happy things more often, when people approach him and ask, "Hey man, are you happy," he can then give them a clearer answer because he's created it.

> **"It's virtually impossible not to experience more of those qualities if you're willing to become more aware of them and then move toward them."**

It can be that straightforward and simple if you take the time to clarify that happiness (or another don't-want-to-answer issue) is a priority in your life and then engage with it. You can take the qualities from your Statement of Purpose and use this same process with any one of them. It's virtually impossible not to experience more of those qualities if you're willing to become more aware of them and then move toward them.

And as you go through this journey, expect that what constitutes your negotiables and non-negotiables will evolve. Over time, interests and priorities naturally change. That's just life. It could be that drive to be successful at all costs shifts into going for greater happiness or exploring more of your creativity. Maybe instead of being available to your clients at all hours, time to paint or write becomes a new non-negotiable for you.

In fact, all of the tools you're implementing now will evolve—your qualities, your Statement of Purpose, your definition of Success. What's the key to managing the whole thing? The level of awareness that you have as you're participating with it. As you engage more deeply with your priorities, you may realize that the goal you're after no longer actually feels like the right fit for you. Or you may discover that it really is something that you've always wanted; it's just that up until now you hadn't made it non-negotiable. You may find that it becomes so important to you now that you're genuinely called to honor yourself enough to put this stuff in your schedule and engage with it.

If you look at my calendar right now, you'll see "Nick Time" scheduled into it. That's my time. I get to choose what I'm going to do there. As I clarify the projects and action steps that matter to me, anything that's not already slotted into my schedule gets dealt with during that time.

What that time also does is give me creative space to consider possibilities and options that may serve my projects or their next action steps. Many people define "productive" individuals as those who go from one meeting to the next, clicking through their day while handling the pressing details of the moment. In that scenario, there is little time or opportunity to pause, to collect one's thoughts and allow space for reflection or inspiration. For myself, I started to increase the quality of my productivity to a much greater degree when I created "quiet" periods within the day. In these pauses I can assess what is transpiring during the day so I may better assimilate the information and deal with next actions prior to rushing to yet another meeting only to wonder at the end of the day, "What happened?"

I encourage you to carve out that time for yourself. It may be a tad awkward at first because you are not used to it. Stay the course. Give yourself the time to slow down and quiet the noise. It's my experience that goodness and wisdom greet you on the other side.

SEVEN

THE POWER OF CLEAR INTENTION

Along with your Value Proposition and Proper Preparation towards achieving success, let's now explore the third element for creating successful outcomes: Clear Intention. This facet works directly with your mind, your focus and your ability to best position you to play in the arena of 100% participation and 0% attachment. Implementing this concept as part of your preparation and mental focus will also absolutely serve you as part of your overarching Negotiation strategy.

We've established that prior to taking action, the mind must be in alignment with that action in order to move in the most effective direction possible. This entails mentally creating plans and strategies so that we then can act on them. In many respects, you've already been doing this, from the creation of your "Why" and then the implementation of your Success game plan. Let's drill down to how you can better support your mind so that it in turn, may better support you.

Drs. Ron and Mary Hulnick, pioneers in the field of Spiritual Psychology, put it this way: *Intentions act as guideposts for us. When I know what my intention is for doing a particular thing or engaging in an activity, I can then consider whether or not I'm on-course in accordance to the result that I'm looking for.*

Remember that we've discussed the power of being present as the best way to positively affect an outcome. Creating a clear intention in advance for what you want to accomplish in a meeting best supports "real-time" focus and guidance during that event. If I know what I would like before I enter the environment, it's easier for me to recognize it when I'm there. Of equal importance, I can also recognize what's not present. When I can see what is not aligned with my clear intention, I can then redirect whatever the interaction is more towards where I want it to go. In the absence of that clarity, I'm at the mercy of what is going on with far less control over the situation. That is not a prescription for success.

As you create your clear intentions in relation to your success, understand that intentions are very different from *expectations* in relation to what you want to achieve. Where one focus supports you in the present moment, the other creates outcome attachments and future fantasies. Pulling away from the present moment doesn't support you in ultimately realizing your objective. Any time I've created an expectation around something I want, all I've done is foster a level of attachment to that outcome that will hinder my ability to "be present." This is one more facet of 100% participation and 0% attachment that can better support your growth and learning as you prepare yourself for an event.

Perhaps you've heard the saying, "Expectation is the Mother of Disappointment." Consider any time you've expected a result and didn't get it. Immediately, you enter a state of disappointment that can last for an extended period of time. It can also dash your hopes and cause you to feel discouraged and defeated. My strong encouragement for you as you proceed along your trajectory of success is that you focus your attention and awareness on the intention of what you want and let go of any expectation around that desire during its pursuit. You will be far better served and stand a far greater chance to achieve what you want.

Do you know that you've already started this process of creating clear intentions? Your Statement of Purpose is a clear intention: *"I am creating my success because I want to experience more _____, _____, and_____ in all aspects of my life."* When you write or speak that statement, you're identifying where you're going and what you want more of.

Consider your current reality: today. As you review the day so far, have you applied your Statement of Purpose as a guidepost to the interactions you've had with yourself and others? Have you remembered to walk into any environment and honor those qualities that you want to experience more? Or did you forget to keep your eyes, mind and heart looking to recognize the signs that align with those qualities? When you look at it from that point of reference, you can start to experience how subtle this game of focus is and how diligent and discerning we all must be if we are truly going to live a life of purpose, as we define it.

A couple of years ago, I had an opportunity to recruit a top-producing agent who was dissatisfied with her current broker. This was a big deal, because not only would I get the agent and her production, I'd also receive validation in the brokerage community that my brokerage was the "place to be." The stakes were high and I might only have one opportunity to secure this person. I had a meeting scheduled with her and was excited to be in pursuit of this talented agent.

As I was preparing myself beforehand, I realized I was getting unusually amped up. It was starting to wear me out before the meeting even started; clearly a sign that I was in "attachment" mode, which wasn't serving my greater intention. My mind was racing off into flights of fancy about all the good that would come from her addition to our firm. I became lost in the future without any hold on what I was going to do to bring her with us in the first place.

I suddenly realized that my attachment to the outcome was completely consuming me and I was in no positive position to be effective during the meeting that was 15 minutes away. Closing my eyes, taking a few deep and easy breaths, I started to come present. And as I did, I asked myself a simple question: "What could I do to create the biggest impact that would serve me and Partners Trust?" After a moment, I reminded myself of one of the core tenets of our company: Service. Our Trust Agreement defined our intention of service and creating trust. That recognition became the key to my focus: I would look for signs and benchmarks to better guide me in ensuring that I stayed in the mindset and consciousness to be of service in this meeting.

That simple awareness started directing my actions. How could I best be of service to this person? Certainly offering information about our company and how it would serve her in making more money would be factored in. From this place of service, my mind calmed even further and I started considering my tone of voice and the questions I would ask to find out how she was doing with this potential change. Then it hit me: She may be scared. She was about to embark on a big career move and she assuredly had many apprehensions about the potential move.

Now strategy ideas started coming forward inside of me. What if I approached this meeting from that place of putting myself in her shoes? Then I'd better understand her fears and concerns and from there, I could better honor them. I had my clear intention and equally important, clear direction. I decided I was going to create the safest environment I could for her and see how I could best support her in making the best choice that served *her* needs.

As soon as I came to that realization, the pressure I was feeling evaporated. I let go of my attachment to my outcome and created a focus—a clear intention—just to be of support. My whole demeanor and tone relaxed. By the time we said hello to each other, I was in complete peace and focused on staying in my intention to be of service and creating that safe space for her. I really didn't need to do anything else. I answered her questions and asked a few of my own and the meeting went beautifully.

Three days later she joined Partners Trust and is with us to this day.

I like this story because it worked out in our favor. Sometimes however, the best of intentions and proper planning don't net a positive outcome. Life is like that. Thinking back to the Success Trajectory graph, remember the Fantasy Trajectory line representing equal action creating equal success. Rather than get disappointed, I encourage you to refer to the Success Trajectory line and trust that each positive action creates a stronger foundation that will ultimately serve you in realizing a greater reality on all levels of your success.

Since our focus for much of this section deals with interactions with others, let's explore ways you can better express your intentions to all parties involved. Let's go back to the foundation we've already laid. Here's a tip that may serve you: Consider that your intentions for a meeting or an interaction are not about getting something; they're about *giving* something.

If my first expression of giving is that of my Value Proposition, imagine how that can start to resonate with the intention of creating a more relaxed environment around me? So, my first intention is to express my best "me." Remember that all intentions start prior to the meeting as part of proper preparation. Identify the components of your Value Proposition as they apply to the environment at hand and you're well on your way to maximizing the possibility. From that foundation, based on the circumstances associated with the conversation, you will enter the environment more poised, ready and able to "read" the guideposts of your intention as the meeting unfolds.

For example, say I'm meeting with a client, and I sense he's starting to drift away. Without a clear intention of focus, I may start to get nervous. When I get nervous, my immediate impulse is to start forcing. My tone of voice and body language reflect tension in this type of non-direction and I start to spiral away from my balance and solid foundation. But because I'm practicing using the guideposts associated with my Clear Intention, I know I'm off-course as soon as I catch myself feeling this. Instead of acting on nervous impulse, I simply remind myself, "My intention is to share the best of who I am through my calm, my tone of voice and my willingness to just stay present."

Once I have my internal mind reset, I can better direct the conversation toward my intended result from a more relaxed place. Restoring my peace, clear that I can't control the outcome or anyone else involved in it, I start to realize that I can redirect that energy more fully on my focus to positively control *my* actions. My questions become directed, on purpose in relation to the reality I see before me: that the client is drifting. From a place of intentionality, driven by a mindset to be of service, my questions are simple, without a nervous energy. Calmly I ask, "Are you with me? Does that make sense? Do you have a question about what I'm suggesting?" Now the conversation can progress, allowing the space for both my client and me to engage in productive dialog without the grip of unnecessary attachment or expectation.

> **"Restoring my peace, clear that I can't control the outcome or anyone else involved in it, I start to realize that I can redirect that energy more fully on my focus to positively control *my* actions."**

One of the most positive choices we can make as negotiators is to enhance the quality of our interactions. The practice of Clear Intention wakes us up to novel ways that we can turn up our quality quotient with the people in our lives and with ourselves. Let's look at how this might play out.

In my professional world, I might have an intention like, "To make sure my client understands that I care about him." So, I craft an email to my client, and before pressing Send I pause to consider, "Have I communicated the message that I'm intending to convey?" Now, I may be purely addressing facts and logistics in my email: "We're going to meet at three o'clock, I'm going to have the stats that you requested and the plan you wanted to hear more about, and I've asked a couple of questions of the other parties involved and they're going to bring that information to the table. Is there anything I'm missing?" Underneath it all, those facts, logistics and questions all convey one underlying message: "I care about you." The simple steps of listening, clarifying the information, taking action and then summarizing what I heard and what I did is high-level communication. That's how I demonstrate my caring.

What kind of service would you like to provide? Would it be useful? Inspired? Or perhaps joyful? What are the qualities or experiences that would better support you and those close to you? Maybe it's appreciation. Or education. Or creativity. Whatever your answers may be, you can start to fold those into your intentions. Stepping into a meeting with this type of forethought can revolutionize your experience and your relationships.

With all of that in mind, let me introduce you to your next opportunity. Pull out the mind maps for the Eight Aspects of your Success and a copy of your Statement of Purpose. Review your mind maps one more time. Re-familiarize yourself with your vision of Success in these areas of your life. If you don't have your maps available right now, simply call to mind the areas of your life that are the focus of your journey to Success in this moment.

Take a minute or two to reflect on the answer to this question: What is my intention for these aspects of my Success? Each area of your life will have its own unique intention. For one aspect, your intention might be about realizing the specific, tangible goal you've identified and are working toward. For another, it might be about experiencing more of the qualities in your Statement of Purpose.

Once you get a sense of this, formulate a simple statement that captures the essence of your intention for each Aspect of your Success. Begin each intention with the words, "My intention is...." There's no exact science to this. Again, you may simply want to restate your goal for this Aspect using this new languaging. The most important thing is that this feels authentic to you. Use your personal imagery and language to craft a statement that feels meaningful and lines up with your definition of Success.

Maybe one of the qualities in your Statement of Purpose is having a sense of freedom in your life. And perhaps one of the ways you experience freedom is through traveling. So, you might craft Clear Intentions for your area of Play or Higher Purpose—wherever this would fit for you—that may sound something like, "My intention is to experience greater freedom in my life. My intention is to travel more often." If there's someplace in particular you've always wanted to visit, you can even specify, "My intention is to travel to the Galapagos Islands."

Or let's say that your focus for Success right now is your Creativity. And one way you enjoy expressing creatively is through cooking. So your Clear Intention might be, "My intention is to cook meals that I love," or "My intention is to express and share my value by creating beautiful and delicious feasts."

This is where the real power of "Intention versus Method" comes into play. Often when we do an exercise like this, our minds immediately jump into the "how" part. Our inner dialogue can sound like, "Wait a minute. That's not even realistic. I'm broke right now. I'm tied down with family obligations. I have an 80-hour-a-week job, for God's sake. I can't have this intention." Stay out of this as best you can when you're doing this exercise. This is not about being pragmatic or sensible; it's about possibility. We're not putting any timelines on this or making any commitments. Just allow yourself to play. And if that kind of inner dialogue shows up, you can simply respond with "Thank you for sharing," and then carry on with your exploration.

Once you have an intention identified for all Eight Aspects, take a look at what you've written. This is the direction you're heading. Clear Intention defines your path. Want some added juice? Include your eight intentions in your regular journaling practice. Remember the suggestion to write out your Statement of Purpose while you listen to the songs on your playlist. If you want to throttle up your journey to Success, include in this mix writing out your intentions daily. The physical act of writing these will enhance your connection and experience in realizing Success.

We're continuing to create our own positive reinforcement here. We're enrolling your Statement of Purpose, intentions and favorite songs as allies on behalf of your Success. Picture yourself taking an action toward your Success, recognizing that the full power of your qualities and intentions are infused into that action.

I'll close this section by issuing a challenge. In the next day, prior to every single meeting that you attend, ask yourself this question: "To what degree am I connected to my Value Proposition, prepared, and clear about my intention for this meeting?" Be ruthless with yourself on this—not one meeting goes by where you don't ask this question. I suspect you'll find that as you work with this question more and more, you'll naturally start making microscopic adjustments that transform into new habits that land you squarely on the most efficient path to your Success.

PART V
NEGOTIATING YOUR SUCCESS

As we enter the final phase of this process designed to empower your negotiating skills and awareness, consider for a moment the foundation that you've created to support you in realizing your success:

You now have a better understanding of your Value Proposition and some very specific tools to support you in claiming your worth and value.

You possess a clearer sense of what Success means to you and have a working road map to achieve your success goals.

You understand how you can maximize your next opportunity by standing taller in your Value Proposition, engaging in Proper Preparation and by creating a clear intention strategy before you even enter the negotiation environment.

Now it's time to build your negotiating confidence so that you can walk into virtually any environment and create the outcomes that bring you greater joy, happiness and success.

CHAPTER THIRTY-
EIGHT

WHAT MAKES A
GREAT NEGOTIATOR?

Having negotiated many deals and been witness to many differing negotiation styles, I've come to the conclusion that a great negotiator simply has the ability to create a level of confidence that what they are offering is what you need.

Think about any recent negotiation where you've either bought something or done something someone asked you to do. Your choice to move forward with that negotiation probably hinged on your confidence level that your purchase or action supported *your* need in the process. That's why you acted; because your need was served. Whether you consciously realized it or not, that negotiator instilled a confidence in you, a peace of mind that made you feel good about the decision you made. When you acted, guess what else you did. You served the needs of the person with whom you were negotiating. However, because your needs were met, you were okay with the fact that the other person's needs were being fulfilled as well. How they got you to your place of peace of mind and clarity to act is the essence of their talent. Either via "selling" you or "educating" you, it worked.

Whether you fully realize it or not, you now have the tools to build that foundational level of confidence in yourself that can directly affect your ability to instill confidence in others and create a greater receptivity to get people to act in alignment with both their needs and yours.

That said, I am not suggesting that you have the ability to make people do things or act against their will. To the contrary, a great negotiator ultimately must deliver the answer, the solution, to another's need and obtain their satisfaction in order to get them to act.

First and foremost, this section is designed to empower you with strategies to discover the needs of others, so you can deliver a presentation that honors those needs. I'm suggesting that your effectiveness in discovering and packaging that solution rides upon your confidence in your own abilities. In turn, that will create the confidence in the person with whom you're dealing. That is the beauty of these strategies. The information and its practical application are going to support your effectiveness as a negotiator in service to your alignment towards success.

Understand that a negotiation is first, a discovery session, and second, a strategy dialog to get both sides more of what they need and want. The greater the needs and underlying "why," the more attentive both parties are towards realizing that solution.

As we transition now to actually negotiating for the experiences and tangible assets that you want, take a moment to consider how you regard yourself as a negotiator. What thoughts pop into your mind? Do you see yourself as a good negotiator or as one who lacks confidence in this area? If you have any apprehension about how you'll do, breathe easy in knowing that you're about to have resources designed to meet you where you are. No prior formal training is necessary. All that's required is a willing mind and a clear intention to lean in and get the most you can out of the material. Make this your approach, and by the time you digest the final page of this book, you'll be in fine shape to step into any arena and successfully represent yourself.

Consider my story. I have no formal training as a "negotiator." I didn't attend negotiating school. No one taught me any standardized technique or methodology. The extent of my formal accredited education is a bachelor's degree from Vassar College. In Drama. Yet here I am.

Moreover, who amongst the great negotiators of all time studied negotiation before they started negotiating? I can't think of one person. And that's because most of the truly great negotiators didn't start out looking to become negotiators. As situations arose, worldly experience taught them their deft touch and artful tact, which means that that skill is available to anyone willing to put in the time to develop it. Including you.

When you think of the people you regard as powerful negotiators, do you see common characteristics? Many of us hold the image that a successful negotiator needs a big, out-there personality—they've got a booming voice and they're good at intimidation tactics. Yet, as an extremely successful negotiator, I do not resemble that at all. However, I have created my own very effective techniques for negotiating positive outcomes for my clients and myself.

One of my heroes, Abraham Lincoln, was a gangly, introverted, small-town attorney who became one of the most profound negotiators the United States of America has ever known. Lincoln never studied "negotiation;" he studied law. But what he did do was apply his talents in concert with his humanity to achieve his intended objectives. And what an exquisite negotiator he was. Consider the herculean task before him: Lincoln committed himself to ending slavery in the United States. Can you imagine trying to negotiate that outcome? From what I've studied of the situation, Lincoln was completely committed to the cause of freedom for all mankind. His "Why" was well defined and his intention most clear.

But when we examine Lincoln's technique, we discover his authentic style of negotiation. Lincoln didn't bully people to get his way. Far from it. Instead he used his formidable skills as an orator, humorist and cajoler—skills learned in the backwoods of Kentucky and later refined in a court of law—to educate those initially against him to see another perspective and to provide clarity that incited them to consider his alternative.

Lincoln was most adept at analyzing situations and the people involved in them; he made it his mission to understand what was important to people and why. You and I now know that Proper Preparation and Clear Intention are absolutely critical components of successful negotiation. Imagine the preparation that Lincoln must have done to meet his adversaries with equally clear, yet opposing intentions, and to develop parallel intentions for what he wanted to achieve with each individual. He succeeded because he knew how to speak to others in a way that honored their perspective while clearly and simply relaying what he wanted to convey.

The foundation that served Lincoln in his negotiations forms the very same building blocks that any of us need as we walk into a room and move closer to our Success. You now have that clear purpose. All you need is the seed of belief that you can do it.

NINE

HOW IS YOUR PERCEPTION DEFINING YOUR REALITY?

Part of developing your confidence as a negotiator is feeling comfortable in as many negotiating situations as possible. As no two negotiations are exactly alike, the more you understand what causes people to act the way they do, the easier it will be to feel comfortable and relaxed. Understand that when you enter a negotiation, part of your preparation is realizing that you may or may not be met with logic, facts or reason. Egos, unrealistic expectations and misguided perceptions are some of the factors that affect people's personalities and thus, the negotiation.

Travel back in time to high school with me, to illustrate a point about perceptions and how quickly they can become hard and fast realities in one's thinking. Let's say your best friend tells you that there's a new kid in school, Bob, and the rap on Bob is that he's creepy. Based on nothing more than the "information" from your friend, you now believe that Bob is creepy. When another friend tells you the same thing about Bob, the reality solidifies further. Doesn't matter that they heard it from the same person. You've got two sources for your "truth," plus the power of your imagination and suddenly you've got a full-blown case against creepy, weird Bob.

But here are the facts: you've never met Bob. You haven't said a word to him or bothered to check out what you've heard. Your entire perception of him is based on hearsay. And that hearsay has led you to formulate a full-blown reality about Bob. Now you can't even look at Bob without piling all sorts of preconceptions on the guy. What's more, you probably don't even recognize this is happening. Your focus is not figuring out whether any of what you've heard is actually true; it's keeping Bob away from everyone near and dear to you and watching out for the next time he goes "weird."

This is a very human behavior and we do the same thing with negotiations. Consider how you determine the value of an object. We tend to formulate solid conclusions based on a perception of that value before we gain enough information through fact-checking and asking questions to assess a more accurate value. We then fight for our perception because we believe it to be true. Why do we do this? The short answer is twofold: First, we have such an attachment to the desired outcome that we create a *perception of value*. Then we justify that perception as truth. We want something to be real so badly that we grab hold of one fact and embellish it into a complete reality. This happens all the time in my business of selling homes.

> "We tend to formulate solid conclusions based on a perception of that value before we gain enough information through fact-checking and asking questions to assess a more accurate value."

Here's how that works. Let's say you want to sell your home. You go on the Internet to see all the homes for sale in your neighborhood. As you check out the photos and compare the pricing and amenities of each home, you begin to formulate an opinion of the value of your home. Your assessment may include commentaries such as: "My kitchen is better than theirs." "My yard is bigger." "I've got a third bedroom." The wrinkle is that with each home you view, you have an attachment to what you want to see. Your focus is to build a case for why your home compares more favorably to the other homes in the neighborhood. Why? Because you *want* your home to be worth more than any other home on the market. This "wanting" creates a filter of perception through which you absorb all the information. Each detail layers upon the last to form the reality you want. After about an hour researching homes online, you've concluded your home is worth a tremendous number and is clearly, "The best house in the neighborhood."

Perception has become Reality in your mind.

However, you don't actually have all the information. The homes you're looking at to determine value are those that are for sale, not houses that have recently sold. It is far more important to gauge the value of your home based on homes that have sold in the neighborhood rather than listed homes. Only after a house has sold can you use it as a viable reference point for the value of your home. Homes listed for sale may or may not be well-priced and that factor can distort the actual value of homes around yours.

The second reason we tend to rely on our perception rather than focus on getting enough information to assess the reality of a situation or valuation is that we don't know an effective way to gain greater clarity. Look back to your comfort zone for a moment. When you are not sure about how to do something, and the consequence could lead to embarrassment or failure, you probably aren't going to be too keen on stretching yourself in this arena. Add the fact that you may not want to hear the truth based on your attachment to your value, and you have zero motivation to be shown anything that may challenge your perception.

Imagine for a moment two sides of a negotiation. Each side has created a perception of value based on attachment and now has justified it as truth. Neither side is willing to listen to the reason of fact because facts may not support the "reality" they've created. If the two sides are not willing to compare the actual foundational facts of the situation as a basis to define the truth, it is very difficult to arrive at some form of agreement.

Then there's the "Right/Wrong" factor. Have you ever walked into a negotiation "knowing" that you're right? Or better yet, the person who greets you is hell-bent on their own "rightness"? In either case, the internal dialog has been had, the information has been evaluated, and the thought has been formed into a comprehensive conclusion. In my experience, when this occurs, it doesn't take long before tempers flare, followed by defensiveness and agitation. Because the presentation started from a defined position—that is, the sense of "rightness"—the righteous person is, by definition, blinded by their position. And when people don't see things going their way, they often create a polarizing position that is met by the other side with an equally opposing position. This classic "I'm right, you're wrong" game does not lead to positive outcomes.

As you progress in going for what you want, you will constantly be faced with perceptions of value. When you consider it a "given" that people enter a negotiation with "inflated" values of their position defined only by perception, either because they truly believe their offering is of greater value or because they're hoping it's of greater value, then you will not be surprised when that shows up. So, accept it. As you do, you'll be in a better position to work through the perception to your benefit.

Patience and persistence, along with effective questioning strategies, are important keys to unraveling such perceptions. We are going to explore ways to diffuse this kind of limited thinking as we move forward. For now, it's important that you understand that you and your negotiating partner may have preconceived perceptions that are affecting your reality. As you can work through those perceptions to get to the reality of *actual value, needs* and *timing*, you'll be better able to avoid the traps of personality and focus your attention on the true solutions to create winning outcomes.

THE VALUE OF HONORING ALL PERSPECTIVES

Consider the concept of honoring. This doesn't necessarily equate with agreement; it simply means acknowledging a person's perception and position, without responding as if they are wrong or out of line. Think about yourself. When you feel heard and honored, you become more receptive to sharing about what's really going on for you. That information is essential to understanding where someone is coming from, what he or she truly needs, and how you can possibly assist him or her. Honoring them will also create the space for greater trust and authenticity down the line in your negotiation.

> "When you feel heard and honored, you become more receptive to sharing about what's really going on for you."

Let's say that you walk into your office on Monday morning only to discover that I, your colleague, believe I am Superman. And, most importantly, I'm sure I can fly. Now, my perception of being Superman is fine in and of itself—as long as I don't do anything that could actually lead directly to harming myself. But if I believe I can fly, and, what's more, I'm ready to head to the roof to prove it, that could end up poorly for me.

So, why should you care? Beyond the fact that you like me personally, I also happen to be the #1 sales associate in your office. You make money off me every time I make a deal, and I can't make deals if I'm dead.

What to do? Consider that the negotiation starts when I share: "Dude, I'm Superman and I can fly!" In that moment, you have a choice of how you respond. One response will honor my perspective, and the other will discount it. Here's how each response could play out.

Let's start with the path chosen by most negotiators: "Nick, you're not Superman and I think you need to take the weekend off." We'll call this the discounting perspective. That response, in conflict with my belief, spurs me into immediate action.

"Oh yeah, well I'll show you!" I bolt from the room and in seconds I'm on the roof. I jump to my untimely demise. End result: You've just lost your #1 producer.

Now let's look at the honoring path. "Nick, really? Wow. That's very cool. How do you know you can fly? Have you tried it yet?" Here, we're asking "perception-checking" type questions with the intention of creating greater clarity and common ground.

"No, not yet. But, I'm sure I can. Want to see?"

"Sure I do. How about you show me right now and let's see how you do it." Note that this is a strategy-type suggestion designed to create greater confidence and clarity.

"Don't you think I should go to the roof for more space?"

"Nah. Just go out front and take a practice flight—to work out the kinks. Make sense?"

"Yeah, you're probably right. Okay."

Now, one of two things will happen. When we get outside either I will be able to fly and you'll have an even more valuable sales associate who can leap tall buildings with a single bound. Or, more likely, I won't be able to fly, and will have dispelled my own perception without harming myself. Either way, you've put yourself in a better position and ensured a more positive outcome by first acknowledging my perspective before you make a conclusion based on your own beliefs.

While a tad far-fetched, this tale has a sound application. No matter what you think you know about the other side of the table, you must have the discipline to first take the time to better understand where that person is coming from and what's most important to him. Hold a clear intention to honor the person's position and perception of value. Remember you don't need to agree with it; you simply need to recognize it and acknowledge it. Once you do, you'll know how to better direct the conversation toward the outcome you wish to achieve.

ONE

SELLING VS. EDUCATING

Most negotiators don't know how to look beyond their own perception of value. Instead they gauge the initial sense of the value of their offering against the value of the other side's offering and start hammering the other side with a variety of selling techniques. When we do this, we enter into the "Selling Zone." This is a space marked by strategies seeking to convince, persuade, sway or manipulate others.

Evolutionarily speaking, we're all animals by nature. It's the job of our reptilian brain to sense things. Our frontal lobe gets involved to figure out the data we're taking in, but everything starts with the information detected by the most primal parts of our brains. We sense danger, we sense calm, and we sense tension in a room. And we sure-as-heck sense when we're being sold. Last time I checked, most people don't like being sold.

"Being sold" usually has some feeling of urgency attached to it, and it activates our internal voice in the form of warnings like: "This is making me uncomfortable" and "I don't know you so I don't trust you." Lack of trust creates polarization.

Negotiations that come from a "sell" consciousness focus on figuring out what you can take from me. This is not a prescription for a successful negotiation.

Furthermore, it doesn't make anyone feel good about themselves in the process. I know this because I used to negotiate from that place. Early in my career I thought this was the only way to get deals done. Hurry up! Force the transaction! Don't wait; they could change their mind!

After a few months of this, I started getting really tired. I started disliking my job. I was getting some results, but not at the level I was aiming for. And I felt as if I was constantly on edge, frantic and out-of-balance.

Then one day it dawned on me that there was another way of doing things. After having been in countless negotiations and feeling like I was beating my head against the wall, I finally recognized that there was an alternative to "selling" that not only served my clients better, but also served ME in a much better way. Once I employed this strategy, I became far more successful in my business and much more effective as a negotiator. This new way was to become an Educator.

Once I learned to slow down and shift my focus to that of Educator rather than Seller, my results soared. Here's the difference I learned:

Walking into a seller's living room with the intention of getting a listing, I entered the environment from a "taking" consciousness. This is fertile ground from which to sell myself which is exactly what I would do. The intention of "What can I do to get this listing?" was really more like "How can I convince this person to give it to me"? I was attached to the outcome. A far cry from 100% Participation and 0% Attachment. Because I had this "take" mindset, I wasn't centered during the discussions. My mind raced with thoughts, trying to figure out if I was saying the right things designed to "get" something.

As I matured and started employing the consciousness of education in alignment with presenting my Value Proposition—to be of service—my entire demeanor shifted. First, I was far more confident because I didn't need to try and force the situation. I entered the environment feeling more relaxed because I didn't need to sell anything. I knew all I had to do was focus on discovering what was most important to the other person to determine if and how I could be of assistance.

Transitioning from discovery to strategy was organic and straightforward, based on the client's specific set of circumstances and needs. This led to building rapport in a much calmer state of mind. The consciousness of education and being of service created far better results. Another wonderful by-product of being an educator is that it created the space to allow everyone the opportunity to better digest all

"As we explore this consciousness of education, we're going to layer in demonstrations of being of service and how the two focuses create a dynamic and effective means of communication and result."

the information and thus make informed decisions.

As we explore this consciousness of education, we're going to layer in demonstrations of being of service and how the two focuses create a dynamic and effective means of communication and result. You'll also see how the foundation of clear intention and proper preparation will fold right into the steps you will learn when you interact with your negotiating partner.

TWO

RECOGNIZING THE MINDSET THAT GREETS YOU

Most of us have been conned, duped or had someone take advantage of us in one form or another. We don't like it and we certainly don't want to repeat it. That very powerful memory creates a protective, preconceived notion that has dramatic impact on our psyches, especially when entering a negotiation. I used to be very guarded when approached by someone I didn't know who offered me an "opportunity." Our protective nature in turn creates our very own Guardian at the Gate in the form of a personality shield. However, if we are going to get more of what we want, we do need to interact and negotiate with others.

After analyzing this dilemma over time, I have developed an approach that can assist you in honoring your guarded position while engaging to get more of what you want and need. The first thing I discovered is that there are two definitive "guard" personalities. We each have both of these on call. Each one is very specific and fairly easy to recognize; this is the good news. Because as you recognize which Guardian at the Gate is in front of you, you'll have the tools and skills to more gracefully honor and speak to that Guardian personality, so that you can better assure them that your intention is not to take or steal anything but rather to assist and educate. As you speak to someone from this clear intention of honoring, you'll see how that Guardian will soften and allow you to get beyond the surface of a negotiation to the underlying matter at hand: their need.

Let's look at these two distinctive mindsets and dissect their personalities so you can better recognize and relate to their guarded perception. The first Guardian has skeptical armor, clad in doubt and distrust. This guardian greets you with characteristics such as furtive or squinting eyes, with arms crossed over the chest, and it speaks in tones of underlying dismissal. Understand that this person is simply protecting himself or herself as they assess you in that moment. Underneath their veneer, they are checking you out and asking the bottom line question, "Are you going to screw me over?"

During initial conversations with this persona, the untrained negotiator can tend to be caught off-guard. Quick perceptions become a reality assessment that the meeting is not going well. Thoughts race and the immediate impressions will be reactive and counterproductive, associated with negative judgments and fears of intimidation. Soon thereafter, the timid negotiator will probably start retreating, looking for the nearest exit, and foregoing any potential opportunity that may or may not be present. Conversely, if you understand that this persona is simply protecting itself from being screwed over, you don't need to be intimidated or concerned by it. You can simply recognize the persona and move toward addressing that concern.

The second Guardian at the Gate personality is far less intimidating but equally potent in its ability to protect itself from harm. This guard greets you at the door, far more welcoming and open. You're offered coffee, tea or water upon your arrival and made to be comfortable. However, this guardian has a very keen eye and is looking to make sure you are going to protect their interests beyond all else. If you do not demonstrate that you can do that for them, they will show you the door and never work with you again. At the heart of this perceptive guarding is the question: "Are you going to take care of me?"

Beyond the persona of each Guardian (Don't hurt me; Take care of me), both individuals want the same thing: Trust. While their respective guards are up, they are gauging to determine one thing: "Can I trust you?" That is the most powerful question of all. I have found my most lasting relationships in both business and friendships are founded on sincere trust. As you develop and apply your Value

Proposition to everyone you meet with a clear intention to be of service, you'll quickly find you can gracefully disarm either Guardian and have more meaningful conversations, which can lead to more successful outcomes.

Please also understand a key element that has to do with all negotiations: If you're in the room, there's a reason. Just because someone greets you with a sneer doesn't mean they don't want something from you. Otherwise, you wouldn't be in the room in the first place. It's easier to deal with and diffuse a person's guarded personality when you realize that they're simply in protection mode.

> "The key is being able to recognize which one it is so that you remain in balance inside yourself and adapt accordingly."

In reality, it doesn't much matter which personality/mindset greets you. The key is being able to recognize which one it is so that you remain in balance inside yourself and adapt accordingly. As we'll discuss in our exploration of negotiation, one of the critical keys to negotiating success is our ability to create rapport and trust. Just because someone's personality has a bit of a bark to it doesn't mean they don't want to negotiate with you.

THE NINE NEGOTIATION KEYS FOR SUCCESSFUL OUTCOMES

Requesting a pay raise. Interviewing for a job. Buying a company. Asking someone out on a date. Offering to provide services for someone. What do all of these life experiences have in common? They involve some sort of negotiation.

While certain types of negotiations have more weight and heft than others (pitching your new invention to an investor is different from asking for extra sprinkles on your ice cream cone), the outcome of every one matters to us. That's why we negotiate in the first place. So it stands to reason that if we want to enhance our success, we'd be well served by developing a skill set constructed specifically to support us in this task.

In the chapters that follow, you'll receive a series of negotiation "keys" that I have refined over the course of my career. Collectively, these strategies are designed to build trust, reveal true motivations and present solutions. Each step builds upon the preceding ones, yet there are no scripts or rigidity here. Each one has its own structure while also giving you the flexibility to express your creativity, share your authenticity and demonstrate your Value Proposition.

Imagine a negotiation as if it were a piece of music. The Nine Keys are like movements in a symphony. In any classical composition, each section of the piece has its own structure and a defined progression from beginning to end. So it is with a negotiation. A beautifully orchestrated negotiation can evolve naturally with grace and ease in the same way that an exquisite piece of music unfolds one note at a time, leaving you feeling more fulfilled and inspired.

Each key contains two distinct components that serve to both define it individually and to weave in with the others collectively, creating an organic structure for your negotiation. Every key contains both an *action* and the underlying *intention* of that action. The action refers to what you're doing in that moment, and the intention is designed to offer you internal direction and guidance that will keep you on-course with the action.

Because negotiations are fluid and don't always go according to plan, you'll be well-served by learning to rely on your awareness and your intentionality to keep your negotiations progressing. In my experience, most negotiators don't know how to create an effective rhythm as they navigate their way through the process. They either get ahead of themselves or don't know when to press forward toward the close. Each intention acts as a clear guide that allows you to recognize when to move the negotiation to the next step and when to hold steady.

As we explore the partnership between actions and intentions, you'll discover the positive impact they have on both your confidence and effectiveness. The more you practice working with these keys and allowing them to serve you, the quicker you'll find your unique negotiating rhythm and stability. As you start recognizing what you're looking for within each segment of the negotiation, you will naturally know when it's time to move forward. And as you become more proficient in your skill, your trust level in your ability will grow exponentially. That's when it starts getting really fun.

Understand that what you're learning here is a type of new language—it's a different way to communicate what you want and how you want to go about getting it. Resist the urge to put pressure on yourself to master these keys right out of the gate. It takes time and practice. As you begin, allow the simple awareness inherent in each key to give you greater strength and confidence. Go at a gentle pace with the knowledge that you're building new negotiation muscles. As you work them, the "language" of your communication through these keys will become more fluid and fluent.

You'll also discover that this negotiating strategy supports you in seamlessly incorporating your value and worth into the entire negotiating equation. This system is designed to support you in effectively educating your counterpart, without having to "sell" yourself at all. For me, that aspect alone is worth the price of admission.

To assist you in anchoring your learning throughout this section, I'll remind you of some of the specific foundational resources we've already explored that can assist you in maximizing each negotiation key. We've worked with a number of tools and concepts to prepare you for this phase. Most importantly, you've had the opportunity to recognize and claim your goodness and your gratitude for who you truly are; that's the ultimate foundation for realizing your success. Now it's time to bring the pieces together into a magnificent whole.

Here they are: nine dynamic-yet-simple, actionable, and highly intentional negotiation keys.

THE NINE NEGOTIATION KEYS AND ASSOCIATED INTENTIONS

NEGOTIATION KEY	CLEAR INTENTION
1. Demonstrating Enthusiasm	Building Rapport
2. Asking Clarifying Questions	Making No Assumptions
3. Defining Your Intention to Serve	Building Trust
4. Illuminating the Objective	Discovering Your Talking Points
5. Recapping the Objective	Practicing Perception Checking
6. Crafting the Strategy	Building Confidence
7. Establishing Your Value	Delivering The Close
8. Introducing "The Pivot"	Preserving Peace of Mind
9. Identifying Next Steps	Confirming the Relationship

As we go forward, I encourage you to reengage with the primary aspect of your success you'd like to develop. As you work through these chapters detailing each action and its associated intention, start applying the keys to your vision of success. Take a look at the mind map for your primary aspect, and review the priorities you defined. Is there any area of opportunity within this aspect of your success that entails a negotiation of any kind? Do you need to ask for assistance from someone in order to move your process forward? If so, I invite you to practice applying these keys to that potential negotiation. You'll better comprehend this approach if you give it tangible application by using a real negotiation in your life.

These nine keys have served me tremendously through the vast majority of the negotiations I've navigated over the course of my career. Each one was paramount to the process of creating Partners Trust. I know that they can serve you as they've served me.

KEY #1: DEMONSTRATING ENTHUSIASM

You've created an opportunity. Awesome! A negotiation is an opportunity to advance your success, regardless of the outcome. Cultivating this mindset will give all your negotiations an expansive and optimistic tone.

Your very first task is to bring your energy to this opportunity. Allow yourself to get excited about it. When you demonstrate enthusiasm, your aliveness creates engagement. And that's a vital resource for any negotiation platform.

Demonstrate that you're genuinely happy to be making this connection. The whole reason you've created this meeting in the first place is because you want to be there, right? Allow enthusiasm to ring from the tone of your voice, the glimmer in your eyes and the firmness of your handshake. Express sincere interest in the person you're meeting and what he or she has to offer.

In *The Seven Habits of Highly Effective People*, Stephen Covey offers a compelling case for the adage, "No one cares how much you know until they know how much you care." This is a great sentiment to keep in mind in this initial stage of the negotiation. We covered this in **Selling vs. Educating**, but it's worth repeating here: It doesn't serve you to lead with the intention of inking the deal, getting the check, signing the papers or whatever it is you're ultimately after. If you do, then the other person will pick up on your fixation and potentially be resistant to it. However, if your only intention at the outset is to connect, and you do that by expressing your enthusiasm for whatever it is that's under discussion, then you're creating a completely different kind of reality. Do you think the other person will enjoy spending a little time with anyone who expresses enthusiasm for what they have to offer? Absolutely.

There are two important coaching points to keep in mind when it comes to demonstrating your enthusiasm. The first one is to match the energy level of the room.

Are you familiar with the rheostat? It's a mechanism that's used to adjust the intensity of a current, like a lighting dimmer switch. Relate to your level of enthusiasm as if it's on a rheostat that you can easily dial up or down. When it comes to meeting people for the first time and expressing enthusiasm, modulation is important. You want to aim to harmonize with the other person's energy levels upon introduction. If you rush into the meeting blazing with excitement, you may overpower the other people in the room and cause those with whom you're looking to build rapport to instead shy away. Conversely, if you enter the room with too little energy, those present may think you don't care or are ambivalent about the topic under discussion. Either too much or too little enthusiasm can be interpreted by people with whom you're meeting as a sign that you lack negotiating skill. That's not how you want to start a negotiation. Match the room or add energy to it by just a degree or two, and you'll start to build a more solid foundation from which to proceed.

Also remember that you'll most likely be met by one of two overarching mindsets: "Are you going to screw me over?" or "Are you going to help me?" Your ability to adapt your level of enthusiasm to match the personality type that greets you will serve you very well at this stage.

The second coaching point for expressing your enthusiasm is to be authentic. Lack of genuine communication is the precursor to a lack of trust, and that's a potential death blow to creating any kind of successful outcome. When we feel uncomfortable or nervous, we tend to over-compliment or force enthusiasm in order to impress the people we're meeting. While it's natural to be nervous, this can quickly become embarrassing or even annoying to others. And more importantly, it tends to undermine both your own self-confidence as well as others' perceptions that you're genuine in your intentions.

If expressed authentically, however, your enthusiasm can be infectious. By *authentically*, I mean in earnest and from your heart. This is not a call for manufactured, invasion-of-personal-space enthusiasm. That's what I call "negotiation repellent." If you start doing that, we might as well call you "Creepy Bob." Don't be *that* Bob.

What to do instead? Use what you've learned. Tapping into your goodness and gratitude and silently repeating your Statement of Purpose are powerful tools you can employ to keep you aligned and authentic during these initial moments. As you feel compelled to share a compliment or offer praise, here's a guideline to bear in mind: authentically share your enjoyment of something or someone in the moment when you experience it. That's the time to comment, and not before. Too often, in our rush to make people like us, we blurt out some pre-fabricated compliment without any genuine sense of appreciation. This tends to ring hollow.

If you're finding it difficult to create common ground, here's a tip. Every so often I find myself in negotiations where I have little connection with the environment or the individuals surrounding me. In those cases, still wanting to warm the waters, I might compliment the color of a wall, a piece of art or a photo, or even the dog lying in the corner of the room. Whatever initial flurry of "ice breaking" comments you choose, make them genuine and authentic if your aim is to initiate a richer connection. That way, if your topic generates more conversation, you can engage in the discussion with sincerity. And bring a positive focus to any initial questions you ask; that will enhance the level of engagement and energy in the room. We all like to talk about things that make us happy. "Tell me what you most love about this [company/employee/book—whatever]," or "Please give me a tour of your new [home/website/campus]" are great places to begin.

With that foundation being laid, let's move into our exploration of the clear intention for Key #1.

Key #1 Clear Intention: Rapport

Building rapport is an essential ingredient for creating any type of positive relationship. Practicing authenticity is both an action and an intention in this case. Focus on expressing yourself genuinely and honoring the other person's temperament—whatever it is—as you make this initial connection. Enter the meeting with the intention to be present and available to assess the energy of the room and its occupants. No glossing over anything here. Take your time and embrace these moments so that the person you're dealing with feels heard and cared for. As you do, you're supporting yourself in staying more fully present and allowing your genuineness to naturally come forward.

Allow yourself to experience a sense of self-trust as you fulfill this intention. Trust that the preparation you've already done will carry you, and allow that to fuel your confidence. From this place of "knowing", you'll better calibrate your energy level based on the mood that greets you. Trust that there will be plenty of time later in the negotiation to present your talents, your worth and your wisdoms. No need to rush into forcing your Value Proposition on anyone. The design of these nine keys creates space for you to present and demonstrate your unique gifts that can serve the greater good of the negotiation. The first guidepost is to build rapport. That's it.

Cue your Gratitude. Remind yourself that this meeting is an opportunity to contribute to your success. Regardless of what happens, you can learn and grow from this encounter. Regardless of the nature of the invitation, the possibility exists to walk away from any meeting feeling better and more inspired, knowing you're fully in the game of creating your success.

When you feel a degree of confidence that you've built a connection, odds are good that you've realized this intention and can move on to the next key. Until rapport has been established, I'd be very hesitant to proceed. If the smiles never come, press forward when you sense there's an openness to continuing the conversation or when you recognize that the other person is thinking about what you have to say. If you hold the intention to meet the other person wherever they are—whether they're ecstatic or grumpy—you'll more naturally pick up on when they're ready for the conversation to evolve.

Key #1 Foundational Practices:

100% Participation, 0% Attachment. This tool will be a component of almost every one of the nine negotiation keys. And we get to this state through...

Gratitude. Enthusiasm is often associated with expressions of gratitude. Before you begin your negotiation, take a moment to reflect on the blessings in your life and to get in touch with what you're grateful for. Remind yourself that regardless of the outcome of the negotiation in front of you, this experience can positively contribute to your Success.

Your **Statement of Purpose** puts you in direct contact with your "Why." Reading or saying your Statement of Purpose before you engage will link you with your most efficient path to your success.

Your **Value Proposition** is the foundation of 100% Participation. Allow yourself a moment to connect with your three goodness qualities from your Value Proposition. This opportunity is a chance to express and share the best of who you are.

Capitalize on the **Proper Preparation** you've done and allow that to bolster your confidence and presence as you step into the negotiation arena.

FIVE

KEY #2: ASKING CLARIFYING QUESTIONS

The rookie mistake most negotiators make is that they *assume*. They assume they know the facts. They assume they know what the other person wants or needs. The classic negotiation killer is making assumptions and then taking misguided action based on them. Whether we do this out of eagerness, laziness or inexperience, we do ourselves a huge disservice when we bypass the pursuit of clarity for the glory of the conquest. Don't let false perceptions lead you astray when you open negotiations.

Early in my career, I'd be sitting an open house on a Sunday afternoon looking for buyers to potentially purchase that property. I'd evaluate everyone who stopped by through an assumptive perception lens. I'd assess them as they approached the front door, and in my naiveté I'd have figured out their entire life story before they ever walked across the threshold. From that narrow vantage point of those preconceived notions, I'd either engage or I wouldn't.

> "Whether we do this out of eagerness, laziness or inexperience, we do ourselves a huge disservice when we bypass the pursuit of clarity for the glory of the conquest."

By boldly assuming all sorts of things, I took myself further and further away from the opportunity to discover what my actual opportunity was with each of them. I didn't realize that some of the people walking through the house could be potential sellers from the neighborhood. I didn't realize that some of the people could even be friends of the seller of the home, coming by to see how well I represented the property. Because my lens was so restricted, I missed all sorts of opportunities. Compound those narrow sight lines with my over-eagerness to perform and I was a walking candidate for "Amateur Negotiator" status.

As you begin to move into any negotiation, you must know where the other person is coming from and most importantly, what they want from you in this negotiation. I cannot emphasize this enough. As a realtor, just because someone invites me into their home doesn't mean they always want to sell it. They may just want to know its value, or what the market looks like in terms of timing to sell. They may want to know if they should rent. Should they develop the property themselves? Who knows what they want? If I walk in the door making assumptions that they want to sell, then my enthusiasm for selling their home may be misconstrued as self-serving or as a lack of care about their needs or intentions, and thus, I've missed the mark.

The solution? Ask questions. Lots of them. Asking clear questions creates an opportunity for discovery and solution. Start with the other person's perception of their reality. Remember the value of honoring someone's preconceptions so that you may better understand them. There's an expression in poker that you "play the hand you're dealt." Before you go too far in a negotiation, you need to know what type of person you're dealing with and what their foundational beliefs are going into the negotiation. Asking questions unearths many of the overt and underlying objectives, perceptions, timing and other outcome-related information that will better serve you and the person with whom you're negotiating as the negotiation proceeds. Acute attention and awareness are critical as you listen to the answers you get. Another essential benefit of asking questions is that, in the answers, you'll get a better perspective as to where you can apply your value proposition and ultimately, your suggestions for a solution strategy.

Key #2 Clear Intention: Making No Assumptions

At this point, all you're looking for is information that will provide you with guidance down the line. Don't over-think this stage. The intention with this step is to ask preliminary questions to better understand the other person's needs and wants. I call this the "first cut" layer of questions. Your only job is to engage in earnest curiosity to develop a greater understanding of how you can contribute to the matter at hand. Your tone of voice can be relaxed and easy because you're not trying to sell anything here. This clear intention will shape your entire demeanor, ideally making you more approachable and comforting.

The truth is, at this stage of the meeting you just want to know why you're in the room. You can do this by simply asking, "How may I be of service?" or "What would you like to get out of our conversation today?" I ask it with a soft smile and a genuine desire to more fully understand the other person's needs. Ultimately, you're the one giving those words life through your tone of voice and smile and the twinkle in your eye.

I've long been intrigued by UCLA Professor Emeritus Albert Mehrabian's studies of verbal and nonverbal communication. He found that if our words, tone of voice and body language don't all match up when we're communicating, then the other person only registers 7% of the words coming out of our mouths. That means the message you're intending to convey is only going to fully land if you're aligned, authentic and honest in your communications. Let that incentivize you to make each of these keys fully yours by being authentic and using the language that's natural to you.

Key #2 Foundational Practices:

Holding your intention to be present and practice **0% Attachment** to the outcome will assist you in staying curious and asking thoughtful questions.

Remember, there are **no tough questions** because you've already taken the time to properly prepare. Your intention for asking questions is designed to give you more clarity so that you can be of assistance.

Know that anytime you utilize this key in a negotiation, you're demonstrating one aspect of your **Value Proposition**; you're bringing forward your caring and your presence through the questions that you ask and the way you listen to the other person's responses.

This is also a great place to practice utilizing your **Inner Guidance**. When you've come to the end of your questions, inwardly ask yourself, "What else would I want to know about this situation?" or, "Is there anything that we haven't talked about yet that would help me be of service to this person?"

SIX

KEY #3: DEFINING YOUR INTENTION TO SERVE

If you do nothing else with this book other than catch the underlying essence of this single key and employ it in full trust of its authentic power, you'll become a very effective negotiator. I could devote an entire book to this key alone; it's that important. Out of all the strategies we're exploring, this one has without question provided me with the most value, because it empowers and supports me in using each of the other eight keys more effectively.

This is such a powerful and foundational key that it could be Key Number 1. However, it's more effective once you've established a foundation with Keys #1 and 2. So don't let its placement detract from its importance.

In my experience, two elements consistently show up in any form of negotiation. 1) Most people feel uncomfortable negotiating on their own behalf, and 2) No one wants to feel stupid or as if they've been duped when a negotiation concludes. Key #3 honors both of these factors by creating an environment that's more conducive to open and honest communication and to considering all of the possible available outcomes.

At this point in the negotiation, it's time to articulate your willingness, above all else, to be of service to the negotiation and in service to the other side of the table.

I realize this may sound strange or unorthodox as this is a negotiation and you, too, want something in return. However, if you can catch the spirit of this ideal and demonstrate your willingness to sacrifice your needs and desires in this moment, it is my experience that you will end up being rewarded handsomely.

The reason is simple: This key has the ability to create a level of trust that becomes a tremendous asset towards ultimately consummating a deal. That said, this is not the time to start sharing your talents or what you want in return. There will be ample time to present your skills and value soon enough. It's just not yet. Right now, your job is to simply and earnestly communicate one thing: Your willingness to be of service. Having shared this concept with my associates at Partners Trust for years, we have a nickname for it. We call this the "Whether you use me or not" Key.

> **"This key has the ability to create a level of trust that becomes a tremendous asset towards ultimately consummating a deal."**

Part of the value of this third key is that it sets a tone for the negotiation. This tone is one of giving. It is also a tone of detachment that more fully empowers the intentionality of 100% participation and 0% attachment. I have come to realize that the person willing to walk away from a negotiation has far more power and influence in the final outcome of a negotiation than the person who is attached to an outcome. This key speaks directly to empowering you to be, genuinely, in that position. It lets all parties associated with the deal know that you certainly have an interest in making a deal, however, you do not have an attachment that would cause you to act foolishly or compromise your position of value. Positioning the key is very straightforward. As all deals are different, here are a few ways you might present the concept for your use.

"Whether I get the job or not/whether we ultimately make a deal or not/whether this works or it doesn't work, please know this: *My intention for our time together is to be of service in making sure that I provide you with enough information so you can make an informed decision that serves your needs."* In my industry, I coach my colleagues to get the message across in this way: "Whether you use me or not as your broker, my intention with our time together is to give you the best information possible so that you can make an informed decision that serves your needs."

When I say this, what have I conveyed? First of all, there is no "sell" in that statement. Instead, I'm sharing with you that I have little or no attachment to the outcome of what we're doing. And beyond that, I'm going to give you information, with no strings attached, so that you can make the best decision for *your* needs, not mine.

Have you ever been approached by a salesperson who kindly said, "Please let me know if I can assist you," and then stepped away? What did you feel in that moment? A little freedom? Space? Support? Whatever the feeling is, odds are that it was positive. No pressure, certainly.

That salesperson's words and actions demonstrate what we're exploring here. Of course the sales person wants to sell you a diamond rings or tinker toys or whatever they're selling because that is their job. Moreover, you also know that the more they sell, the better they do. Bearing that in mind, consider the spirit behind the salesperson's offering and how effective it is inviting you into a deeper level of engagement *if* that's what you'd like. Those nine words not only set a positive tone; they also act as a table-setter for the potential negotiation to follow. They're expressing, "When you're ready, I'm ready. And not before." The experience of freedom, ease and greater trust are all possible when someone communicates with us in this way.

As with all the keys, you can tailor the language to apply to your circumstances in whatever way works for you. There are no scripted statements in any of this dialoging. This key is a mindset; a state of consciousness. Regardless of whether you're negotiating for a new job or a raise in pay, or talking to a customer in your auto repair shop, speaking these words in earnest creates an environment of greater transparency and honesty in your communications.

Key #3 Clear Intention: Building Trust

Your effectiveness as a negotiator grows in direct proportion to your ability to create an environment of trust among all the players in a negotiation. Genuinely demonstrating your willingness to play at this higher level is the best strategy I know for paving the way toward greater trust and alignment. From that place, you're in a much stronger position to share and demonstrate your value proposition.

That said, heed this warning: If you don't truly believe in and embrace the outlook underlying this approach, your 0% Attachment facade will crack at some point in the negotiation and one of your actions or comments will give you away.

When that happens, any trust and good will you've created up until that point will evaporate and the meeting will take on a hollow demeanor. Conversely, if you can keep your focus and hold true to this "whether you use me or not" intention, it will begin to separate you from your competition. Dramatically.

"Easy for you to say, Nick, but I've got bills, mortgages, family obligations, student loans. How am I supposed to authentically personify this mindset when I'm feeling the pull of my immediate needs?" Excellent question!

Here's my answer: Start with practice. Practice focusing on being as present as possible while in the negotiation and trusting in your preparation, your clear intention and your ability to execute these nine keys. Next, consider your current reality at this point in the negotiation: You don't yet have what you came for. And if you don't have what you came for, the truth is you can't lose it. Does that make sense? Getting attached to an outcome that doesn't exist yet is not only unproductive, it's counterproductive.

What I'm suggesting is a way, a proven strategy, that can serve your ultimate objective far better than the road of attachment, urgency and lack. I understand that the bills still need to be paid. The mortgage still exists. For sure those realities are most present. However, if you consider that you've created an opportunity to utilize a strategy that can get you a better result than your current reality, isn't that worth exploring? The key here is that you need to employ this philosophy fully in order to get maximum value. That's why I start by saying, "practice it." Work it, and it will start to serve you. Maintain the discipline of staying present, knowing that this is the most potent thing you can do to realize a positive outcome. From the mentally and emotionally free point of 0% attachment, you're in the best position to achieve what you want.

In my experience, the more I can remain neutral in my attitude, intention and presentation, the better I'm able to focus on my clear intentions and stay present with what's happening in the moment. Please understand that neutral doesn't mean "disinterested." On the contrary. I've been professing the power of enthusiasm as the best way to show caring and interest. But when it comes to discussing strategies, gathering information or presenting myself, I want my tone of voice and body language to communicate the energy of neutrality. If I'm amped up or overly encouraging in the presentation of any strategy, it can be construed as "selling," and that is not part of my execution strategy.

All of that said, I do recognize that what we're talking about is rarified air. I'm no different than any one of us. I have bills that need paying, too. But allowing your focus to drift to the bills will only yank you out of the state where you have maximum effectiveness.

Here's a mindset that has worked for me as I've built this muscle over the years. I call it "suspended reality." While I'm in the midst of the negotiation, I give myself permission to pause my immediate need level for as long as I'm engaged in the moment of a negotiation. If this idea speaks to you and you want to give it a shot, set a Clear Intention to be present for your meeting and to release any attachments you might have to the outcome, knowing that as soon as the meeting is over, you can go right back to being attached. All you're committing to do is to practice this concept and see if it serves you.

Remember that the intention is to create more trust. Refrain from interpreting any positive signs as indications you can now rush or get attached. If you sense the meeting is going well, simply trust that and let it go. Stay the course, fully aware of what the other side is sharing with you and how you might potentially deliver value for them.

Furthermore, keep the intention to *not* start talking about yourself just yet. Key #7 is going to give you ample opportunity to bring your talents and value into the equation. During that time, you'll have the intention to focus on securing a deal or creating agreement with the other side of the table. For now, remain a sponge, soaking up as much information about the other side as possible. When you approach the process this way, you're positioning yourself to realize your greater Success. That's how you can achieve the power of this concept for your full advantage without manipulating anyone else in the process.

I look at my track record of success and I attribute my results largely to this key and to the strategy of 100% participation and 0% attachment. Most often the by-product of employing "whether you use me or not" is that the other person starts to drop their guard. By the time we complete this beat, the intention is that we've quelled the concern of either mindset of, "Are you going to help me?" or "Are you going to screw me over?" Consider both mindsets for a moment, and let's see how that statement impacts each one.

For the "Don't screw me over" filter, here's how their mindset may start to shift: "You're not trying to take anything from me right now. That's good. Not sure if I trust you yet but at least you seem to be straight up. Okay, I'll continue listening to you." And for the "Care for me" filter: "This is like music to my ears. You're not pressuring me, you're giving me information that helps me and I get to make my own decision. I like you. You can stay. Keep going, please."

When there's greater trust present, communications become more candid, authentic and caring. And that's tremendously fertile ground in which two people may come to an accord that serves them both.

This key also supports you in taking better care of yourself on your own journey toward your Success. If you find yourself dealing with a difficult personality, you can also give yourself full permission to end the negotiation at any moment; any time you enter a meeting and your inner dialogue tells you, "I don't need this negotiation. Furthermore, I don't like dealing with this person. I'm done with this negotiation." The mindset of "I don't need this" is the self-honoring side of Key #3.

I've stated that the ultimate strength in any negotiation is the willingness to walk away. That's an authority that comes forward with experience. If I've got enough clients, then I'm not at the mercy of any one of them. If I have very few clients, then I may have to kowtow a little bit. The more you claim your value and worth and step into the authenticity of who you are, the more that will resonate and you'll start to attract like-minded clients.

Key #3 Foundational Practices:

100% Participation, 0% Attachment. If you authentically play at this level, it's my experience that people will flock to you. But first you've got to have trust and faith in yourself. And faith begins with...

Gratitude. Gratitude gets you closer to a state of 0% attachment because you're more thankful for your life as it exists currently. Practicing gratitude before any negotiation will give you a strategic advantage. It creates a tremendous by-product: greater calm—a useful thing to have when you're negotiating. When you focus on what you're grateful for, you're also connecting with a sense of abundance. And when you feel abundant, you'll feel less needy or lacking. That's a hugely empowering perspective from which to launch any negotiation. Walk into any room in touch with the gifts and blessings in your life, and you'll be amazed by how graceful Key #3 becomes. We covered this in our chapter on gratitude and its authority over lack, so take a look at that chapter if you could use a refresher.

When it comes to staying connected to the mindset of 100% participation, try repeating your **Statement of Purpose** before you enter your negotiation. That's your direct connection to your "Why." You might also want to review the **Mind Maps** for each of your 8 Aspects of Success as a way of linking up with the holistic picture of your success. Taking this step can be a great way of gaining perspective by reminding yourself that you've already created lots of opportunities in many different areas of your life and that the negotiation before you is just one of many.

KEY #4: ILLUMINATING
THE OBJECTIVE

Key #3 is meant to create an environment that potentially dissolves any myths or assumptions that your interests are solely self-serving. The action of Key #4 is to ask a deeper cut of questions for the benefit of the person with whom you're negotiating, as well as for your own.

If you've been authentic in your presentation thus far, you will have created more comfort at the negotiating table. When a person feels comfortable with you and considers you as a resource that may be able to help them, odds are they will start to tell you more of what's really going on with their situation. That is what you'll need if you are going to assist in creating strategies that can be of real assistance. That is the first important aspect of asking deeper questions from an intended place of service.

There is another important benefit from gaining a deeper knowledge of the person's needs, timing, dreams and goals. You are also part of this equation with specific needs of your own, among them knowing how you can assist in meeting your negotiating partner's real needs. When you have a clear understanding of what someone needs, you are better able to start giving insights that will support you down the line in presenting your unique value and skills.

In Key #2, you got an initial perspective of what the other side needs and desires. In Key #4, you have an opportunity to expand on the information you already have. As with Key #2, the action of asking questions serves your intention of using the shared information to assist you in creating a negotiation strategy that serves their interests—and yours. However, as with the previous steps, this is still *not* a time to start presenting your attributes or talents. When someone is sharing important and perhaps sensitive information about his or her situation, the last thing you want to do is start giving the impression that you have a vested interest. I've seen many negotiators start pressing themselves into the dialog at this stage and all it tends to do is shut off the flow of information that you still need.

You can initiate this key by asking the other person, "What are you looking to achieve?" This works in any type of negotiation. In my professional world, my colleagues and I ask the question this way: "What are you looking for in your broker?" Another way of asking this could be, "What do you want from the expert who's going to help you accomplish your goal?" Or if interviewing for a job, "What are you looking for in the person you hire?" Or you can expand the other person's thought process by asking, "What if I could give you what you're hoping to achieve here? What would the process look like for you?"

If I'm in negotiation with you, I must find out how clear you are about what you want, how you're going to achieve it and what you're willing to give in return. For example, if you're looking to hire a service provider, do you know what you're looking for from that provider? I always ask this question of my new clients because up until that point, they haven't fully considered it. I know that may sound strange but I see it all the time. Remember, most people don't like to negotiate for themselves because they don't know all they need to consider. As you become more facile with this process, you'll see how often you assist others in gaining greater clarity while facilitating deals.

Often when I ask someone what he or she is looking to achieve, they'll give me a long list of what they're *not* looking for. That information is equally as helpful. It's also an indicator that they've probably had a previous unpleasant experience that they don't wish to repeat. When I start hearing these types of answers, it's easy to recognize the protector type of "Don't screw me over." As you are familiar with that point of view, you know how to adjust your presentation.

Often in a negotiation, the other side of the table doesn't fully know everything that is available to them in the final negotiation. They know the broad strokes of what they're looking to achieve but not all the nuances of value available to them to finalize a deal or relationship. You gain major ground when you are the person who educates someone to this additional value. With that, you have introduced greater value and the ability to expand that value base as you begin packaging your offer.

Let's use the home sale negotiation as an example. You are the realtor. The seller told you he wants to sell. He told you he wants one million dollars for his home and he's adamant about that number. This is the "first cut" of his negotiating position. However, as we start to go deeper into the seller's motivation and need, we find other aspects of why the seller needs to sell. And in those aspects, we find our nuances that also have value as part of a bigger package. For example, if he can't stand living in his home for whatever reason, then the value of getting out of it may override his attachment to getting every last dollar out of the sale. Or perhaps the sale of the home gives the seller the ability to invest in a business that could yield a much bigger return than the equity in the house. These two additional pieces of the selling puzzle offer far more opportunity to present a value package down the line of the negotiation that actually will serve the seller more than their initial adamant position of "I want $1,000,000 or I'm not selling."

Here's another helpful question designed to expand someone's perspective about the broad scope of value available to him or her in a deal. "Once you have what you want, what will you do with it?" Many times, a person involved in a negotiation focuses solely on the front end of what they want instead of the complete picture. By asking this open-ended question, you achieve two critical gains: 1) you create an opening for that person's greater clarity and 2) you gain key information as to what's most important to that person and how you can speak directly to your ability to deliver what they need. You want enough information so that you feel comfortable saying to them, "I see the fuller picture of what you want, why you want it and when." Once you've got this data, you've got a solid opening for both their and your success.

Key #4 Clear Intention: Discovering Your Talking Points

In support of this action, you're looking for your "deal points" and "perspective points." Deal points are logistics and packaging. Examples are creating agreements wherein "You want X for your product" or "I'm starting you at this position at X amount of money." Perspective points activate and reactivate the motivation to act and are used throughout the negotiating process—not from a place of forcing or coercion but as a way to get people to move beyond their position, that might include fears and apprehensions associated with any new reality.

Consider that a consummated deal changes a person's reality, which also creates change in their lives. Change means shaking up comfort zones and, as we've discussed, can make people retreat or pause. Look back at our home sale example with a prospect who won't sell his home for less than $1,000,000, but also can no longer stand living there. Because you've asked questions to reach the underlying motivation, you can employ a perspective point of reminding them why they may benefit from accepting an offer of $975,000 and having the associated value of freedom to move on. In this case, the intangibility of "freedom" has tangible value.

> **"The effective use of perspective points creates a clear point of reference that offers broader insight and value that could make someone feel better about moving forward even though they didn't get everything they initially thought they wanted."**

The effective use of perspective points creates a clear point of reference that offers broader insight and value that could make someone feel better about moving forward even though they didn't get everything they initially thought they wanted. When defining aspects that make a good negotiator, consider that your ability to create a sense of peace as often as possible throughout the negotiation is a very important aspect of your skill and talent. Perspective points used to create that sense of peace are invaluable.

Urgency and need come in many forms. Take your time as you navigate this step. I've made reference to the "first cut" when dealing with peoples' responses to these discovery-type questions. Be courageous enough to initiate a meaningful dialogue, and then be present with the person as they respond. Too often, early into the fact-finding moments of a negotiation, as negotiators think they understand what's going on and what's at stake, in their excitement and enthusiasm, they drop into assumption mode. As in Key #2, this point in the negotiation can tempt amateur negotiators to rush and push through faster than its natural, organic unfolding. All that leads to is derailment. Trust that until you have a clear understanding of what is at stake and what everyone needs, you need to keep seeking more information, so that when you do turn the corner to start crafting your negotiation game plan, you're on solid footing.

Remember one of our initial premises: *Until you recognize your value and claim your worthiness to achieve success, you'll either sabotage or deflect your ability to receive it.*

From that perspective, think about how far you've come on achieving success. Now that you have so much more information and support in creating your success, understand that many of the people you negotiate with have their own limiting beliefs and concerns that can show up during a negotiation. I've touched on the idea of change causing people to pull back or away from a negotiation for all sorts of reasons. If you sense resistance, don't be thrown by it. Instead, bring your compassion and understanding.

Your focus is to understand someone's true motivation and how you can better assist them. Remember your tone of voice as you proceed so that you can keep the negotiation process on-course. Stay aware of this dynamic. Lift your perspective above the "personality" level that is in front of you and ease the other person into their expansion. Consider your Perspective Points. You can remind him or her about the ultimate need—the real "Why" they're seeking to achieve. You can remind them that this step is part of the path to meeting that need. You can ask them, "What's stopping you in this moment? Is there something you're not clear about? Is there a concern?"

You want to drill right down to it so that you get to the heart of the issue at hand, and then remind them of their greater need as a way of offering a level of clarity and comfort. You might even say, "Remember your need is the reason for doing all of this. You're taking this next step in order to meet that greater need." In my experience, a statement like that reconnects people to their motivation and starts the wheels in motion again.

Key #4 Foundational Practices:

Think of this key as the process of assisting the other person in **Defining** *their* **Success**. Here you get to utilize the skills you're learning in this book as a resource to assist others. I'd say that becomes part of your Value Proposition.

Key #2 helps you discover their "Why." Now harness the power of **Intention Versus Method** by helping them discover their vision. Walk the other person through a mental **Mind Map** of their ideal experience. It's premature to get into strategy discussions just yet, but you can share with them your ability to create "The How" through "The Why" when the time is right.

Use **100% Participation, 0% Attachment** to stay present, curious, and refrain from making assumptions about what you think the other person wants or needs.

EIGHT

KEY #5: RECAPPING THE OBJECTIVE

The simple action of summarizing and repeating back what you've heard up to this point in the conversation gives you the opportunity to ensure that you've clearly understood what's been communicated. Equally importantly, it gives the person you're speaking with the opportunity to get clear about what they've just shared. Remember, when someone has a need and they're approaching you to see if you can help them meet it, they may not have all the details worked out yet. They don't know everything that's involved in the process of achieving their goal. But they probably have a sense of what they do and don't want. By helping them clarify this, you continue to build and reinforce their sense of trust and confidence in you.

The process of playing back what you've heard for greater clarity is called Perception Checking. This skill has been beautifully presented to me through the work of Drs. Mary and Ron Hulnick at the University of Santa Monica. When I'm practicing this key, I simply say to the other person, "What I heard you say is…" and then I tell them what I've heard so far. After recounting that, I ask, "Is that accurate?" or "Did I hear you correctly?"

Taking this step does three things for you. First, it demonstrates that you were present with the other person and you were listening fully. Second, it reinforces your caring. They get that you are listening with purpose. We *love* it when people get us, don't we? And third, it allows space for the other side to acknowledge that you heard what they wanted to convey, and gives them the space to clarify or add anything either one of you might have missed. This is also their opportunity to say, "Oh, and I forgot to tell you this part." In this way, everyone involved in the conversation gains understanding about what matters to the person who's seeking to have their needs met. And if there are multiple parties taking part in this negotiation, then using this key is your opportunity to ensure that everyone is on the same page before you move forward.

Key #5 Clear Intention: Practicing Perception Checking

The objective here is to demonstrate your ability to listen fully and clearly articulate that you hear and honor the other side of the table. Perception Checking is a basic tool utilized in psychology, psychotherapy and conflict resolution. Ultimately our intention is to build greater trust and goodwill among all parties, which is the powerful result of using this key.

Perception Checking also helps you avoid missing something that could cause you to create a separation between you and the person with whom you're negotiating. Any time I articulate a piece of information that is off-base or misinterpreted, I begin to create a divide between me and the other person. And unless that misinterpretation is addressed, that divide widens. The longer the inaccuracy festers, the bigger the divide gets.

The other person's body language will always tip you off when this is happening: When they stop engaging with you, either because they begin to look away or their face takes on a quizzical look, these can be signs that they're no longer mentally with you. If you sense that behavior is showing up, here's what I suggest you do. Stop talking, look right at the other person and say, "I'm picking up that what I just said didn't make sense or you may not have understood me. Is that accurate?" In that moment, you're bringing the other person back. Everything stops so that you can stay on the same trajectory together. You don't need to rush any moment in this process.

You can even add, "It's important to me that you're clear about what I'm saying." No one wants to look foolish, right? This is particularly important if you're beginning to be seen as having any level of authority regarding what's under discussion. If the other person doesn't understand you, then they may start to shy away from the conversation. And guess what the result of that is? Their inner 8-year-old takes over—the one who thinks like this: "I don't understand what he's saying. He scares me. I don't like it. I don't want to be with this person anymore." Then the adult version of them looks you in the eyes and says, "Thank you so much. I'll get back to you." And then you never hear from them again. You thought it was going so well! What happened? You weren't present, so you missed the moment where you lost them.

My biggest asset when it comes to fulfilling this intention is Being Present. Before I communicate anything to anyone else, I've got to allow space in the meeting for nuance to appear, for reflection to occur, and for observation of what is *really* going on as the meeting is taking place.

Key #5 Foundational Practices:

You know it's coming: **100% Participation, 0% Attachment**. Keep practicing this intention throughout every step in the process.

Stay connected to your **Value Proposition** here. Know that your questions and ability to listen are part of your demonstration of the value of the service you provide. Allow yourself to relax and enjoy this part of the process.

Check in with **your Inner Guidance** as you ask the other person questions and listen to their responses. Is there anything else that needs to come forward? Is there something you heard that you didn't quite understand or would like clarity about? Is there some random question that pops into your mind? Take a risk and ask that question if you sense that it may serve either one of you in gaining clarity.

NINE

KEY #6: CRAFTING THE STRATEGY

There are many different types of negotiations, with a variety of complexities and associated risks. Regardless of the circumstances, at some point in any negotiation, the time comes to transition from asking questions and fact-finding into crafting a strategy that eventually leads to a deal. Part of your role as a negotiator, either for yourself or on behalf of another, requires your ability to assess the information you've received and use it to assist you in creating that strategy.

For those of you who don't play in the field of negotiation on a regular basis, I realize this may sound a bit daunting. Fear not! Know this about creating a strategy: it is not an absolute science. There are many ways to create a sound strategy and they don't all entail you being an expert in the field right away. Your execution of these nine negotiation keys provides a tremendous leg up and will serve you in ways you don't even realize yet. No matter what your level of negotiating acumen, let go of the pressure to perform right now as you assimilate this key. Let's look at this from a few vantage points.

These days, most of us use mobile GPS apps to navigate our driving routes from point A to point B. And yet, we are still provided with several route options to get there, depending on timing and convenience. The path of a negotiation is very similar. The route options you consider are just like the choices you have to realize the desired path for your negotiation. Let's say your client (or you for that matter) wants to move quickly to achieve an outcome. What options are available to you to "cut to the chase"? How does money factor into the equation? Do you pay the price on the table to get what you want right away? Maybe. Are there other terms that you can quickly give away to demonstrate movement to accelerate your "good will" to get more of what you want? Possibly. Choices are like playing cards in your hand. The more choices you recognize that are at your disposal, the more powerful your hand is. Being able to see the choices that present themselves in your negotiation makes you a better and more potent negotiator.

Choices also serve another important role in negotiations. Articulating potential choices with colleagues when formulating a strategy creates the ability to dialog a situation for mutual benefit. "What do you think about this strategy? Or that one maybe?" Dialoging gives you the opportunity to explore the merits of each possible choice. Discussing choices between you and your clients also gives everyone the opportunity to weigh in and offer their thoughts. This freedom to dialog opens the doors of everyone's creativity in finding solutions so you are no longer burdened with having to figure it all out on your own. One of my favorite aspects of negotiation is engaging in the creative process of exploring choices to come up with an effective strategy that everyone on my team aligns with. Once the strategy is defined, you become better aligned to execute it.

As you transition from fact-finding to strategy creation, understand that the information you need in order to present viable, solution-oriented choices comes from the questions you asked as part of Keys 2 and 4. That is why I've been so adamant about you staying present during those information-gathering sessions. As you were listening to the information that was being presented to you, realize that you were being given great resources that you can now use to your advantage. The needs and objectives that you were hearing in the early parts of the negotiation now become your opportunity to consider potential strategies that you can explore. I so enjoy the creativity associated with this key, because each negotiation has unique qualities and being able to cultivate solutions becomes part of the artistry of a negotiation. As you gain trust and confidence in this area, this becomes one of the really enjoyable aspects of any negotiation.

Some of you may doubt that an actual dialogue can exist when you're dealing with two potentially adversarial positions in a negotiation. Here's where Keys 1, 3 and 5 come to your aid. Working those Keys, you've been establishing rapport and trust. Those assets are of tremendous value as you enter this stage of the negotiation. Remember that people enter a negotiation with someone because they want or need something from that person. You've created an environment that is most conducive to get the other side of the table to work with you. If their need is real and they sense that you've got something that can assist them, they will want to dialogue with you to come to an amicable accord. Knowing this can relieve even more of the pressure of feeling like you're alone in creating a strategy. As crazy as it sounds, my experience is that the other side of the table will start to work with you because there is a level of trust that your intentions are good and that you're willing to honor them to the best of your ability.

> "Remember that people enter a negotiation with someone because they want or need something from that person. You've created an environment that is most conducive to get the other side of the table to work with you."

Since no two negotiations are alike, recognizing when to make this shift takes a bit of practice and intuition. Part of that intuition activates as you "read" the room to see that the other side of the table is ready to hear a potential strategy to move the ball forward. As you've been developing your rapport during the initial stages of the negotiation, you'll start to see and sense the other side's receptivity to hear what you have to say. They may even ask you directly for your thoughts. Theory in this instance can only take you so far. When you're present in the negotiation and focused on being of service, the "when" of moving forward will organically materialize, and your transition will be more easily recognized.

Here are some recommendations to more effectively present your strategy suggestions when you feel the timing is appropriate. I realize that I've encouraged you not to speak or share your thoughts about your value and skill during the initial steps of this negotiation strategy. That doesn't mean you don't consider where your talents could be of service as you're listening and how you can apply them when the time is right. While I'm listening to their issue, I'm present with what they're saying *and* I'm reflecting on how I can share potential ideas, relevant experiences and suggestions to help them. The reason I tend to hold off from sharing my perspectives is because I don't want to break the flow of communication that is coming my way.

Also, remember that prior to walking into your negotiation, you've done your preparation homework. If statistics are relevant, you've got them to assist you in clarifying an effective strategy when you need them. If research is necessary to help educate the other side gain greater perspective and clarity, you've done it. If you're applying for a job, you've checked out the company and the person interviewing you to get as much information as possible so you know where there are similarities and connectivity. You've also considered in advance and answered those "tough" questions that may be asked so that element is covered. If you've used all of what you learned as you listened during the initial Five Keys, you could already have the foundation of your strategy to build upon at this time in the negotiation.

Next, use the resources you've confirmed through your perception checking. Here you're essentially saying, "Let's take everything you just shared with me about what you want, and build a roadmap for getting there." Now you can summon your Value Proposition and begin to infuse it into the game plan that serves all parties. As you articulate your strategy, remember the concept of "Selling vs. Educating." Do your best to present your ideas and suggestions from a place that educates about the plan's benefits and doesn't sell them.

This brings me to another point about how you can be a more effective educator. If you ask my team at Partners Trust, they all know that the best way to educate is either through facts and/or stories. And here's why.

When I present factual information to you, the only thing in question is the validity of the fact. Using a home valuation analysis for reference, if I tell you that in the last 6 months, only one home has sold in your neighborhood, that is a pretty compelling piece of information. And if I add that currently there are 10 houses on the market in the same area, that adds yet another dimension to my presentation. Were you to hear those two facts about the activity in your neighborhood, you'd have a pretty clear understanding that the market is slow. Conversely, if I don't have facts and only present you with my perception of the market that "Boy the market is really slow," do you think my presentation has the same impact? Based on the fact that my job is selling houses for a living, could it be construed that I have a vested interest in convincing you of my point of view? Could that undermine the authenticity of how you receive the information? When someone just gives their perception of something, it usually causes you to wonder if the information is influenced by the presenter's agenda, which doesn't instill trust. But when they lead with the facts, their conclusion has far greater authority.

Stories are an equally useful way of sharing information, but they achieve their objective from a different vantage point. We've looked at stories within the body of this book as a way of relating to a situation or event. Stories also give us the ability to package information in a way that we can better understand and relate to it.

When it comes to negotiating outcomes, using stories as reference points creates associated perspective points that serve very well. I've used stories as a method to get people to see an expanded perspective; for better or worse. And depending on the outcome of that story, I can assist people to realize that their current choices and positions may or may not be serving them.

We all relate to other people's experiences and use those third-party experiences to our advantage, especially when we don't want to travel down a road that ended badly for someone. Here's an example. I had a buyer for a client and we'd received a counteroffer from the seller. At first, he didn't like the counter; actually he was offended by it. Because I'm the kind of negotiator that honors a client's upset, I appreciated his position and asked what he'd like to do about the counter. After listening for the next five minutes about what a bad person the seller was and how my guy was no longer interested in the house, I asked if I could tell him a brief story about another client who had been in a similar situation. With steam still erupting from his ears, he grudgingly agreed to hear my story.

I started by saying that my past client, a buyer, was equally upset about a counteroffer of $10,000 more than he had offered on a house he and his wife liked. I went on to share the similarities between my past client and this current situation. I noted my past client really wanted the house but couldn't get beyond his upset with the seller's counter and chose to walk away from the negotiation. Three months later, the buyer still hadn't found a house and his wife was ready to divorce him. This client was miserable that he had let $10,000 stand in the way of his owning a house he liked, based on principle. He ended up kicking himself for months. What's worse, the house sold less than two weeks later for more money than my client could have purchased it for.

When I finished my story, my current buyer smiled at me and asked, "What should I do?" Not being an advisor/negotiator who tells my clients what to do, I asked him a question back. "Are you okay if you end up down the same path as my previous client or would you like to buy this house?" My buyer weighed his options, signed the counter offer and bought the house. There you have the power of a story to give people a broader perspective about value and what is of importance to them.

Here's a tip on how to distinguish between selling and education when utilizing Key 6. If I speak to my own need, it'll likely be construed as self-serving. If I speak to the other person's need without any reference to me, my point of view becomes more engaging and is perceived as "educational." Whenever I disagree with a position taken by someone I'm negotiating with, I'm very precise in how I word my objection. I'll say, "That may not serve **your** interests." Not, "**I** think that's a bad idea," or "**I** wouldn't do that if I were you." Note the difference in how I deliver my message. I'm focusing on them and their objective instead of on my thoughts.

What's most entertaining is the look on the other person's face when I say, "That may not serve your interests." They look at me as if to say, "What do you mean, 'it may not serve my interests?'" That opens the door for me to further explain my point—without coming across as if I have any agenda or self-serving interests. In truth, I don't in that moment. The statement is made genuinely with the intention of getting the person to move off a position that appears to be off-course with achieving their goals.

In negotiations, it's easy for anyone to get lost in the forest, hugging a tree of righteousness, when what's really needed is to gain altitude for more efficient forest navigation. A good negotiator can be that elevator into the treetops of perspective through neutral education. It starts with our own detachment.

An important component of crafting a successful strategy is making sure that you take the opportunity to share your Value Proposition as it applies both to the purpose of the meeting (Key 2) and to helping the other person have the experience they want (Key 4). In real estate, it's rare that buyers or sellers think as clearly as brokers and agents do when it comes to making wise decisions about buying or selling a home. This is not a slight on buyers and sellers; it's simply a reality, as buyers and sellers are usually more attached to outcomes than their broker.

I have complete compassion for the fact that they have tremendous emotional investment because a home is where they have been or will be living with their families. Yet most negotiators in our field don't know how to separate the emotion from the process of moving the deal forward. Furthermore, they have no game plan to sort through that difference so they start forcing their position and opinions onto an already volatile situation. And as soon as you start to layer your need, or the perception of your need, into this type of situation, you erode the trust you've built.

No matter what the negotiation, your action of crafting a strategy starts by presenting thoughts, options and choices based on the information you've been given. This will support people in seeing the wisdom of your ultimate proposal. Offering choices and options gives people the chance to breathe and assess. It also gives them the freedom to see a path that gets them to where they want to go without any force or coercion. Consider for yourself when someone gives you options vs. only one path. Whenever I hear, "You've got only one choice," I start resisting and fighting. Let's say I have a $1,000,000 seller, adamant to get his price. I can deal with him in a couple of ways. If my first option is to tell him he'll never get $1,000,000 for his house, do you think I stand a good chance of working with him? Probably not. However, if I agree with him that "we can absolutely start at that price. However, what if we don't get that price? What would you like to do then?" I know the person wants to sell the house as quickly as possible. How long will he want to stay at that price if no one brings him an offer for $1,000,000? My question is posed in such a way that I want him to consider the alternatives if he doesn't get his price.

As you dialogue about options and choices in pursuit of your strategy, incorporating relevant facts and stories greatly helps to create more clarity about which option makes the most sense. I can certainly provide my $1,000,000 seller with facts about value and tell him positive and negative stories of past clients who held firm for a price that either won or lost. Again, my presentation of information is not geared towards my gain but in the spirit of assistance and education, for the benefit of the client. This application works for almost any type of negotiation. Any time you can infuse consequences as a measure against a person's need, you'll start to assess the true desire at hand and how you can better guide them, beyond their own positions, to a more successful outcome.

In the options, facts and stories you provide, you also get to infuse the qualities of your Value Proposition as part of your grander strategy. Consider that every strategy has a person who becomes the vehicle to get it done. The qualities of your Value Proposition are what give texture and color to the ultimate strategy you and your negotiation partner agree upon.

Reflect on the qualities and talents of your Value Proposition. As you craft your strategies, consider how you will employ and empower your value through the execution of the strategy. How do your organization, humor, diligence and caring positively affect the execution of the strategy for the benefit of your client? As you educate the person with whom you are negotiating by demonstrating your abilities and caring, you start to distinguish yourself from your competition. Because you are so clear about what you bring to the table and your capabilities, it becomes much easier to layer them into your strategy and thus create greater confidence in the person considering working with you. That's how this works. Candidly, there really isn't much more magic to it than that. The more you practice and articulate your skills, the easier it is for others to recognize them, relate to you and want to work together.

Key #6 Clear Intention: Building Confidence

Your ability to craft a strategy that fulfills the other person's needs both demonstrates your abilities and showcases your value. In doing this, you're helping them to realize they can rely upon you to meet their objectives for Success as they've defined them.

Understand this: there's only so much goodwill in any negotiation. Goodwill translates to trust and respect—qualities that grease the wheels of negotiations. I work very diligently to make sure I establish and nurture goodwill wherever, whenever. This takes time and patience. Rushing, assuming, and forcing are all actions that erode goodwill, and therefore trust and respect. When that happens, you'll lose the momentum and goodwill you've created.

Stay attentive. Don't get cocky. Make sure you continue to perception check and verify that your strategies are appropriate and on-course. Don't assume that people are hearing you or getting the value of what you're offering. Check in with the other person and ask questions such as, "Do you see the value in what I'm suggesting?" or "Is it clear how what I'm giving you matches up with what you said you were looking for?" Present, ask for confirmation, get it, continue forward, and repeat. This key point is of paramount importance to achieving your desired result.

Utilizing the Nine Keys will also instill goodwill and confidence in yourself that you can draw upon as a tangible asset during a negotiation. I was recently dealing with a business manager in the sale of his high-profile client's condo. He asked me "Why aren't you asking five percent more for this unit?"

"We're already pushing the envelope," I said. "We're basing our price on a single sale that hasn't even closed yet. If that sale doesn't close, then we have no foundation whatsoever for this price. Our strategy is to communicate that our number isn't an *asking* price; it's a *selling* price because we can point to that sale and say, 'That's why this condo is worth this price.' Why add wiggle room when it's already going to be an aggressive sale?"

The business manager said to me, "I appreciate that. I just wanted to talk it through. You've given me the information and I support your recommendation. Thank you."

In that instance, my facts created the peace of mind for this business manager to proceed.

Know that there may be challenges to your strategy. Let that be just fine. Consider that a challenge is a demonstration of engagement. It's also a great opportunity to flesh ideas out further for your collective benefit. As long as there is dialogue, we've got a negotiation. Stay true to your Value Proposition and your understanding of the needs of the person with whom you're negotiating. Steady as she goes while you navigate your way through this important facet of your negotiation.

Key #6 Foundational Practices:

100% Participation, 0% Attachment: Continuing to practice this will keep you calm and focused as you integrate all you've heard into a new strategy to achieve the other person's goals. Remember that your intention to stay present will give you a strategic edge.

Value Proposition: Focus on the intersection between their needs as you understand them and your assets, skills, gifts and goodness. Remember that you're demonstrating in the moment how you *apply your Value Proposition to everything you do*. It's important to share how your Value Proposition will be of assistance to the other person and enhance the journey to the outcome they're seeking.

Selling vs. Educating: Stay focused on the data you can share—both quantitative and qualitative—that illustrates the value of your strategy for achieving the desired goals. Keep the conversation focused around facts and stories that reinforce the value of the strategy you're proposing.

Proper Preparation and Answering the Tough Questions: You'll be thanking yourself for all the preparation you've done when it comes time to utilize this key. You'll be ready to deal with most objections or curveballs that the other person throws at you, once you start articulating your vision.

Developing a good strategy is a wonderful exercise in creativity. If you've applied all the Keys up to this point you may even find this step fun and satisfying, because you'll have all the resources you need to accomplish it.

KEY #7: ESTABLISHING YOUR VALUE

We've established that creating a strategy comes as a result of dialoguing options and choices until all parties agree on the best course of action. However, the best strategies can fall flat if there isn't a competent individual or team executing that strategy.

This Key is where you have the opportunity to establish yourself as the right person for the job or present your product/service as the best solution. Now is the time you get to offer your unique value in a way that defines you as the last integral part of the equation for success, the person who will make it happen. Are you ready to have some fun?

Let's say you're looking for a position with a company. You've heard what the employer needs because you've employed the first six Keys. Consider that the employer has given you a shopping list of what they want and now all you need to do is apply your talents to show you can deliver what the employer is looking for. If the employer has stated that they need someone dependable, you are prepared to articulate all the ways you demonstrate "dependability" from your arsenal of talents and your Value Proposition.

Do you see how easy this becomes? Because you've utilized each Key up to this moment to establish the objectives and the clear path to success, now all you need to do is deliver on that need from your proper preparation, your Value Proposition and through your Clear Intentions of what you are willing to bring to the job. Imagine being an employer sitting across the table from you. How happy do you think you'd feel if someone applying for a job knew all the facets of the job and articulated their ability in specific context to what you were looking for?

Once you've shared your Value Proposition, take the opportunity to perception check; to discover how it resonates with the other person. Taking this step adds value to the negotiation process beyond simply determining whether or not the other person is interested in moving forward and working with you. As you do this, your "shared values" focus can come forward through the negotiation. Why is this important? If you're looking to engage with the other person in any form of partnership, it's critical that your basic values align if you want to reach your goals together. When you take the time to clarify this, you create another opportunity to build meaningful rapport and foster deeper trust and understanding between you. This exchange lifts everyone involved, and it's also a tremendous differentiator. You're building a powerful connective tissue between everyone involved in conversation while continuing to instill confidence and peace of mind.

You can begin this qualifying process by asking the question, "Of the others you've spoken to, has anyone else presented themselves in the way that I've presented myself today?" As always, you can customize this wording to use whatever makes sense for you based on what you've heard in this conversation as you've utilized the other keys. Another way of wording the question could be, "Has anyone else given you as cohesive a strategy for achieving your objectives or articulated their value proposition to you this way?" Or, "Have you felt this same level of safety and trust with anyone else you've met with?"

Remember the task at hand. Asking questions gives you the opportunity, first and foremost, to Perception Check that you're on the right course. And then, at this stage of the negotiation, remember to stand strong in your Value. When it comes to developing into an effective negotiator, the most strategic quest you can undertake is to fully and authentically claim your Value Proposition. Asking this question also gives the other person the opportunity to assess and acknowledge the significance of what you've provided for them.

No matter what the profession or product, we know that we have to demonstrate our worth. This is a given. That said, you must be prepared to answer the question "Why should I hire you or buy your product?" If you're not willing to take on that level of responsibility (defined as "response-ability: the ability to respond"), you might as well not even show up.

Since you know these types of qualifying questions are coming, you can turn those "why you?" questions to your advantage. When I was learning that, I chose to use those very questions to establish my talking points designed to distinguish me from the competition. Here's some context as to how I would establish my worth when speaking with a potential client.

The foundation is simple. First I defined what I knew to be the most important aspects of my job. I knew it was very important to be an **Ambassador** for my clients as an extension of them in representing their home. I also knew I needed to be an effective **strategist** to create a game plan for the marketing and sale of the home. And lastly, I knew that I needed to be an effective **negotiator** to protect my client's interests and to get them the best deal possible.

> "No matter what the profession or product, we know that we have to demonstrate our worth. This is a given. That said, you must be prepared to answer the question 'Why should I hire you or buy your product?' If you're not willing to take on that level of responsibility (defined as 'response-ability: the ability to respond'), you might as well not even show up."

Aware that questions about these qualities would come, I chose to define how I demonstrated each of them. What's more, if the qualifying questions didn't come, I took it upon myself to initiate the discussion to make sure I established these all-important points. I did this by suggesting what I'd look for if I were a client trying to buy or sell a home. My delivery was always easy and straightforward with no attachment to an outcome. "If I was in your position, my primary goal would be to secure someone who's an adept and confident *ambassador* and representative, a *strategist* on behalf of my goals, and an effective *negotiator* for the outcomes I want. And I would absolutely want to know how they would do each of those things."

Here is where my preparation brought me huge advantage. Beyond the ability to offer a compelling presentation, I went one step further by putting myself in the client's shoes to make the information more digestible. And because the information was comprehensive and thoughtful, designed to serve the needs of the client, it made it easier for the client to be receptive to it.

Once I'd established this new bar of professionalism on my terms, I used my next question to separate myself from the competition. The question is simple and designed to provoke thought. "Have you asked anyone else you've spoken with about how they negotiate? Or what type of Strategist they are? Or how they demonstrate being an Ambassador on your behalf?" With those questions, I established for my client the awareness that a new benchmark may exist and I was the one delivering on it. And with this raised bar, I'd set a tone that everyone else being interviewed would then have to meet.

Imagine being the next agents being interviewed by this potential client and being asked, "What makes you a great Ambassador, Strategist and Negotiator?" If they're not prepared to address those qualities, picture the client watching them stumble over their words and comparing their answers to the comprehensive and confident responses you gave. Do you see how you can empower yourself and thus separate yourself from any competition when you understand, through proper preparation and the previous six Keys, how to make them work for you?

Forget being a realtor for a moment. Whatever position you seek, whatever company you want to purchase or sell, you can apply your assets to the need of the other side of the table by the way you prepare for the meeting with a clear intention, having defined your Value Proposition. And in so doing, you establish a compelling argument as to why you are the right person to execute the strategy to get the job done.

The work you've done using the first six keys becomes the ingredients for the "wedge" that you drive between you and the competition by applying Key 7. You've already crafted a strategy as a way of showing the other person you are the one to complete the task and now you've articulated it. If they're clear that no one else has offered them what you have and they like what you're offering, isn't it inevitable that you're going to, at the very least, take a next step with this person—if not fully secure your relationship with them as a trusted advisor and ally?

The truth is, if you're not able to craft a good strategy for them, then you're not the right person to execute that strategy. But if you craft a comprehensive strategy and then ask, "Has anyone else created a strategy like this for you?" and the other person says "No," then, really, is there any reason why they shouldn't hire you?

Their answer is your opening to move ahead.

Now, the other person's answer may be, "Yes, someone else has offered me something comparable." If that is the case, acknowledge that you're playing in a very professional arena. When I've received that response, there's really only one more question to ask. "What will be the defining factor in making your decision?" Once again, using the resource of these Keys, I circle back to see if there is a way that I can find an opening to further articulate my value. Be prepared that there may be times when there is nothing more to be said or done. Those are the moments where I call upon my gratitude for the opportunity to practice my skills in a real situation. I thank the person for their time and the opportunity to be of service. In the absence of anything more to do, all I can do is wait to see how it goes.

Some people won't care about quality at all—regardless of the logic and caring behind it. Sometimes the only thing people want to hear is, "I can get you more money for what you've got than anyone else can." In these situations, what you have to offer won't matter at all because they only want to hear what they want to hear. Even if there's no evidence to back up that claim, people will get so hypnotized by the idea of getting what they want that they buy into it. That can be a prescription for failure and frustration for them and you don't want any part of that.

In the world of real estate, clients are easily seduced by a realtor assuring them, "I can get $1.8 million for your home," when the real number is $1.6 million. They won't care to question the fact that three other brokers have told them that $1.6 million is the fair market value for their home. Strategically, they need to check their source. But many people won't.

If I'm in a situation like this, and a seller says, "Someone told me I can get $1.8 million for my house," I respond, "Wow! Really?" I'm not going to be intimidated by that statement. I'll start over with Key 1 and bring my enthusiasm to this part of the conversation. Then I move back into Key 2, let go of my assumptions and start asking questions. I might say, "Tell me, did that person show you data to back up that value? Because I've got all the sales in the neighborhood based on square footage and lot size and condition." If the other person says, "They didn't give me anything. They were just enthusiastic about the house," then my response would be something like, "That enthusiasm is going to be checked by buyers who are looking at where to spend their hard-earned dollars. And they're going to be evaluating your house relative to the competition. Enthusiasm is going to wear off very quickly in the face of that."

I'd then employ Key 3 and say, "Whether you use me or not to facilitate this deal for you, I want you to have enough information so that you can make an informed decision that serves your purposes." If I know they need as much money for their house as possible and I understand all the moving parts necessary to achieve that end, all I need to do is educate them more fully as to the best ways to get that result. If, after I've shared with them all the options and strategies to get the job done, they still want more for their house than is realistically achievable in the current market condition, I then have the choice to either walk away or take the opportunity as part of a larger business strategy for my benefit. However, because I'm in "suspended reality" of the philosophy of Key 3, I can be more candid and truly try to educate the seller that their desire may not serve *their* best interests.

Then I'd kick into Key 4 and say something like, "I get a sense of why we're here, but what is it that you *really* want to get out of this? Is the objective to *list* the house for sale or *sell* it?" Next, I'd shift into Key 6 and use facts and stories to educate them about the strategy they're entertaining. "Do you want to showcase your house and have a lot of people walk through it, only to get feedback from your broker telling you that people are having trouble with the price? There's nothing tactile or tangible that says that you're going to get $1.8 million for this house. The only way a seller in this situation could possibly get that number is by pricing it in the realm of realistic values and then have buyers coming to you and driving the price up because you have multiple bidders for your property. In my experience, you're not going to create a multiple bidder situation if you come on the market 5-7% over what the market will bear. If there's a sale that I don't know about, I'm happy to look at that and re-evaluate. But in the absence of that, I don't see this as an effective strategy."

Don't be afraid to have conversations like this with people. These are the dialogues I frequently have with clients. A professional is someone who dives into their craft to such a degree that they're even prepared to challenge a client's perception that may not be serving them. It's all based on the foundation of authority and credibility. I'm communicating to them, "I've done my homework and I have your best interests at heart."

Key #7 Clear Intention: Delivering the Close
Delivering The Close is really another form of Perception Checking. Closing

is like saying, "Do you understand what I've shared with you? And has anybody else raised the bar to this level?" If they have, then you've created a level playing field with your fellow competitors. And if they haven't, then you've distinguished yourself from the field.

Often, people close themselves. All I do is to help them see the options, and then put together the moving parts so that they can get what they want and need. I show them the way and watch them walk that path. If I try to push them, they'll resist, kicking and screaming. But when they proceed with clarity and understanding on their own, they claim greater peace of mind that they're choosing this as the next best step for themselves. It's always their call.

This is also true of the series of closes that take place within any deal. We're always speaking to the next best step forward. We're communicating, "Given the situation, based on whatever conditions are in play, this is the best course of action I see for those conditions. Would you like to go forward?" I find it is often more effective to invite the opportunity to move forward through a question rather than a statement: "Okay, we're moving forward."

In order to have these kinds of conversations, you need to be able to rely on the strength of your Proper Preparation. If I walk into a negotiation and I understand most of the scenarios that could unfold during our discussion and have strategies to achieve a myriad of outcomes, that's as close as I can come to knowing the answers before the questions are even asked. As long as you set the table in a way that unlocks the door to trust and clear communication and create an aligned strategy that best positions all parties in the strongest negotiating position possible, you've done your job.

At the end of the day, we can never really have all the information about what's going on with the other side of the table. Sometimes deals won't come together, and we'll never find out why. Who can know the true inner motivation of anyone else unless that person is willing to openly and authentically share it? Sometimes *they* don't even know what their true motivation is.

There will be times when deals don't come together for reasons well beyond your control. When that happens, do your best to be easy with yourself. See what you can learn from the situation and let the peace of mind come through your knowledge that each opportunity is a chance to learn and grow.

Key #7 Foundational Practices:

100% Participation, 0% Attachment: Set your intention to remain neutral when you utilize this key. This is the easiest place for attachment to creep in. Stay anchored in your Value Proposition and in your Gratitude.

Proper Preparation: Doing thorough homework is the remedy for any concerns or anxieties when it comes to rolling out this Key. Preparing as best as you can always ensures that negotiations unfold more smoothly. It also supports you to feel like you've taken your best shot at Success, regardless of the outcome.

Answering the Questions You Hope No One Asks: Remember that by having those answers ready to go, you're giving yourself the ability to stay more fully present, free of any need to distract your mind from the nuanced verbal and non-verbal communications that are being shared with you. You also have the ability to really take charge of the negotiation by putting these forward.

Your job is to present your value. If you've done that well, then you have been successful regardless of what the client does after that.

KEY #8: INTRODUCING "THE PIVOT"

The rhythm and flow of a negotiation is often unpredictable. Depending on the amount of time it takes to consummate the deal, there can be a host of twists and turns that can show up, all categorized as "Unexpected." And when the Unexpected shows up, beyond your best efforts to craft a clear and comprehensive agreement, all sorts of chaos can ensue.

The Unexpected can be new information, a change of emotion, interruptions, delays and a variety of other factors that alter the timing and flow of a negotiation. When that flow is disrupted, it can have a marked effect on your final outcome. How you deal with this information and its effects in real time often defines both your ability as a negotiator and the outcome of the deal. During these moments, we all must "Pivot" or adjust our position, based on the new information to either move towards or away from the fruition of a deal. Let's start with a quick war story that created quite a "Pivot."

I had a buyer very excited to purchase their first home. We were working through our due diligence, evaluating the information we were given from the seller while bringing in our own inspectors to make sure the house checked out; all for the buyer's peace of mind.

All was going great until about a week before the closing date. We had already removed all of our necessary protections in the contract and the loan was in place. One morning, the seller's agent called to casually say, "Just wanted to let you know that a couple of years ago, someone died in the house."

"Excuse me?" I said.

"Yeah, the seller thought you might want to know. No big deal."

I would describe this as "new information" to say the very least.

None too pleased, I had to tell my client immediately. One thing I know about death is that people have very definite opinions on the subject. For my client, it *was* a big deal. Before he was willing to move forward, he wanted to know all sorts of information about the circumstances—when it happened, how it happened and why. Clearly, the timing of this information created tremendous distrust on my client's part toward both the seller and their agent. "What else has he not disclosed to me?" my buyer asked. And I couldn't answer. Now my client's head was spinning. And because there truly was no way of soothing his apprehensions about other potential issues with the house, the buyer cancelled the deal.

So in this case the "Pivot," based on the new information, was to terminate the transaction under a provision in the contract that allowed for the cancellation. Had the seller presented us with the information early in the negotiation when they were supposed to and shared all the facts associated with the disclosure, odds are my client would have been able to work through it. But the fact that information came in the form of "Oh, by the way..." at the very end disoriented my client in a manner that could not be overcome.

In my years of experience, almost every deal I've worked on included something unforeseen showing up that made us all stop to reassess the situation, the deal and our desire to move forward. Once I accept that "something" as a potential reality, I'm not as thrown by it when it materializes.

As I take this course of action for myself, I also work to manage the expectations of my clients when I'm negotiating on their behalf. I define managing expectation as *honoring people with the intention of education through clear communication.* In the midst of the enthusiasm that we've come to an agreement, I still caution my clients that we've got a long way to go before we fully celebrate. I let them know that there are many moving parts to be worked through and that as we proceed, there may be some moments where we encounter snags. I assure my clients that if obstacles arise, we'll deal with them in partnership, the way we've dealt with everything else to date, to best protect and take care of them.

The fact that you've applied the first seven keys of an effective negotiation will have lasting, positive impact at this moment. Most clients don't really understand what my caution means and sometimes it can momentarily dampen the mood. However, the fact that I proactively alerted them to this potential reality ultimately makes my client feel more confident in my ability and my knowledge of the workings of a transaction. Once clients get a better understanding that I'm just preparing them for a possibility, any momentary "mood dampening" is replaced with greater peace of mind.

Now that expectations have been managed, let's look at some of the ways to best deal with the unexpected when it shows up.

First, remind yourself or your client that you talked about this potential development and it has now arrived. That won't make anyone feel a whole lot better, but it helps. The first challenge when dealing with anything unforeseen is getting a better handle on what the issue is so that a clearer assessment can be made. Move quickly and diligently through your fact-finding to demonstrate your caring and to create peace of mind with your client. Creating peace of mind is your primary intention at this stage. Know this: Dealing with the unexpected is simply another opportunity to cycle through the Keys of Negotiation. Claim your confidence in having the tools and techniques to work through this new development for the benefit of all involved.

Start at the beginning with Key 1 as you look to find answers and information to see if this new "wrinkle" is a little issue or a big one. Little issues can be worked through relatively easily so that the deal can get back on track. Big issues, as with the story I told above, have been known to stop a deal in its tracks and dismantle it. In either instance, you will be met with the opportunity to Pivot, one way or the other. And that is what any Pivot is; an opportunity to demonstrate both your ability as a negotiator and your caring for the other person in the negotiation.

There's an expression: "When one door closes, another door opens." It's a very optimistic saying that I like a lot. If new information is the possibility of a "closing door," the Pivot you create will provide the ability to either reopen that door or choose a new one.

If you've put a tremendous amount of work into a deal only to find that you may need to start all over again, that saying may not resonate the same way for you. I understand. I've Pivoted clients out of many deals only to begin again from Square One. It can be frustrating and time-consuming. However, consider the alternative. If I've just been given new information about a house that causes my client to recoil, my first concern must be to honor the concerns of my client. As an example, say the foundation of the house is crumbling and the cost to fix it is $50,000 that my client doesn't have or want to spend. That is pretty much a deal-killer. If my Pivot is to try and convince my client to stay in a deal that they don't want, guess what my client's next Pivot will be: fire Nick.

As you consider your options in the face of new information, whether for yourself or a client, know that your actions, choices and presentations going forward are defining moments for your relationship and the deal at hand. Faced with your new reality, the best thing you can do is to stay relaxed. Don't make the mistake of assuming that the goodwill you've created so far is going to sustain you. As I've already stated, start from the beginning with Enthusiasm. Depending on the nature and timing of this new information, enthusiasm may be the last emotion you or your client may feel. Yet, the situation is what it is. How you emotionally deal with it will ultimately serve to further the negotiation or cripple it.

"Whatever new information shows up, it usually has direct impact on all parties involved in a negotiation. Your aim is to distill the information and present it neutrally to your side of the table in a way that speaks to their needs."

I've referenced the mindset of managing expectation and emotion. Whatever new information shows up, it usually has direct impact on all parties involved in a negotiation. Your aim is to distill the information and present it neutrally to your side of the table in a way that speaks to their needs. Remember, we're not selling here—and that applies to unexpected information as well—we're educating about what is now a new facet of the negotiation. From there, you and your client can huddle up and dialog to evaluate the information to see if the deal still aligns with your objectives.

Sometimes new information can enhance your position greatly and affect how you continue your discussions. New information may be a sign of weakness from the other side and that could give you the ability to reduce your offering. It's fun when that happens. Other times, new information may necessitate upping your ante. Suddenly, you could have more competition for what you want and depending on how badly you want something; you may need to extend yourself. Either way, new information is just that: information. How we deal with it greatly affects our next course of action and by managing expectations and going through our strategic beats in order, we stand the best chance of creating and negotiating successful outcomes.

To that same point, be aware that anytime there's a Pivot in the deal, the other person's original self-protective mindset will likely rear its head again. New information tends to push people toward their predisposed patterns, whether that's, "Those jerks are trying to take advantage of me," or "Oh no. What are we going to do?" Your job is to communicate that you are there for your client and will guide them through in a manner that serves them. The best way I know to serve my clients when I'm in the midst of a Pivot is to communicate with them. Often. Emotions are heightened with new information. Distrust runs rampant and emotions associated with disappointment tend to make people act more rashly. This is where your next action as a good negotiator comes in. When people are agitated, they look for soothing. They want to be honored, especially in a negotiation where they are looking to you to take care of them.

Whenever I'm faced with working through a new issue or piece of information, I go into hyperdrive of information communication. I do this because I've found that lack of communication leads people to form their own opinions and conclusions. If someone starts feeling that they're being played, then they'll convert their positive emotions into negative ones until they just spin out. I'd say it's akin to "jilted lover" syndrome.

To circumvent this, always err on the side of over-communicating. Even with the other side of the negotiating table. If you're in a Pivot and your client is taking some time to make a decision about next steps, communicate this to the other side of the table, even if you have nothing new to report. Staying in contact keeps all parties connected emotionally—which is very important in these highly sensitive moments of a deal. I know this because I've had instances where I didn't stay engaged and my clients' minds went to the worst possible outcome. That made it very difficult to restore the deal. At the end of the day, my client may choose not to go forward with the deal. As his negotiator, my job was to stay engaged with the other side until he was ready to make his decision. Conversely, if my client wanted to stay in the deal, my constant communication served him in maintaining the goodwill moving forward.

Ultimately the motivation a person has as they enter into a negotiation will be a key factor in whether the deal closes or not. Think about it: If you want something bad enough, new information or a delay of its timing may only be a minor setback. Unless, of course, the information is crushing. Then motivation is crushed along with it. I will add that I have experienced Pivots where the client gets so mired in their own fear or concern that they over-react, relative to the severity of the situation.

In these instances, if the person you're representing gets stuck in their negative mindset during a Pivot and you need to get them back on track, you can always reconnect them with their ultimate motivation. Start with Key 3: You can say to them, "Whether we get to the end of this deal or not is entirely up to you, but..." (now to Key 2) "you said you wanted this specific goal. And..." (on to Key 4) "remember that you shared with me what the experience of reaching for that goal would look like for you. You can still get there." And then to Key 5, "I'm checking with you now; is that still accurate for you? And if so, what are we doing here—are we sticking with your vision or are we letting it go?"

Creating a more elevated perspective using these Keys will greatly assist you in giving your client an opportunity to breathe and come back into alignment with the greater purpose of the deal. Your ability to assess a situation and Pivot through the unexpected can maintain more grace and flow that keeps interested parties engaged with the ultimate outcome of Success.

Key #8 Clear Intention: Preserving Peace of Mind

Successfully navigating unexpected developments leads to a tremendous sense of calm regarding your ability to be a good steward for yourself and/ or your client's interests and objectives. Peace of mind is the natural result of managing expectations—and emotions—along the way. That is one of the true measures of a good negotiator. Because the truth is, sometimes things get weird. People miscommunicate. Someone makes a mistake. Accidents happen. In those moments, it's important that we leverage our own ability to respond to the situation. Have a Clear Intention during a potential Pivot to stay connected to your Value Proposition. Trust that you have the inner and outer resources to work through the situation at hand and stay *your* course. If a deal is meant to blow up, let it blow up. The fact that you've maintained your value and held true to your intentions of service and the execution strategy to deliver on that will help keep you clear of most blowback.

Orientation vs. Disorientation will have a direct impact on peace of mind. Your intention is to create re-orientation in the midst of a Pivot. You start by assessing the situation and seeing if there is still alignment with the initial intended objective. Consider how you feel when you are oriented about something. You have the information about it and that creates clarity. Clarity creates peace of mind and we now know how important that quality is when moving all parties forward in a deal. Conversely, how do you feel when you're disoriented? Confusion usually creates some form of unease inside of you, moving you into an associated protective rigidity that causes you to question everything. This state of mind does *not* serve anyone in the pursuit of a deal and therefore you want to stay as clear of this debilitating mindset as possible.

Key #8 Foundational Practices:

100% Participation/0% Attachment: Dealing with the unexpected will test your attachment to the outcome of a deal more than any other aspect of negotiation. Remember that cool heads prevail. If your emotions heat up and your ego starts to run rampant, slow things down. It's okay if you don't have all of the answers right now. Practice using your *Discernment* to communicate what you do know as clearly and neutrally as you can in a timely way.

Recognizing the Mindset That Greets You: Whatever attitude you encountered in your initial meetings will likely show up again here. Be on the lookout for it. And when it shows up, remember that your only job is to re-establish trust and rapport with whomever you're talking to. You've already created a strong foundation based on your cumulative interactions up to this point. Offer reassurance that you have the person's best interests at heart.

Perception Checking: Again, you want to slow things down during a Pivot. Make sure you accurately receive and deliver all of the new information that's showing up. If the person you're representing expresses concern, you can say something like, "It sounds like this is bringing up a sense of uneasiness for you. Is that accurate?" Listen and be present with them. As you explore options together continue to make sure that whomever you're speaking to—whether it's your client or the other side of the deal—is on the same page with you.

Your Success Defined: Remind everyone involved of their "Why" for doing this. Given the new information and the options before you, is the path you're on still a healthy and viable route to the client's success?

Selling vs. Educating: Ultimately, the decision on whether or not to move forward rests with the person you're representing. Use your expertise and experience to assist them in navigating this unknown territory on the way to their Success. Remember the intention is to create peace of mind for your client, and that's true regardless of the outcome of the Pivot.

Bottom line: Being prepared for the unexpected showing up is required. Letting it throw you is optional.

KEY #9: IDENTIFYING NEXT STEPS

Negotiations end in one of two ways: You either make a deal or you don't. Consider any negotiation you've had of any importance. Was the negotiation accomplished in one shot or many steps to reach a decision about a deal? Negotiations with any sort of value take time, great attention to detail and consistent energy to complete. Consider all the steps we've discussed to date and the nuances within each one. Negotiations are delicate business and as you realize just how intricate they are, you can better understand why so many people shy away from them.

Presumably you now understand the value of establishing relationships with trust and confidence. Abilities need to be confirmed and objectives clarified so that the individual you're dealing with can better determine whether or not you're the right person to assist them in their goal. Each of the ongoing meetings, conversations and related actions are meant to further confirm or deny that all parties are on an aligned course. Therefore, I'm suggesting that each one of these events is a micro negotiation unto itself. The negotiator who can effectively string each micro meeting to the next micro meeting to keep the ball rolling is the negotiator who will more effectively orchestrate positive outcomes.

As we consider this final stage of our Nine Negotiation Keys, understand that this Key has great importance because it creates the bridge to keep your negotiation flowing from one step to the next. Realizing its importance and how you integrate it with each step of your negotiation will become part of your talent that makes you an effective negotiator. Building these bridges occurs through the creation of Definitive Next Action Steps.

> "Each of the ongoing meetings, conversations and related actions are meant to further confirm or deny that all parties are on an aligned course. Therefore, I'm suggesting that each one of these events is a micro negotiation unto itself."

A Definitive Next Action Step has two components that, once established, create maximum effectiveness. First, one or both parties of a negotiation agrees to complete a specific action prior to the next meeting. Second, a specific meeting time is agreed upon between all parties of the agreement in order to keep the larger negotiation moving towards resolution. I realize that this may sound obvious to a seasoned negotiator. However, I can't begin to count the times I've been involved in deals where a meeting concluded and the people involved weren't clear about what the next action was because it wasn't properly defined. For those of us fully employing each of these Nine Keys, understand that you haven't completed a negotiation stage unless you have a Definitive Next Action Step, agreed upon by all parties, that keeps your negotiation moving. This is especially true when you are at the beginning stages of your negotiation, when you're only dealing in conversations and there is no written document yet. Your only guideposts for moving the agreement forward are what you say to each other.

Let's take a most basic premise to illustrate my point: Your next negotiation is creating a lunch appointment. For our definition of this negotiation, you've got two parties involved. You both have an intention to be together. You understand your "why" and "how" to achieve your objective. If, at the conclusion of the initial conversation, you don't create a definitive next action step, which involves someone agreeing to make a reservation at the designated restaurant and the two of you agreeing on when you're having this lunch, that lunch may not happen. That's true for any sort of negotiation.

For example, I'm your realtor. You are a home buyer trying to decide whether or not you want to work with me and you want to see properties in a certain neighborhood. We talk, and I go through my Keys and their intentions. At the end of the conversation, knowing that my intention is to create a Definitive Next Action Step, I make an offer that needs your acceptance and commitment to keep us connected. Remember the offer needs clear action and associated clear agreement as to when we will meet again.

I begin building my bridge: "How about this? May I pick you up on Thursday at 3:00pm? I'm happy to drive. We can get into the three properties you want to look at and can see which, if any, you like. Does that sound like a good plan?" If you agree to this, we have our Definitive Next Action Step and our negotiation will continue forward with efficiency and on purpose. That's the completion of that particular negotiation.

Then I go to work to create the schedule of showing the three houses you want to see so I'm prepared for our next meeting. The next negotiation begins when I pick you up again at 3:00pm to see the first house. Where the discussions go during that outing becomes our next negotiation. And so it goes, until you ultimately have what you want and I ultimately have what I want. With each micro negotiation, the intention is to cycle through these same Negotiation Keys and conclude with a definitive next action step to keep the relationship connected and progressing.

Understand that we do not have any written agreement here. Our "contract" to stay connected is only a verbal communication at this point. However, because I've established a connection, a clear action and received commitment from you, the buyer, I have a far greater likelihood that you will stay engaged with me until that next meeting where I can continue building my rapport and mutual trust to nurture the relationship.

Conversely, what if I ended the conversation with "Okay, I'll call the agents for the three homes you want to see and we'll connect later?" That's weak and vague. The only connection we have is that I'm doing something without asking for a commitment from you to reconnect with me. This lack of commitment doesn't keep me connected with you fully because we have no agreement to reconnect. Do you see the difference? It is imperative that you create clear terms of engagement into the future in the absence of a written contract or you might as well consider that you don't have a client.

How many times, in the absence of a clear next step, have you reached back to someone and they never got back to you? The reason this happens is usually because you weren't specific enough in asking for what you wanted to keep that connection. That's on you. Now you've just entered another aspect of having created, promoted or allowed a reality that doesn't serve your greater good. I understand. We've all concluded a conversation and not proposed a clear next action step. We knew we should have but for whatever reason we let the conversation end without asking for what we wanted. Cue Comfort Zones and fears of asking perceived "Tough" questions. See how it all circles back when we have a greater understanding of how we might tend to "operate" in our worlds. To all of these apprehensions that have stopped us up until now, consider how creating a definitive next action step can proactively shift you forward towards creating more of what you want.

> "Recognize your value and claim your worthiness to achieve your success so that you may experience more of the qualities you want to experience in your life."

The first key, as always, is awareness. You have that now. You also know the two elements necessary to create a definitive next action. Have faith that, as with any negotiation, if there are two people in a room engaged in conversation, they want something from the other and they are looking to see if that person has what they want.

If you've been doing the exercises, by now you know your value. You know what you want. You are clearer in why you want it and how to go about getting it. You have negotiating skills that elevate your ability to negotiate above the vast majority who are still in fear of negotiating. You have plenty of resources to ask for what you want and create the definitive next action steps that bridge your negotiations to successful outcomes. It's time you...

Recognize your value and claim your worthiness to achieve your success so that you may experience more of the qualities you want to experience in your life.

Key #9 Clear Intention: Confirming the Relationship

If you're moving forward in partnership, this is your transition from "theory" to "reality." Utlizing this key creates the connective tissue of the negotiation to keep all parties actively engaged and in agreement during each micro negotiation of the overall negotiation. This is the time to be very definitive with your commitments and your enthusiasm to deliver on the results that you've discussed during the meeting. Now is the time for crystal-clear focus and communication.

This is the most tangible intention we work with. You want to know where you stand and what's next, as in, "You're going to do this. I'm going to do that. We're going to do those things within a prescribed period of time. Great. I look forward to seeing you next time." It takes about 30 seconds. However, in the absence of this clear communication consider that any progress you made in your meeting maybe nullified without it.

Also, regardless of the outcome, take a moment to *enjoy* the fact that you've presented yourself in a meaningful way and that you're on the road to creating the personal Success that you've defined for yourself.

Key #9 Foundational Practices:

Creating Your Road Map: Take the strategy you've crafted and start breaking it down using the structure you applied to your own vision of success. Identify the projects that can have the biggest impact for your client, and flesh them out until you identify the next step you can take to move toward each one.

Clear Intention: Practice Clear Intention as you move forward. Define your intentions before any meetings related to the negotiation at hand. Use your intentions to help you create high-quality actions and focus on achieving positive outcomes for each subset of this deal.

Little Things Done Consistently...: A deal is a sequence of small actions taken until the goal is achieved. That's it. Start small, keep the ball rolling in the direction of the "Why," and do each thing in excellence. You'll create a major impact.

Scheduling Your Success: This deal is now one of your Non-negotiables. Remember the power of your schedule, and use it to keep you accountable in consistently taking actions toward your and your client's Success.

When everyone knows and agrees to the next step, everyone is moving closer to their desired outcomes.

THREE

THE DYNAMICS OF A NEGOTIATION

I can't imagine anyone entering a negotiation who doesn't want to come away from it feeling that they got a good deal. And, more importantly, that they didn't feel taken advantage of. Yet, as much as we try to gain clear-cut answers to satisfy our desires of winning while allaying our fears of being taken advantage of, we're never going to truly know if we got the best possible deal and gave up the least we had to. That is the crazy-making part of this negotiating game.

I can't tell you how many times I've questioned myself after a negotiation, wondering if I could have done better for my clients or myself. The ink wasn't even dry on the contract and my mind was already racing through different scenarios about this turn and that pivot where perhaps I could have done better. It's taken me years to relax into a more peaceful state of mind, realizing I don't necessarily need to know whether I could have done better or not because many times, that is unknowable.

In this final section of our negotiating segment, let me offer you an awareness that may give your ever-turning mind greater peace. It will assist you to more fully engage in your negotiations and walk away from each of the remaining negotiations in your life feeling perhaps more content.

The plain truth is that when dealing with negotiation, variables such as motivation, urgency and market conditions, make it impossible to establish objective parameters of "good" and "bad." Your motivation/urgency to get what the other side has to offer uniquely define what "value" is to you/your client. So why try to objectively quantify subjective variables after the fact? Your need drove you to act just as their need drove them. In the moment of agreement, both parties gave what they felt they had to give to gain the value they wanted in return.

When you can see from this elevated perspective, you begin to better understand the folly of trying to quantify any facet of your gain. Often part of my job as a negotiator is to reflect that expanded perspective of value to my clients. When I do that successfully, they can better understand and feel good about their choice because they know it supports their greater intention as to why they entered the negotiation in the first place.

> **"So why try to objectively quantify subjective variables after the fact? Your need drove you to act just as their need drove them. In the moment of agreement, both parties gave what they felt they had to give to gain the value they wanted in return."**

We've all heard the idea of "Win/Win" negotiations. The Win/Win philosophy, in my opinion, is designed to create a greater sense of peace around the final outcome of a negotiation. And while the intention to make people "feel" good about the outcome of their negotiation is noble, I agree with Jim Camp, author of *Start With No*, that creating Win/Win negotiations are not part of the objective. Feeling good about how your deal turned out is not the objective. Getting what you want and need from the other party is the objective. Plainly put, I've managed hundreds of negotiations to agreement and yet neither side of the bargaining table felt good about it. Buyers usually end up feeling they paid too much and sellers often feel like they coulda/shoulda gotten more. Despite the fact they both received enough value to accept the terms of the agreement that brought them to the negotiating table in the first place.

With that sobering fact, let's be clear. *Honoring your needs is the primary objective of a negotiation.* Based on an assessment of need from the other side of the negotiating table, you can create deals designed to serve both parties. That said,

THE DYNAMICS OF A NEGOTIATION

BUYER	THE DEAL ZONE	SELLER

START
POINT

START
POINT

it's also fine to take full advantage of a negotiating situation for your benefit, and the nine keys give you every opportunity to do that.

To more fully explore this construct, look at the chart above.

We have a buyer and seller. For the purposes of this discussion, it doesn't matter if the negotiation is for a tangible object or a service. We're just looking at the fabric of any negotiation. The first awareness to have with any negotiation is that two parties begin a dialog because they each want something from the other; otherwise, why meet? If, at any point, one side no longer sees value in what the other side is offering, the negotiation ends. That said, as long as each side continues to engage, there remains something that each side wants/needs from the other. Keep this in mind: As long as the other side is still talking, they ain't walking.

Good, bad, or indifferent, negotiations tend to be regarded as "sport." Two sides, armed with their own perspectives and perceptions of value, engage in battle seeking to gain advantage over the other side. Volleying back and forth, both sides look for weakness and the opportunity to strike the winning blow that renders the other side into submission. Winners and Losers are declared and depending on which you are, you feel great and victorious or bad and defeated.

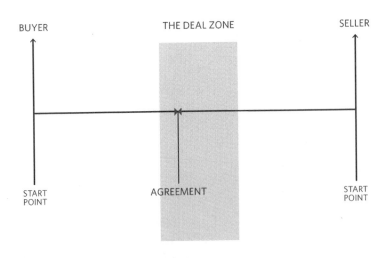

However, we've already established that "winning and losing" can't be accurately defined, so don't fall into that ego trap. No matter what personality greets you on the other side of the table, I encourage you to look past their ego and focus your energy on discovering their need so you can use it to your advantage when the timing is right. Remember that your objective is to honor your need while doing your best to honor their need as well. Because when both sides' needs are honored, you will stand a better chance of creating an agreement that will last. And that is a great prize.

Looking at our next chart, you see that there are two arrows originating from the buyer and seller that come together and meet.

These arrows represent movement derived by give and take, compromise and urgency towards agreement between the two parties. This movement toward a common ground, a field of play where a deal can be reached, is what I'm calling the Deal Zone. There are many theories and strategies presented in countless books on negotiation, promoting ways to get people to move into the deal zone. Some promote "Sell" tactics and "Manipulation" strategies to force the other side to act in accordance with your wishes. To me, this is all nonsense. You can't truly force or manipulate a person to act without resorting to unethical or illegal activities; something I would not do for any reward. However, consider the power and effectiveness of Education vs. Selling.

Consider that a person's motivation to act and their associated need level combine to become the engine that propels them toward a common ground. The way you, as a negotiator, can further ignite that movement toward an agreement is through your ability to educate, to provide greater perspective as to why moving serves their greater interests and objectives.

If I know you want something and I explain to you, in a manner that gives you comfort and confidence, why acting a certain way will give you a better chance to get what you want, you'll probably act. The skill with which the information is presented so that the other party may best understand it is what defines a good negotiator.

Taking a closer look at the Deal Zone, notice that there is an area of latitude that makes up the zone; it's not just a finite line. Each end of the zone spectrum represents the respective party's threshold point in which they would consider the bare minimum for them to enter into an agreement. The deeper either party proceeds into the deal zone represents the more they need to and/or are willing to give in order to reach an agreement.

We've established that coming into any agreement is not an exact science due to the number of variables such as time, value/scarcity and motivation. Therefore, we must allow for some sort of margin wherein parties come together and deals are made.

Here's an example: I've cut my hand and it's bleeding. You have Band-Aids and I don't. I've got an important meeting in 5 minutes. I'm dressed in a suit and a white shirt. The last thing I want to do is enter the room bleeding and/or walk in the room with blood on my shirt. So I ask you how much you want for a Band-Aid. As you ponder your response, you look to all of the above-mentioned variables and probably see that I've got a definitive need and the associated urgency. Could you get $100 for a 10¢ Band-Aid? Probably. That showcases the elasticity of what makes up the potential latitudes of a deal zone.

Back to our discussion on creating greater peace and acceptance; the ultimate deal you make ideally serves your greater intention. Based on motivation and need, look back at the deal zone chart and consider where the final deal was made. Who got the better deal? The buyer is certainly closer to the buyer's starting point than the seller in this example. But is that the only defining measure as to who got the better deal?

I urge you not to fall into the trap of assumption. In looking at that graph, you don't have all the information necessary to formulate an answer. You don't know the motivation of the parties. You don't know if the Seller would have come further down in price if pressed or the Buyer would have paid more. And you never will. At the end of the day, the Buyer paid a price for the object or service and the Seller was willing to move that far away from their starting point to meet them at a point that was acceptable—to them first, and then to the buyer.

Consider our Band-Aid negotiation. What if the Buyer who paid $100 for the Band-Aid was so relieved that they walked into the room feeling greater confidence and thereafter secured a $1,000,000 fee? That sense of relief and confidence becomes the real value, transcending the $100 cost. That Band-Aid made him a fortune, and was a good deal for the Seller as well.

How can you know when a negotiation is successful? If a deal is struck. That means both parties received something in the range of what they needed. That was the objective going in to the negotiation, so "Mission accomplished." Don't waste your energy focusing on the perception of winning or losing a negotiation. Instead, consider why you're entering the negotiation. Hold steady to the construct that you are going into that negotiation based on a specific motivation, aligned with a greater intention beyond that negotiation. Strike the deal that supports that greater intention and feel good that you've engaged in a negotiation that supports the greater purpose. That's the best way I know to process and assess any negotiation.

DOES THIS STUFF WORK?

"Does this stuff work?" is a great question. The best way I can answer it is with a story and then a question back to you. Here's the story.

An agent named Nicole joined our Pasadena office four years ago. Right after she came on board, she attended the Value-Conscious Negotiation series I was teaching to our Partners Trust associates. We met together during that time, and I asked her how much money she wanted to make in her first year in the business. She said, "$250,000." I remember thinking that number seemed a little aggressive for her first year, and, wanting to manage her expectations, I told her as much. We discussed her goals and at the end of the meeting, she said, "Okay. I'm going to make $142,000." It was such a specific number that it stuck in my head long afterward.

Fast-forward to the end of that year, when Nicole approached me after another workshop. I'd been watching her apply these principles over the course of the year and it was fun to see her again. She walked up absolutely beaming, extending a piece of paper toward me. It was her commission statement showing her earnings in her first year both with us and in the business. She had made $142,000.

Now, here's my question concerning whether this works or not: "Will you work it?" Or are you sitting on the sidelines saying, "Prove it to me?" You define your reality. You get to use your discernment in whatever way works best for you. What I've seen is that when we hang out and wait for proof, opportunities to use these principles and tools will keep sailing by us.

These techniques, and especially the way I have organized them to support each other and produce synergistic results, have worked for me. I have seen them work time after time for the people I have shared them with who take them to heart. Having said that, if you wanted to get from Los Angeles to New York City, and I gave you a brand-new jet all fueled up and ready to go, it wouldn't get you there until you got in, fired it up, and flew it across the country.

My encouragement? Dive in, check it out for yourself and see if it works. If it doesn't, report back. You can prove me wrong—I'm really open to that. Another option could be to have an intention that this stuff does work and prove me *right*.

> "If you wanted to get from Los Angeles to New York City, and I gave you a brand-new jet all fueled up and ready to go, it wouldn't get you there until you got in, fired it up, and flew it across the country."

If you've found yourself hanging back, here's an easy way to lean into this: Write down an awareness related to your Value Proposition, Proper Preparation and Clear Intention prior to one of your meetings. You could even give yourself a quick 1-10 rating before the meeting as a reference point. Then check yourself again after that same meeting and write down how it went. If you capture your thoughts both before and after, you'll be more acutely aware of the impact these tools have had.

The power in this pre- and post-analysis resides in its ability to give you real-time data as to whether you're on-course or off-course with your journey. Make your hypothesis, then experience it for yourself. Doing that, you'll have your own answer to the question, "Does this stuff work?" One thing's for sure, though: If you think something won't work, and you never try it, it definitely will not work for you.

AFTERWORD

Congratulations on getting this far. Reaching this point can be your first completion.

Reflect for a moment on your level of awareness about yourself and your success when we began this adventure. Has it changed? If so, what's different? Take a moment right now to consider the difference between where you are now and where you were when you began this journey. Acknowledge yourself for the wins along the way—for continuing to show up, for the steps you've taken, for the growth that's occurred.

Where do you go from here? That's up to you.

Consider that you now have the means of identifying where you really want to go ON YOUR TERMS. You have methods for creating a doable, step-by-step roadmap for getting there. And you have the golden key—negotiating from the foundation of serving—that will ignite the engine of a vehicle that makes reaching your destination a practical reality. What's more, you have ways of getting around obstacles you might place in the way of your progress.

I will leave you with these final thoughts:

• Good things happen to good people.

• You are a good person.

• What better foundation for building your success do you need than that? Whatever you choose to do, I wish you the very best.

Nick Segal
Santa Monica, California
March 8th, 2018

BUT WAIT...
THERE'S MORE!

You now know literally everything you need to achieve what you want in your life. However, if you have questions, would like encouragement, or are interested in additional resources for getting over the speedbumps and hurdles that tend to show up, we're on it.

Our website, **onyourterms.net**, is filled with useful material that will help keep you energized and moving at the rate you want to go. You'll find new content designed to assist you in your quest for success, including blank forms you can download and use for the exercises in this book. In the Ask Us section, you can request answers to questions about situations you're encountering as you work the techniques we've introduced.

Do check out the site. In exchange for your time, we'll give you a free e-Book with a wealth of information that complements what you've read here.

Reading our book may have seemed like a completion. Yet we hope you consider it more like the beginning of a new adventure. We'd like to continue to be your guides—and perhaps your colleagues and friends—as you move forward.

Visit **onyourterms.net**, discover more resources, and get your free e-Book.

NICK SEGAL

A nationally renowned executive, prized speaker and celebrated innovator, Nick Segal has had an immeasurable impact over his three decades in real estate. Fervently committed to raising the bar of professionalism in the industry, Nick has developed two prominent real estate companies from the ground up: growing DBL Realtors, acquired by Sotheby's in 2004, from 12 to 650 agents, and founding Partners Trust, acquired by Pacific Union International after achieving more than $11 billion in sales in only eight years. While serving as CEO of Partners Trust, Nick received both the Realtor of the Year and William May Garland Awards.

To support the success of his associates and others, he began a parallel career designing and facilitating workshops for those who would like to have more of what they want in life. He has facilitated countless workshops and coaching sessions in Los Angeles and across the U.S.

Nick and his wife Laura, a life coach and Nick's facilitating partner, live what they teach. They thoroughly enjoy the success they have created from their lovely home base near the beach in Santa Monica, California.

LAURA SEGAL

Laura Segal is a life and business coach dedicated to supporting individuals, groups and organizations in experiencing greater joy and freedom in their lives. She holds a master's degree in spiritual psychology from The University of Santa Monica.

PRAISE FOR *ON YOUR TERMS*

I love the dimension of this book. You can think of 'Terms' as in crux or essence of negotiating the best deal possible. And, you can also think of 'Terms' as in the depth, or essence, or level of caring that you experience during any negotiation regardless of outcome. The first will often enhance your bank account. The second will always enhance the quality of your life. Nick is communicating how to have both in every deal.

Ron Hulnick, Ph. D., President,
University of Santa Monica
Co-author with Mary R. Hulnick, Ph.D. of
Remembering the Light Within: A Course in Soul-Centered Living

This is a handbook for professional and personal success in the 21st century. Nick offers significant keys for establishing good relationships, a road map for effective negotiations and a truly heartfelt process for achieving business success and personal fulfilment. For a graduate starting their career, or anyone feeling overwhelmed in this rapidly changing world of business and finance, *On Your Terms* is a must read.

Anne Naylor
Coach and Motivational Speaker

A modern day *Think and Grow Rich*. Based on his success in business and life, Nick Segal compellingly answers the question, "Are you worth it?" The answer is yes, which makes this book well worth reading.

Mark K. Updegrove, Director of the LBJ Presidential Library and
Author of the newly published *The Last Republicans:
Inside the Extraordinary Relationship Between
George H.W. Bush and George W. Bush*

Made in the USA
San Bernardino, CA
22 August 2018